THE CLOTHES ON OUR BACKS

THE CLOTHES ON OUR BACKS

How Refugees from Nazism Revitalised the British Fashion Trade

ANNA NYBURG

VALLENTINE MITCHELL
LONDON • CHICAGO

First published in 2020 by Vallentine Mitchell

Catalyst House,
720 Centennial Court,
Centennial Park, Elstree WD6 3SY, UK

814 N. Franklin Street,
Chicago, Illinois,
60610 USA

www.vmbooks.com

Copyright © Anna Nyburg 2020

British Library Cataloguing in Publication Data:
An entry can be found on request

ISBN 978 1 912676 91 0 (Paperback)
ISBN 978 1 912676 25 5 (Cloth)
ISBN 978 1 912676 26 2 (Ebook)

Library of Congress Cataloging in Publication Data:
An entry can be found on request

All rights reserved. No part of this publication may be reproduced in any form or by any means, electronic, mechanical, photocopying, reading or otherwise, without the prior permission of Vallentine Mitchell & Co. Ltd.

Contents

Acknowledgements   vii
List of Illustrations   ix

Introduction   1

Chapter 1 | German and Austrian Fashion between the Wars   4
Berlin and *Konfektion* | Jewish Clothiers | Vienna | Paris | The German Textile Industry | Press and Publicity | Photography | Training

Chapter 2 | The Nazi Destruction of Germany's Clothing Industry   31
Nazis Come to Power, 1933 | Nazis Target *Konfektion* | 'Aryans' and Jews | *Judenrein*: the Jews Disappear from Germany | The *Anschluss*: Austria is Annexed into the German Reich

Chapter 3 | Britain: New Home to the Refugees, Ancient Home of the Knitting Trade   43
Great British Woollen Traditions: Pringle and John Smedley | Possible Destinations for Jewish Refugees? USA and Palestine | *Kindertransports* | The Great Northern Trading Estates Miracle

Chapter 4 | War!   60
Refugees into Enemy Aliens | Rationing, Making Do and Mending | Paris and Couture during the War | Bureaucracy

Chapter 5 | Showing Off   69
Refugees at 'Britain Can Make It', 1946 | Festival of Britain, 1951 | The New Window Display | Export or Die! *The Ambassador* Magazine and Hans and Elsbeth Juda | Refugee Photographers at *Vogue* | Refugee Graphic Designers in Fashion

Chapter 6 | Refugee Stories — 85

- Hats off to Otto Lucas: Gay, Glamorous and German — 85
- Ettinger: Bags of Style — 95
- The Little Refugee Kangaroo: Kangol — 101
- Making Sparks at Marks: Hans Schneider brings Dior to the Masses — 110
- Over Here and Underwear: Silhouette — 118
- Textiles and the Refugees: Colour, Texture, Pattern — 127
  Elisabeth Tomalin | Jacqueline Groag | Tibor Reich | Zika and Lida Ascher | Miki Sekers | Bernat Klein
- Otto Weisz at Pringle and the Twinset — 146
- Mr Berdach, Mr Churchill and the Bow Ties — 158
- Buttoned Up: Hornflowa, Lucie Rie and Issey Miyake — 164
- Mr Noskwith, Bletchley Park and Charnos Silky Stockings — 168
- John Smedley's Mysterious Klothilde Ehrenfest — 172
- Francis Steiner and Tick-a-Tee Children's Wear — 176
- Hans Schneider and the Arts — 180
- Illo, the *Kindertransportee* at M & S — 188
- Launer, on the Arm of Her Majesty — 192
- Double Two Collars the Shirt Market — 196
- Frank Usher and the Frocks — 203
- Lord Kagan and Gannex — 209
- The Fabulous Kroll Dynasty — 214
- Jerseycraft: Mr Bratman of Wakefield — 222
- *Kultur*! Textile Refugees in Opera, Theatre and Visual Arts — 228
- Djanoglys — 231
- Landsberger: Bags of Ingenuity — 236
- Eva Aldbrook: Fashion Illustrator in the Golden Age — 241

Conclusion — 245

Bibliography — 257

Index — 263

Acknowledgements

I would like to express my special gratitude to Professor Charmian Brinson and to Neil Taylor for reading the manuscript and for their helpful comments, as well as to Rahel Feilchenfeldt for her constant support. Also thanks to Chiara Barbieri for her kindness in formatting the manuscript for me. My gratitude is due to all those who gave up their time to be interviewed or to put me in touch with interviewees: Eva Aldbrook, Rolf Andersen, Richard Balfour-Lynn, Julian Barnes, Freddie Berdach, Ralph Blumenau, Gerald Bodmer, Leila Croft, Sir Harry Djanogly, Richard Donner, John Donner, Robert Ettinger, Stanley Grant, Nic Harris, Thomas Heatherwick, Professor Simon Kroll, William Kroll, Ralph Land, Sam Reich, Katherine Shock, Nick Sigler, Monica Stark, Frank Steiner, Adam Sykes and Stefany Tomalin. Susie Hopkins was especially generous with her time and with information. Others helped by correspondence, in particular: Prof. Andreas Hillert, Klaus Jahnke, William Kaczynski, Sean Leon, Peter Lobbenberg, Neil MacGregor, Nadine Meisner, David Nieper, Frederick Michael Pick, Oriel Sonnet, David Weisz, Ruth Williams and Professor Rachel Worth.

For their support through help with research and providing contacts I would like to thank Monica Bohm Duchen, Rachel Dickson, Celia Joicey, Sarah MacDougall, John March and Rachel Taber. For her help in editing and proofreading the manuscript, my thanks to Sally Wood. The Association of Jewish Refugees kindly allowed me to place a search for subjects in their *Journal*, a call which resulted in many correspondents all of whom I wish to thank. Various archives and libraries were a vital source of information and I am grateful to their staff, including The Victoria & Albert Museum , especially Alexia Kirk, the London College of Fashion, Magdalen College Oxford (especially Ben Taylor), the Tate Gallery archives, the Wiener Library London, the Marks & Spencer archive, Leeds (especially Katie Cameron and her colleagues), the John Smedley archive (especially Jane Middleton-Smith and her volunteers), Live Borders Heritage Hub (especially Zilla

Oddy), and Hawick Museum and Shona Sinclair. Their volunteer Gordon MacDonald was also most helpful.

To all those who gave me images or gave me permission to use their images, I am very grateful. These include Eva Aldbrook, Ralph Land, Peter Lobbenberg, Nick Sigler, Freddie Berdach, Richard Donner, Jenny Kagan, Adam Sykes, The Museum of London, the Wiener Library London, Magdalen College Oxford, Charnos Hosiery, Roman Originals, Pringle of Scotland, John Smedley Ltd, Silhouette, Marks & Spencer, Kangol, Launer London Ltd, Ettinger London, Tibor, Heriot-Watt University Heritage Service and their archivist Helen Taylor, and Sekers Fabrics Ltd.

To the many others who helped or supported me in any way with this project, I am deeply grateful.

I wish to thank the Martin Miller and Hannah Norbert-Miller Trust for its generous financial support for the publication of this book.

List of Illustrations

1. Linkers at work in the Sigler factory, courtesy of Nick Sigler
2. Otto Lucas, courtesy of Rolf Andersen
3. Otto Lucas pillar box hat, courtesy of the Museum of London
4. Ettinger pouch, courtesy of Robert Ettinger
5. Gerry Ettinger (right) at press launch, courtesy of Robert Ettinger
6. Kangol wool Monty beret, courtesy of Sean Leon
7. 'Paris inspired' article, *St Michael's News*, p.2, 29 April 1955, courtesy of The M & S Company Archive
8. 'Television, The Dress Designer and Dressmaker' article, *Sparks*, p. 22, April 1957, courtesy of The M & S Company Archive
9. Hans Schneider at office party, *Sparks* p.22 April 1957, courtesy of The M & S Company Archive
10. 'Radiante' corset, courtesy of Peter Lobbenberg
11. 'Silhouette' swimwear, courtesy of Peter Lobbenberg
12. Hosiery factory H. Sigler in Chemnitz, courtesy of Nick Sigler
13. Thomas Heatherwick with printed scarf from Elisabeth Tomalin's archive, courtesy of Thomas Heatherwick
14. Tibor design 'Spaceflight', 1957, the same year as the Sputnik satellite. Courtesy of Sam Reich.
15. 'Aldo 01' Sekers, courtesy of Sekers
16. Bernat Klein printed dress, image courtesy of Heriot-Watt University Heritage Service, image by Douglas McBride
17. Anne Crawford – Twinset, courtesy of Pringle of Scotland
18. Vintage Pringle advertisement, courtesy of Pringle of Scotland
19. 'Wabena' Bowties, courtesy of Freddie Berdach
20. Walter Berdach, courtesy of Freddie Berdach
21. Hornflowa advertisement
22. Charnos vintage advertisement, courtesy of Charnos Hosiery
23. Charnos 'Killer Figure Hourglass Control Tights', courtesy of Charnos Hosiery
24. John Smedley design, 1938, courtesy of John Smedley

25 John Smedley, contemporary advertisement, courtesy of John Smedley
26 Tick-a-Tee advertisement, ca. 1960s, courtesy of Francis Steiner
27 Hans Schneider with 'Mutti', Anne Ayars and Kathleen Ferrier, courtesy of Magdalen College Oxford Archives
28 Hans Schneider with Russian dancers, courtesy of Magdalen College Oxford Archives
29 Illo's grandfather's shop, courtesy of the Wiener Library, London
30 Illo with her mother, courtesy of the Wiener Library, London
31 Launer bag, 'Traviata multi-cal F2', courtesy of Launer
32 Queen visits Launer factory, courtesy of Launer
33 Double Two vintage advertisement, courtesy of Richard Donner
34 Double Two label collage, courtesy of Richard Donner
35 Frank Usher vintage advertisement, courtesy of Roman Originals
36 Frank Usher advertisement of 1989, courtesy of Roman Originals
37 Lord and Lady Kagan with Gannex coat, courtesy of Jenny Kagan
38 Joseph Kagan with Harold Wilson, courtesy of Jenny Kagan
39 Natasha and Alex Kroll, courtesy of William Kroll
40 Frank Bratman as a young man, courtesy of Adam Sykes
41 Molyneux outfit. Drawing by Eva Aldbrook, courtesy of Eva Aldbrook
42 (Left to right) Simon Djanogly, Jack Djanogly, Edward Sieff, Moshe Sharett (second Prime Minister of Israel (c. 1960), courtesy of Sir Harry Djanogly
43 Landsberger twins in Berlin, courtesy of Ralph Land
44 Soscha Landsberger, self-portrait, courtesy of Ralph Land
45 Eva Aldbrook hats, courtesy of Eva Aldbrook
46 Eva Aldbrook Molyneux outfit, courtesy of Eva Aldbrook
47 Queen visits Launer factory, cutting cake, courtesy of Launer

Introduction

German fashion? How many names spring to the minds of British or American fashion fans? Jil Sander may be known to them, and surely Karl Lagerfeld is German, but they probably do not know that the American-sounding Betty Barclay was actually founded by one Max Berk in Heidelberg in 1938. There are also still some German brands trading today which had their roots in a darker time: the seemingly British shoe and boot company, Doc Martens, was created by an enterprising doctor who had served in the German army, the Wehrmacht, and whose name was Dr Klaus Märtens. In 1945 he had the idea of using leftover rubber from the former airfields of the Luftwaffe to make extremely hard-wearing boots which became popular with British working men.[1] It is ironic that this example of turning the sword into a ploughshare itself turned into the boots adopted by skinheads and extreme right-wing groups given to violence in 1970s Britain. Happily, Doc Martens have now settled into a fairly mainstream brand worn by students, workmen and others as a democratic form of clothing, much like denim jeans.

One brand with a more sinister story is that of Hugo Boss, for Boss was the businessman who made the brown shirts for the early members of the National Socialist (Nazi) party. His company then made the black shirts for the SS and designed the Hitler Youth uniforms. Some might say he was just a businessman doing his job and providing employment – all true. But Boss used slave labour during the war, not something any company could be proud of.[2] The company has changed hands many times since, but the dark story lives on.

This is a history of German fashion too, but it is also about a special group of refugees during a time of great movements of refugees from outside Europe to Britain and other European countries. It is a reminder that people who come to this country under straitened circumstances do not only take, but also give: they provide labour and employment, they create wealth for the national economy using their different skills and expertise. And the German-speaking refugees from

Nazism gave us an unexpected bonus: they enriched our cultural lives too, particularly in the arts and music, one even founding his own theatre, finding that there were none locally. They sponsored galleries and exhibitions, as do their children and grandchildren today.

It is also a tale of clothes, those most personal of items. In their suitcases, the refugees brought a piece of their home with them, clothes which perhaps were the size and shape of their relatives, perhaps still with a lingering smell of their perfume or pipe smoke about them. How precious they were, especially when they were the last reminder of dear ones left behind in the desperate rush for safety in Britain.

In this book the refugees' stories are told: their origins are tracked down where possible; the tales are told of the persecution forcing them to flee to Britain and of their struggle to make a living here in the difficult 1930s, only for the Second World War to break out. This research is incomplete and some of the stories have gaps in them. Their documents may have been destroyed in the war (either by Allied or Axis bombing here or in Europe) or, in some cases, their families and companies did not keep records. This means that the trajectory of the refugees from Nazism who made their mark on the British fashion industry can for the most part be seen in traces.

Here we find that the outstandingly successful milliner Otto Lucas left a legacy of fabulous hats, like the ones he sold to Greta Garbo or the Duchess of Windsor. It is easy to find them in the Victoria & Albert Museum, London or in New York where he sold thousands. He appears briefly, in some memoirs, smiling out of photographs, yet his voice is strangely silent. Where are his letters? His diary? Who knows his story? Then, by contrast, there is the story of the charming Mr Gerhard Ettinger, whose beautifully crafted leather wallets are still made today under the auspices of his son, Robert, and collected by Japanese connoisseurs. Exceptionally, the story of Hans Schneider, Head of Design at Marks & Spencer is recorded in rich detail, including his friendship with Benjamin Britten and Peter Pears, his involvement with the Bolshoi Ballet, his work and relationship with the artist John Piper.

On the whole, this story should be seen as a garment made of exquisite lace, the tiny holes are a part of the fabric itself and none the less appealing for them. Those stories which are more complete can guide us towards filling the gaps in others less so, for after all they have much in common.

This is not a closed chapter of history by any means, as several of the refugee companies are trading still, not a few under Royal Warrants. But it is a new chapter of fashion history: it is the untold story of how the refugees from Hitler clothed, employed and enriched us in more ways than we might have expected.

Notes

1. https://www.campaignlive.co.uk/article/great-british-brands-dr-martens-originally-using-rubber-salvaged-luftwaffe-dms-attained-cultural-significance-linked-football-punk/154761, accessed 8 January 2018.
2. https://en.wikipedia.org/wiki/Hugo_Boss, accessed 8 January 2018.

CHAPTER 1

German and Austrian Fashion between the Wars

Berlin and *Konfektion*

This story of German fashion started in the Weimar Republic, the regime which followed Germany's defeat in the First World War. Despite the political uncertainty of the period (1919–33) and the tremendous swings both upwards and downwards in the economy, the Weimar Republic was a time of activity and innovation in nearly all areas of cultural life. This was the time when German cinema flourished, when actresses like Marlene Dietrich made their name. The huge UFA film company produced films for the silent era while in the theatre Berthold Brecht's plays were performed using ground-breaking ideas, such as his *Verfremdungseffekt*, the alienation technique designed to create an educative distance between audience and players. Staging and costumes changed also in an attempt to show symbolically rather than literally where the action was taking place and what the characters were like. Photography boomed, soon taking its place alongside illustration in fashion journals and starting to appear in picture books. There were the satirical cabarets, known to us now through Christopher Isherwood's *Goodbye to Berlin*. There was new music, new architecture, new graphic design and then there was fashion.

Fashion exploded in this period in Berlin to a degree few of us can imagine, for it was a phenomenon. It belonged to a moment of liberal lifestyles and sexual freedom. The reason may have to do with the new cult of individualism, because in the 1920s clothing had become democratised. No longer did women have to go to expensive dressmakers to have new clothes made. Weimar women were changing: they had the vote; they went out to work in offices and shops, they had enough money to be consumers of fashion, albeit the less expensive variety. Moreover, they were themselves involved in fashion as journalists, illustrators, photographers, models, saleswomen and makers of clothes in all levels of production.[1] Now they were using public transport to get to work, as well as taking part in sporting activities such as cycling or tennis. They needed to be able to move freely. From the early garments in the first decade of the twentieth century which no longer featured a sharply nipped-in waist, dresses evolved quickly, becoming shorter, flimsier and increasingly made out of new, easily washable synthetics. Almost everyone could have more clothes and look modern. Bobbed hair and bobbed frocks were everywhere. Suddenly, in Berlin, which was the centre of the trend, there were fashion magazines, but also fashion film magazines, films showing fashion, films in which fashionable actresses acted, fashion teas, fashion shows and above all, fashion companies. These were not for the most part couture houses but instead what in German is called *Konfektion,* or in French *prêt à porter* (ready-to-wear).

The sexual freedom of the era, which was also expressed in fashion, applied to gay men too. Homosexuals, then as now, played their part in the success of the clothing trade and Berlin was a city where they could live and work in freedom. Homosexuality was a term apparently dreamed up by an Austrian and Germany was the home of research into same-sex relations.[2] Sigmund Freud's work was just one part of this new area of scholarship, which remained largely Germanic until after the Second World War. By the late 1880s, police unofficially tolerated homosexual activity, in stark contrast to the draconian and cruel measures taken against Anglo-Saxon men, Oscar Wilde being only one. No wonder then that gay men flocked to Berlin where there was a vibrant scene until the Nazis put an end to it. There was literally no other city like it, having as it did in the 1920s and early 1930s gay clubs, gay magazines and gay films, all allowed. Several gay men working in the German rag trade were also Jewish and forced to flee from the Nazis and come to Britain, where homosexuality was strictly illegal still, a double burden.

However, notwithstanding the liberal climate, in Germany as in Britain, there were some echelons of society where homosexuality was frowned upon, and that included some upper-class Jewish families. One who felt that he had to hide his sexuality was Wilfrid Israel, the grandson of the founder of the Nathan Israel department store in Berlin, for which he was groomed to take over as MD (see below). His biographer noted on his sexuality, 'For the Berlin-Jewish community, this was unmentionable. The famous permissiveness of Weimar Berlin did not touch the Berlin merchant society in which Wilfrid spent most of his time.'[3] Ironically, this secrecy which he was forced to cultivate stood him in good stead later in his life's work which was to rescue thousands of German Jews during the Nazi regime (see Chapter 2). Like a spy, he was able to dodge and dive, to move between Nazi officers and politicians. He was half British too, which added yet another thread to his ability to be chameleon-like. He died in 1943, never able to express the 'love that dare not speak its name'.[4]

Given this general mood of freedom of expression in Berlin, was there a difference in what people wore in Germany and Britain in the inter-war period? One person who can help with a comparison was Alice Newman, a German refugee fashion illustrator and designer who first came to London in 1936 where her husband was trying to get his medical qualifications recognized so that the family could settle in safety in England. She had come from Berlin and had excellent training, both at the Berlin Charlottenburg Kunstgewerbeschule (KGS for short) and at the famous Reimann School (see below). Her first impression of the clothes she saw was that they were mostly of dark fabrics, using lots of felt, and very conservative.[5] For the most part, however, British and German clothes were fairly similar and any difference was not obvious to the eye. The real distinction between the clothes lay in the origins and influences behind the look of the clothes. In Germany, fashion was political.

German clothes had evolved through foreign influences. First came a reforming movement of the 1890s in Germany, part of which is a story preceding the refugees and their world but linking Germany and England through the name of Jaeger. Nineteenth-century Germany, the country that gave us pilates, homeopathy and many health diet regimes was also taking a long, hard look at clothing and finding it unhealthy. Gustav Jäger (1832–1917) was a naturalist, interested in entomology, chemistry and anthropology. The system of clothing associated with his name originates from *Die Normalkleidung als Gesundheitsschutz*

Linkers at work in the H. Sigler factory, Chemnitz (courtesy of Nick Sigler)

('Standardized Apparel for Health Protection', 1880), wherein he advocated the wearing of rough fabrics, such as wool, 'close to the skin', objecting especially to the use of any kind of plant fibre. The teachings of Jäger inspired the creation of the Jaeger clothing brand, which shed its health clothing image along the way.[6] Jaeger was established by British businessman Lewis Tomalin as 'Dr Jaeger's Sanitary Woollen System Co Ltd' in 1884, importing the clothes first from Germany and then five years later producing the garments in Britain.

By coincidence, Tomalin was the family that one of the most successful German Jewish émigrés, Elisabeth Tomalin née Wallach (on Tomalin, see Chapter 6) married into. Jaeger's writings about the value of wearing animal fibres (not cotton) next to the skin had attracted many, including explorers such as Ernest Shackleton, who wore their undergarments. Jaeger had received its first Royal Warrant by 1910. The next generation of Tomalins, Lewis's son, brought modern design to Jaeger clothes in the 1920s, now worn by the new breed of young women who worked in shops or offices, independent and earning, as well as people from other social classes. Their advertisement of that time claimed 'You can no longer tell a shop girl from a Duchess, thanks to Jaeger'.[7] One of the most famous fans of Jaeger was George Bernard Shaw, who apparently always wore wool next to the skin under his tweed suits. Perhaps this advertisement was what inspired his play *Pygmalion*?

An important step towards liberating German women from their restrictive clothing had come with the first really innovative shapes seen in Paul Poiret's designs. This Parisian designer (1879–1944) was truly groundbreaking: in the first decade of the twentieth century, designing the earliest examples of loose, flowing clothes for centuries, often based on foreign garments such as kimonos and made of silk and similar lightweight fabrics. European and American women loved his exotic clothes, hinting sometimes at the Ballet Russes which were all the rage then, and indeed Poiret's dresses invited the wearer to dance and sway to show off the movement of the fabric.

Clothes, which are a reflection of social and sexual movements, are an important sector of the economy too. Ever since Germany was united in 1871, clothing had been one of their major export items. As one fashion historian noted: 'By the time World War One erupted, annual domestic clothing sales had increased to 250 million marks [from 100 in 1890]. And remarkably, fashion-related export sales were more than quadruple that amount.'[8] No wonder then that when the Second World War broke out only nineteen years later, the government was keen to keep such major revenue coming in to fund the expensive war machinery.

Jewish Clothiers

At the heart of this explosion of making and buying clothes in Berlin at this time were the protagonists of the *Konfektion* success – Jews – for it was above all Jewish Germans in the interwar period who shaped the fashion scene. As one author explained, Jewish women were over-represented among designers, photographers, consumers and shopkeepers.⁹ The whole trade, *Konfektion,* was markedly Jewish, although there has been controversy about the exact percentage of clothing production companies typically active in Berlin's busy square, the Hausvogteiplatz, that were owned by Jews. Uwe Westphal, a researcher who has devoted much of his professional life to campaigning for recognition of the destruction of this creative and lucrative industry by the Nazis (having to have police protection in the face of possible threats of violence for his efforts),¹⁰ maintains that no more than 49 per cent of the companies were Jewish owned, as compared to official Nazi figures of around 90 per cent.¹¹

Nevertheless, that 49 per cent was still an over-representation, given that Jews only made up about 1 per cent of Germany's population at that time, with a somewhat higher percentage in the large conurbations such as Berlin. Jews were well placed to succeed in this field for historical reasons. In the Middle Ages in what was to become Germany and in parts of what later became the Austro-Hungarian Empire, Jews were excluded from many economic activities, such was the deeply embedded antisemitism and fear from Christian traders that Jews would take 'their' trade. For example, Jews were never allowed to join the guilds necessary to carry out a particular craft.¹² They were certainly forbidden to sell or make new clothes. It was this ban which led them to do what they were allowed to: they sold second-hand clothes, pieces of used fabric, even rags, which is where the expression 'the rag trade' comes from.¹³

Pedlars of such goods wandered throughout Central Europe in the medieval period and were a familiar sight on the roads and at fairs. It was a very hard life, but there were very few possibilities for them to feed their families and this was one of them. Before the Industrial Revolution new clothes were hard to come by, with no mass production of fabrics, with the garments laboriously hand cut and sewn, so that second-hand clothes were much in demand. Jewish pedlars walked through the countryside and its villages selling their wares. By dint of traipsing for miles around German lands, the wandering Jews got to know their customers, their needs and tastes, and who would buy what and for how much.

It was in the nineteenth century that in Prussia at least Jews were finally emancipated, a process which had started after the French Revolution. Once Germany was unified into one country in 1871, Jews at last acquired their freedom after centuries of being officially treated as inferior and unworthy of equality with Christians. Of course, antisemitism never disappeared, and the exclusion of Jews from many professions continued unofficially.[14]

Jewish traders in second-hand cloth were ideally placed to set up shop at the end of the nineteenth century, once they were allowed to, and this they did with gusto. From small tailoring shops and fabric stores, many quickly moved up to the next logical step that was the latest development in retail – the department store – and they took these stores to the next level. The first of these had been set up in Paris and the way of life in such shops was described in novels like Zola's *Au Bonheur des Dames* (*The Ladies' Paradise*). They tended to be rather Rococo affairs with much gilding and swirly, theatrical décor. Soon, the phenomenon spread throughout Europe. It was in the German provinces in the nineteenth century that the first department stores in Germany started life with Wertheim, Karstadt and Tietz becoming household names, and based on the ornate French model.[15]

Often these stores had been founded by Jews from the Eastern provinces (what is today Poland or Russia), who made their way west as their prosperity grew. Although Wertheim and Tietz outlived 'Aryanisation' (see Chapter 2) and survived into the new millennium, Karstadt alone still trades today. Other retail giants in their day were Gerson and Manheimer.

A different version of these department stores sprang up in bigger German cities in the 1920s. They were sleek, modernist buildings, designed by the likes of Erich Mendelsohn, who was later to flee to safety in Britain where he designed buildings including the fabulous De La Warr Pavilion in Bexhill-on-Sea, with co-architect and another émigré, Serge Chermayeff. In Germany it was Erich Mendelsohn who built a chain of stores for the entrepreneur Salman Schocken.[16]

The Schocken brothers had started out as humble merchants in the Eastern provinces, doing well and moving up the economic and social ladder swiftly. Their department stores in cities like Chemnitz and Berlin were organised on scientific lines so that staff, customers and goods alike could move around in the optimum ergonomic way.

Additionally, these stores were not just devoid of ornament and utterly state of the art, they featured what was really an early form of corporate design. All the fixtures and fittings, down to the uniforms of the staff and the stationery, were designed by the architect and his team. It is only recently that researchers have begun to realise what a rich source of social documentation such stores provide. They were like theatres where the world of fashion played out, because it was in these stores that clothes were sold, shown off in fashion shows, and worn by modish customers and salesgirls alike. In the late 1920s, Kaufhof, Schocken and the other large stores were employing between 10,000 and 20,000 people. In Berlin, the capital of Germany and the biggest city, which was the epicentre of fashion, the best-known store was Nathan Israel.[17] By the 1930s it was one of the largest stores in Berlin and was referred to with pride as the 'Berlin Harrods'. So Jewish Germans were not only successful entrepreneurs in the clothing sector but were innovative merchandisers, bringing new business practices and a fresh look to the industry.[18]

Vienna

Vienna was the second German-speaking city of fashion after Berlin and had been the capital (with Budapest as a secondary capital) not just of Austria but of what was left of the Austro-Hungarian Empire after the First World War. It still had the magnificent Baroque buildings and the decorative beauty missing from some German cities. The Austrians' defeat in the war had caused the disbanding of the Empire and now countries like Hungary and Czechoslovakia became independent, leaving Vienna an ornate and monumental capital of a small country. The interwar period was known as the First Republic following the abdication of the Emperor and was a time, like the Weimar Republic, of huge social, political and economic change. The social-democrat regime that presided over the capital earned it the name 'Red Vienna', a city where the arts flourished. But even before the First World War there had been an unusually rich and active cultural scene, dominated by the presence of new twelve-tone music by Arnold Schoenberg, the sometimes scandalous paintings of Gustav Klimt or Egon Schiele and the similarly shocking plays of Arthur Schnitzler.

The fashion scene in Vienna between the wars was somewhat more conservative than in Berlin, perhaps luxury more than modernity sums up the prevailing taste. However, there had been a creative period just before and after the First World War, in the form particularly of Emilie Flöge (1874–1953) and her sisters.[19] This enterprising woman had been one of the painter Gustav Klimt's many conquests, but had realised early on that their partnership would be better as a creative one rather than a romantic one. She produced in her studio garments that reflected the Paris fashions of the time, a looser more flowing interpretation but not one that went to the extremes, still unpopular at that time, of the unstructured 'reform' look. (Some *Konfektion* shops in this city had their origins in tailoring firms who had made uniforms for the vast Austro-Hungarian army or for the Imperial Court.)[20] Jewish tailors from *shtetls* in the far-flung borders of the Empire often made their way through the generations to the capitals, Vienna or Budapest, where there was plenty of demand for their work. Viennese style was also influenced by an abiding love of English dressing: tweeds, wonderful woollens and excellent tailoring.

Added to the mix were the Austrian traditional *Trachten*, the Alpine costumes with loden greens and greys, embroidered Alpine flowers and tailored suits. The look and feel of Vienna in the 1920s is recreated in a memoir by Trude Kanter, a Viennese milliner of that time. In Kanter's *Some Girls, Some Hats and Hitler*, the narrator describes her life and work in the city before she, as a Jew, is forced to flee to London when the German Army marches in.[21] In the book, she often describes the outfits that she wore in pre-war Vienna: 'In those days, it was considered chic to wear Tyrolean outfits for sport and travel. Emerald-green braid ran down each side of my slim, grey flannel skirt. My grey flannel jacket had a tiny emerald green stand-up collar, wide revers and cuffs. The buttons down the front were made of horn.'[22]

Local costume, *Trachten*, was worn commonly even in big cities like Munich, not just for festivals but as street wear: embroidered dirndl skirts and bodices, as well as lederhosen and traditional hats with *Gamsbart* (chamois beard) for the men. This fashion even travelled to Britain, becoming all the rage there too, as illustrations from *Vogue* and other journals of the time testify.

Importantly also, sports clothing was developed in Austria because of the mountain sports that were enjoyed in the Alps, skiing in particular. Long, loosely-knit jumpers were flexible and allowed for free movement while keeping the skier warm. So many fashions have developed from sportswear of course, with men's formal tailcoats being a form of riding coat, the split back section making it possible to straddle the saddle. And one only has to think of the current craze for tracksuits and trainers, which would never have been worn as street wear before the 1970s. Sporty knitwear was something that the Austrian refugees brought to Britain.

As she relates in her book, Trude Kanter fell in love with Walter, the man of her dreams, with whom she would eventually escape to Britain. At the start of their relationship they began to frequent Vienna's best cafés, Demels for example. 'Walter wears a dark grey bespoke flannel suit; hand-made white brogues with black toes; a white silk shirt; a tie. No doubt all of this came from Knize, his tailor. How handsome he is.'[23] Knize was not only the source of the most sought-after menswear in Vienna but was part of the mythology of Vienna – the artist Oskar Kokoschka bought his clothes there in exchange for his paintings.

Knize provided a magical shopping experience, one which was due largely to Ernst Dryden (1887–1938). Dryden was originally Ernst Deutsch but as an ardent anglophile changed his name, thereby at the same time making it less obviously Jewish. He was a ground-breaking designer, illustrator and entrepreneur whose career in Berlin and Vienna (and later New York and Hollywood) links these periods of heightened cultural activity and indeed he contributed much to them himself.²⁴ The story of the writing of the biography of this multi-talented Jewish artist came about in a Hollywood way that seems appropriate for one so glamorous. Two abandoned trunks of letters, photos and magazine covers were found by the author, Anthony Lipmann, who was distantly related to a woman who for decades was the object of Dryden's affections, Hello (Helena) Budischowsky. Lipmann sums up Dryden's career, saying it 'grew out of the ferment of Vienna in the last days of the Austro-Hungarian Empire when writers, musicians and architects, as well as the new psychoanalysts, contributed to the life of that city in a way that has not been seen before or since'.

Returning to Vienna after a stint in Berlin as a poster artist, Dryden, walking through the park one morning, immaculate as ever, was stopped by a lady who demanded to know where his clothes were from. Hearing that he had designed them himself, Gisela Wolff summoned him to work for her menswear company, Knize. Dryden was happy to accept and started to think about the right look for this company. The elegant Austrian had often visited London and loved what he saw. Not only did he admire the quality of the suits but he liked the modesty of the British non-advertising, where instead of chasing after clients, tailoring firms quietly inserted the words 'Made in England' or 'By Royal Appointment' which spoke volumes for themselves. Dryden devised a clearly-lettered logo for Knize. The store had been designed by the most famous Viennese architect, Adolf Loos, whose motto was 'ornament is crime' and was consequently an elegant building with simple lines. Dryden added to this look, creating an identity, using the lettering everywhere including in brochures and on labels, much as the German entrepreneur Salman Schocken had done for his department stores. Dryden used the theme of the ultimate gentleman's sport, polo, as a theme. Indeed, the contemporary American designer Ralph Lauren acknowledged his debt to Dryden when devising his own anglophile range, 'Polo'.

Dryden created a series of men's toiletries, a first for those days. One of the lines, which came out in 1924 was the men's eau de toilette 'Knize Ten', a fragrance featuring notes of leather, patchouli and sandalwood. Still sold today, it is worn by connoisseurs all over the world who enthuse that it is the perfect adjunct to an impeccably tailored suit, such as one from Knize in Vienna. The inspiration behind the name, which also accounts for its longevity, is explained by one contemporary critic:

> Ten is known as the highest player-rated handicap in polo. For Dryden, polo was the symbol of English elegance. Dryden also designed the packaging for the 'Knize Ten' fragrance line, which still exists today in the same timeless design. The shoe designer, Manolo Blahnik, for one, names the fragrance as his favourite, in fact his father and grandfather had loved and worn it too. [25]

The shop Knize, too, still trades in Vienna and has many famous names on its list of clients: Marilyn Monroe, Josephine Baker, Marlene Dietrich, Billy Wilder and King Juan Carlos of Spain all bought clothes there. After Gisela retired, the Wolffs' son Fritz took over the store along with his wife, Hello Budischowsky, and spread the Knize brand to other cities including Berlin and Paris, something which was possible thanks to Dryden's creation of the Knize identity. After the *Anschluss* (the German occupation of Austria in 1938) Hello, who like her in-laws was Jewish, moved to London where she again set up shop.

Paris

Konfektion operated in the 1920s and 1930s in Berlin and Vienna, in some cases in 'vertical' firms, that is to say where all the different processes happened under one roof. However, the design of clothes took place for the most part in Paris, the centre of *haute couture*. High fashion had its origins at the end of the nineteenth century with couturiers such as Worth and Paul Poiret. From then onwards, Paris was synonymous with couture, enjoying an interwar Golden Age with designers such as Coco Chanel, Schiaparelli and Lanvin. For this reason, German and Austrian buyers, copyists and businessmen (as well as British and American ones) flocked to Paris for the twice-yearly collections to see the new designs. But there was a dilemma here for

German clients – France was still the enemy. Although the Franco-Prussian war was some thirty years back, feelings of enmity lived on. Had they known it, the First World War was only a year or two away and the two countries would be yet again at each other's throats.

The love-hate relationship with French fashion which had started even before the twentieth century continued to be problematic up to and including Hitler's Third Reich, so could and should German women adopt the new loose fashions of Poiret? In Poiret's favour was his friendship with the Berlin *Konfektion* magnates H[errmann]. Gerson and V[alentin]. Manheimer, both Jewish and both major trendsetters whose influence could make or break designers.[26] This is, no doubt, why Poiret launched his models in Berlin in 1911. The outbreak of the First World War, however, meant that his success was short-lived, as it was considered unpatriotic to buy French fashion and in any case, immoral to flaunt fashionable clothes while German blood was being spilt on the killing fields of Europe. In 1916 the association for women's clothing manufacturers began a campaign to make Berlin, not Paris, the centre of fashion production.

But in the interwar period, going to Paris for the new collections was an exciting and creative adventure. Trude Kanter describes in detail getting the sleeper train to Paris and arriving at her hotel, which would have been full of her fellow countrymen at this time of year.[27] The challenge was to see the new models and be able to recreate the design back home without taking photographs or sketching, crimes for which they would have been forcibly ejected from the salon. Her friend Mitzi, another milliner, gives her useful hints for when they are allowed to handle the new hats: she is to use the length of her thumbs and fingers as measuring devices, and to memorise the colour, shape and trimming. Such procedures would take place under the shrewd eyes of Madame, the salon *diréctrice*, who was just waiting to pounce on possible plagiarists. In all the salons of Paris, Germans and others were frantically rushing to the toilets after the show, sketching as fast as possible the details of the models before they were forgotten. The hotels were buzzing with foreign designers and buyers, drawing and phoning the office back home. Some even rushed from salon to train station, to get back to Berlin before their rivals. The Paris trips were also associated with 'goings on', then as now people took advantage of being away to have sexual relationships outside their marriages. Gay men did too, like Mr Kohn in Uwe Westphal's fictional but well-researched account of *Konfektion* in the Nazi period.[28]

However, the 'corrupting' French influence was only one dilemma for the German authorities of the 1930s. Berlin's greatest triumph in the clothing sector was the Jewish *Konfektion* houses – they were the ones that brought style, taste and income to the sector. But yet again, Jews were being made the main scapegoats for Germany's defeat in the First World War. Although in reality, Jewish Germans had volunteered for military service in their thousands, anxious to prove that they were as German and patriotic as their Gentile neighbours, the antisemitic press and nascent fascist groups labelled Jews as cowards who had let Germany down on the battlefield and off. This, despite Iron Crosses and other military distinctions awarded to Jewish soldiers being proof to the contrary. (In the Third Reich, Jews with military distinctions were initially spared persecution, but this was short lived.)

By the 1920s and into the early 1930s, as in Britain and France, as well as the shorter skirts, waists were dropped, long necklaces and scarves were worn and hair was cut short. Geometric shapes in clothes and as pattern on textiles reflected the influence of the new Bauhaus school (see below). Berlin fashion was more extreme than elsewhere in Germany; it was here that one saw monocle-wearing vamps and cross-dressing women (and men), but elsewhere clothes looked much as they did in Britain, with variations in their knitwear and underwear (German apartments had central heating before British houses did) and there was a general love in Europe for sporty knitwear, fine and warm.

The German Textile Industry

There are no clothes without fabric of course, and textile manufacturing and design was an area in which Central European refugees excelled. When forced to flee, they would bring their technology, colour, new pattern traditions and textures to British life. After centuries of linen, wool and cotton, now in the twentieth century, in continental Europe at least, synthetic fabrics arrived on the market, something which seemed at the time like the Holy Grail of textiles.[29] Nowadays of course, the consumer sees natural fibres as desirable, allowing the body to breathe (unlike polyester for example, which causes the body to perspire and does not allow the sweat or heat to escape easily through the fabric) and also having an organic quality which distinguishes them from synthetic fabrics. These desirable qualities, however, were not sought after during the 1920s and 1930s, when most families did not possess a washing machine, when much work was dirty and people lived in coal-heated homes and the air was smokier and dirtier than now. Garments which would wash easily and dry quickly, possibly then requiring no ironing, were what women dreamed of, and it was almost exclusively women who were expected to carry out this work then. Anyone who would like to have a better feel for how important this almost mythical new fabric was in those early days should watch the film *The Man in the White Suit*.[30] The British Film Institute website explains the plot:

> *The Man in the White Suit* relentlessly works through the implications of an apparently desirable scientific breakthrough – the invention of a dirt-resistant, unbreakable fabric – by a timid genius of a chemist, Sidney Stratton (Alec Guinness), so nondescript that even his own colleagues barely notice him. Sidney's invention at first excites his boss, who spies a commercial advantage – until he realises, along with his business rivals, that clothes that never wear out would mean the death of the entire industry.[31]

Different countries researched different methods of producing fibres: some from organic products like wood, processed chemically to make it develop long fibres, referred to as regenerated fibres, and these included viscose, lyocel and others. Synthetic fibres come from inorganic materials and Britain produced the first polyester in this way using coal tar, although it was a German refugee who first saw its potential for clothing (on this see Double Two). It was also Britain which first came up with acrylics, the main producer being the Courtauld firm. America had led the field in experimenting with mineral oils, producing nylon during the Second World War, which was then used to make strong parachutes. By the end of the war nylon's potential as a textile for making women's stockings was realised and demand soon rocketed. Before then there had only been the extremes of silk for the wealthy, or wool, lisle, distinctly unglamorous and ill-fitting for the great majority of women. As will be seen, the war was a make or break time for many manufacturers, and synthetics were part of this story.

Press and Publicity

Then as now, people enjoyed reading about fashion as well as buying and wearing fashionable clothes. More than any other publication, it was the German magazine *Die Dame* which was the source of the latest trends, of the most elegant pictures, of the best-written articles. It has been called a more erudite version of *Vogue*. Again, here it is Ernst Dryden's story which helps us recreate the journal, which is a necessary link for not only did *Die Dame* cease trading in 1943, but very few copies are extant. Fortunately the cache that Dryden's biographer Lipmann saved also contained some rare covers designed by Dryden, who worked for the magazine for seven years.

Along with *Elegante Welt* which differed in that it was exclusively a fashion magazine, *Die Dame* was the most popular and widely-read journal for those who wanted to know the latest in clothing styles, but also in literature and social habits, and who wanted their illustrations to be state of the art, whether photographs or hand drawn. It featured work by authors such as Colette or Stefan Zweig. At its height the circulation was around 60,000 per issue. The publisher was Ullstein, a giant concern owning book and newspaper publishing departments as well as a printing works (and its own fleet of aeroplanes) and was created and owned by the Jewish Ullstein family, some members of which would escape to England after the Nazis seized the company.[32]

Ernst Dryden produced covers for this prestigious magazine while he was living in Paris, so he was ideally placed to report on the *haute couture* scene. As a fashion designer himself, he could give particularly nuanced descriptions of clothes seen in the salons that season. He was given free rein in that respect and all doors were open to him; after all, not only was he a connoisseur but he had designed for Coco Chanel personally. Moreover he could remember designs with his photographic memory, drawing them later and sending them straight to Berlin where they could be copied by the *Konfektionäre* to sell in their shops. This was how most Germans got their taste of Paris, just as if they were looking through shop windows, probably unable to afford the trip themselves.[33] Dryden drew heavily on his beloved muse, Hello, for inspiration for his sketches as she was to him the embodiment of the New Woman – petite and with a boyish figure and cropped hair.

Another contributor to *Die Dame* was Vicki Baum, an Austrian Jewish writer who later emigrated to the USA where some of her novels were adapted for films. In Berlin, she understood the fashion victim of the Weimar period, just as well as did Peter York, the English author who recognised and satirised the Sloane Ranger tribe in London in the 1970s. One article by Baum in *Die Dame* from 1927 focused on her 'friend' Yosi, who was a 'copyist'. Not a secretary or an illustrator but simply someone who copied others: she had her hair bobbed the minute other women did; she flips through fashion magazines; goes to fashion teas and wonders why oh why can she not stand out in a crowd, just for once?[34]

Photography

In the 1920s and early 1930s, the relatively new craft of photography gained in popularity and developed technically too. Here, companies like Leitz produced the first lightweight hand-held cameras. Also, Germany was probably the first to have popular magazines illustrated by photographs, the *Berliner Illustrirte* from Ullstein being the best known. Photojournalism was born in the Weimar Republic, in Berlin in particular, from where several of those who really invented the profession were forced to flee to England or America. One of the best known of these was Stefan Lorant, who was the founding editor of the iconic *Picture Post* weekly news magazine in Britain to where he escaped as a left-wing anti-Nazi. Photogravure, which was a relatively new technique (used later on the *Picture Post*), meant that photos could be reproduced almost endlessly without reduction in quality. The images were prized for their rich, dark but nuanced blacks, which made for dramatic shots ideal for photojournalism.

The possibilities for photography as a commercial medium began to become obvious from the 1920s onwards and as one researcher of the period noted, photography revolutionised the representation of fashion. Technically it was now possible to create a more accurate depiction of clothes compared to sketchy illustration. In addition, the new photography became part of the change whereby German and Austrian women increasingly found work opportunities.[35] Photography could provide a freelance career for enterprising women who could set up their own studios. In those days, fashion photography was created by photographers who chose the models and the clothes, set up the scene for the shoot and then sent the photos to a magazine or newspaper, sometimes using an intermediary agent for this purpose.

Two who made their name in commercial photography and who typified the pioneering women engaged in this activity were the founders of ringl + pit, the lower-case names being stylishly modern. Their real names were Ellen Auerbach and Grete Stern, daughters of respectable Jewish middle-class families. Choosing a short, memorable working name became a fashion; Yva (Else Neuländer-Simon) was one of the best known of these. In a charming film, the two women, ringl and pit, now in their eighties, talk with honesty and much humour about how they set up their photographic studio and invented ways of showing off clothes or other products for commercial use.[36] In the film ringl tells how she went to the Bauhaus for a year to study under the Master of Photography there, Walter Peterhans, but found that the rather abstract photos she took in that period were 'less fun' than the ones she took later for the studio. In a sense, their time was a Wild West of commercial photography: the women point out that, in one shot, the model is holding a product, but that the hand in shot actually belongs to one of the photographers standing behind her – they had to be inventive.

Mme D'Ora was the pseudonym of Dora Kallmus, a Viennese photographer who established her studio in Vienna in 1926. Although she had been the first woman admitted to study photography at the Viennese training college, the Lehr-und Versuchsanstalt, she was not allowed to use the chemicals for developing photos because of her gender.[37]

A significant proportion of the women who made successful careers in photography were from Jewish families both in Germany and in the former Austro-Hungarian Empire; in fact it has often been noted that Jews have been significant movers and shakers in photography.[38] For this reason, it was inevitable that in the Nazi period Jewish photographers would emigrate, often to Britain, where some of them at least set up their practices and made their mark on British visual culture (see Elsbeth Juda and others in *The Ambassador*.) Two of the greatest fashion photographers were Horst P. Horst and Edwin Blumenfeld, both of whom founded their careers in Germany but eventually fled to America after some work for London enterprises.

Training

The fact that so many refugees from Nazism were able not just to find work in Britain in the Hungry Thirties but also to succeed, excel even, must be due in part to their excellent training. Indeed, Britain gained not just highly-qualified employees among the refugees but, if the British employers were open to innovation, then they could have an introduction to new products and new business practices. In Germany and Austria there were different routes into *Konfektion*: only one being the traditional apprenticeships, a practice which goes back to the Middle Ages in both Germany and Britain and still continues today, although less so in Britain. However, increasingly in the twentieth century, apprenticeships no longer took place under the guidance of a master tailor in Berlin or Vienna, but instead in a ready-to-wear factory.[39]

Then there were the applied art schools or vocational colleges specifically for textile or tailoring training. Two of the best known of these were the Kunstgewerbeschulen (KGS) or vocational arts schools, one in Charlottenburg, Berlin and the other in Vienna. Similar in ethos to the British Central School of Arts and Crafts (now known as Central St Martins), both provided practical as well as theoretical training. The KGS Wien (Vienna) has an especially illustrious history as its teachers were largely artists or craftsmen working for the Wiener Werkstätte (WW), the studios which dominated the applied arts scene not just in Vienna but in its time across the world, where jewellers, furniture makers, ceramicists, theatre designers and others produced fabulous work.[40] The WW had come into being, with the support of the Scottish Rennie Mackintoshes among others, as a result of the artists' Sezession movement which signalled a break with traditional art of the nineteenth century.[41] The fashion department of the WW was established in 1910, but it took time for the new styles to trickle down into mainstream clothing. Just some of the former students of the KGS Wien who had to escape to safety when the Nazis annexed Austria were the textile designers Marian Mahler and Jacqueline Groag (on Groag, see Textiles), and the ceramicist Lucie Rie (see 'Buttoned Up'). Its prestige is still great and it is no coincidence that the Chanel designer Karl Lagerfeld chose to teach there for two years.

The Bauhaus school had been established in 1919 and is world famous perhaps because after its closure in 1933 some of its teachers and alumni went not just to London but to other countries including to the USA. There they were able to re-establish Bauhaus-like schools, thus perpetuating its design ethos. It has often been said that the art and design scene in Britain was just too conservative in the 1930s for the avant-garde *Bauhäusler*, as the students were known, while America was more forward looking. In fact, there was no fashion department at any of the three incarnations of the school, in Dessau, Weimar and Berlin, the last location of the school where it finally closed down in 1933. The authorities were not only minded to exclude Jewish students but accused the Bauhaus directorate of 'cultural Bolshevism' as many of the staff and students were left wing.

In any case, the Nazis equated Jewishness with Communism, so that they could close down the school for either reason. However, although there was no fashion design course at the Bauhaus, there was always a textile department, one section which admitted women, as surprisingly some courses were closed to female students even at such an *avant-garde* institution. These textile courses were experimental and produced innovative work. Weavers such as Gunta Stölzl and Anni Albers created geometrical designs recognisable as the Bauhaus style. One graduate who came to England to escape the Nazi regime, as an anti-Nazi who was not Jewish, was Margarete Leischner (1908–1970). Having found the Bauhaus a useful playground in which to develop her knowledge of materials, a fundamental part of the Bauhaus training, she became a skilled structural textile designer (as opposed to a surface designer, for example of prints). In 1948, Leischner took over as Head of Weaving at the Royal College of Art in London where she revolutionised the rather folksy weaving practice, updating it to make it fit for the industrial work that RCA graduates would undertake.

So, rather than providing fashion graduates who came to Britain as refugees, the Bauhaus was a source of talented and multi-skilled manpower for a variety of economic activities such as textiles, as in the case of Margarete Leischner. However, some were active in what could be called supportive sections of fashion such as photography. Lucia Moholy trained at the Bauhaus where her husband, the photographer László Moholy Nagy, also taught (see above Photography). Having become a *persona non grata* in Germany, the talented Moholy came to England, where she later taught Elsbeth Juda to take photographs. This tuition enabled Juda to create a career for herself as a freelance fashion photographer for *Vogue* and other prestigious publications, as well as meaning that she was well equipped to become the art director on her husband's journal *The Ambassador*, credited for doing more for British fashion and textile exports than any other publication. (On this see Chapter 5.) The Bauhaus was also noted for its unusual *Vorkurs*, the foundation year, still emulated in British art schools today, which provided its students with an unusual versatility in allowing them to move from one medium to another.

There were also several specialist trade colleges like the Lette Verein in Berlin. Established in 1866, Lette was a technical school for girls which rose to the challenge in the 1920s of bringing new design and excellence in dressmaking skills. Similar in some respects to the Lette Verein, the Reimann Schule, later called the Reimann School,[42] is a relatively unknown school which deserves wider recognition and was actually a refugee itself. It was established in Berlin in 1902 by Albert Reimann, an educationalist and talented gold- and silversmith who had started out by offering children's classes in crafts. Because the Reimann family were Jewish, the school was forced to flee along with many of its teachers and students to London in 1936, where Heinz Reimann, Albert's son, re-established the Reimann in 1937 in the Westminster area for all too short a time. By 1940, with the Blitz at its peak, it was impossible to make the school viable and in 1941 the building was flattened by the Luftwaffe. Meanwhile, the Berlin version had been first 'Aryanised' (that is, taken over by non-Jews) in 1935 and then, irony of ironies, bombed to smithereens by the Allied Bombers. The Reimann was the very embodiment of a kind of cultural transfer, bringing state of the art German practice through its refugee teachers and students to British students, even in the short time it existed.

While the Bauhaus was the world-famous seat in Germany of *avant-garde* art and design, the Berlin-based Reimann, equally modern, focussed more on the vocational training, priding themselves in turning out highly employable designers, photographers and craftsmen. However, there was a certain amount of cross-pollination with the Bauhaus and teachers moved from one to the other. Like the Bauhaus, the Reimann had a photography department then, which in Britain was a rarity at that time. One who took a part-time course in photography at the London Reimann was the novelist Agatha Christie, who was intending to be of help to her archaeologist husband with her new skill. She had not reckoned, however, with the trendy, quasi-surrealist style embraced by the Reimann, and her abstract arrangements of rusty nails were a source of puzzlement to her husband. Who knows whether it influenced any of her stories…[43]

Also, the London Reimann was the very first to have a course in window display. Inevitably, some Berlin alumni escaped to Britain when the school was 'Aryanised' in 1935, becoming 'Kunst und Werk' (Art and Work). Another famous alumna, of the London school at least, was Annely Juda, the gallerist, whose mother had been a fashion student at the Berlin Reimann and had inspired her daughter to study in the evenings at the London Reimann School.

Unlike the Bauhaus then, the Berlin Reimann had its own fashion departments. In the school's early days, just after the First World War, Reimann's fashion department grasped the opportunity to celebrate German fashion, a reaction to defeat by France. But this represented a phase which was soon replaced by a more international outlook. Nevertheless, the school received praise for their patriotic efforts in this field. Needless to say, this praise counted for nothing once the National Socialists were in power and starting to persecute Jewish Germans and destroy their livelihoods.

Hildegard Kölling took over the fashion department from 1928 to 1934, marrying Heinz Reimann, son of the founder, along the way.[44] She introduced the notion that cutting was an essential skill, engaging a teacher who had been at the famous Wiener Werkstätte studios for this purpose. Students should not cut against the fabric, and any details added to the garment should evolve organically from the process of construction of the dress. The fabric and the garment, the colour and line should all be in harmony. And it was not just pattern-cutting that helped the Reimann to its leading position: Albert Reimann had been the first to see how the new, fast-changing fashion business needed support from fashion illustrators who would no longer be mere copyists. As well as having a solid grounding in life drawing, the new generation of fashion students would *create* elegance, for creativity was now an integral part of the syllabus. Kölling also emphasised the role of developing a personal note, a trademark style for each student.[45]

All of these developments in fashion, textile, photography and window display needed a showcase, and the school provided just that with its annual and much celebrated costume ball, the Reimann Ball.

Accounts of these spectacular affairs could be seen in the school's house magazine *Farbe und Form* (Colour and Shape), a feast for the eyes in itself thanks to the great graphic design skills of the students. Posters for the ball survive too in German archives. One who designed costumes for this fantastic event was the ubiquitous Mr Ernst Dryden, the designer of posters and clothes and at home wherever there were fashionable young women.[46] Dryden also taught poster design from 1912–14 at the school, as one of the best known artists in this field.

* * *

Pre-war Austria and Germany were countries where new art and design flourished, along with technical developments in different fields, in a time of both boom and disruption. Some Jewish entrepreneurs and designers, while revelling in the success of their companies, initially tried not to think what the implications of Adolf Hitler's takeover in January 1933 would mean for them. Surely, they thought, this madness, these torch parades, the chanting and displays of antisemitism would not last? Were they just another manifestation of the instability of the Weimar Republic? But for those who refused to see the real threat of Nazism to themselves, their families and livelihoods, the doors would clang shut and it would be too late to escape.

Notes

1. M. Ganeva, *Women in Weimar Fashion* (Rochester NY: Camden House, 2008), pp. 2–3.
2. http://www.dailymail.co.uk/news/article-2847643/Berlin-liberal-hotbed-homosexuality-mecca-cross-dressers transsexuals-male-female-surgery-performed-Nazis-came-power-new-book-reveals.html, accessed 31 July 2017.
3. N. Shepherd, *A Refuge from Darkness, Wilfrid Israel and the Rescue of the Jews* (New York: Pantheon Books, 1984), p. 55.
4. A quote attributed to Lord Alfred Douglas, Oscar Wilde's lover and commonly thought to refer to homosexuality.

5. This section from U. Westphal, *Berliner Konfektion und Mode: Die Zerstörung einer Tradition 1836–1939* (Berlin: Heinrich & Co, 2009), pp. 161–165.
6. https://en.wikipedia.org/wiki/Gustav_J%C3%A4ger(naturalist), accessed 12 July 2017.
7. E. Ewing, *History of Twentieth Century Fashion* (London: Batsford, 1985), p. 135.
8. I. Guenther, *Nazi Chic? Fashioning Women in the Third Reich* (Oxford/New York: Berg, 2004), p. 42.
9. Kerry Wallach, 'Weimar Chic: Jewish Women and Fashion in 1920s Germany', in Leonard J. Greenspoon (ed.), *Fashioning Jews: Clothing, Culture and Commerce*, Studies in Jewish Civilization, Volume 24 (West Lafayette, Indiana: Purdue University Press, 2013), p. 113.
10. U. Westphal, *Berliner Konfektion,* p. 250.
11. Ibid., pp. 89–100.
12. R. Kremer (ed.), 'Preface' in *Broken Threads: From Aryanization to Cultural Loss – The Destruction of the Jewish Fashion Industry in Germany and Austria* (Vancouver: Berg, 2007), p. 20.
13. The Yiddish term for rags is 'Schmatter' or 'Schmutter', still used today to refer to clothes selling.
14. For example, R. Kremer, *Broken Threads*, p. 22.
15. C. Schramm, 'Architecture of the German Department Store', in R. Kremer, *Broken Threads*, p. 30.
16. On Schocken, see A. David, *The Patron: A Life of Salman Schocken 1877–1959* (New York: Metropolitan Books, Henry Holt and Company, 2003).
17. On Wilfrid Israel, see the film *Wilfrid Israel: The Essential Link*, Director Yonatan Nir, 2016.
18. Once the Second World War broke out, these spectacular, modern buildings, no longer in Jewish ownership, were used as distribution points and eventually destroyed by Allied bombing. It was a sad end to the exciting but short-lived era of modernist retail.
19. On Flöge, see for example M. Greiner, *Auf Freiheit zugeschnitten. Emilie Flöge – Modeschöpferin und Gefährtin Gustav Klimts* (Vienna: Verlag Kremayr & Scheriau, 2014).
20. One such was the family of Otto Bassell, later Burton, who fled to England but who never managed to recreate his successful Viennese textile company in Britain. On Bassell, see A. Nyburg, 'Textile in Exile: Refugee Textile Surface Designers', in M. Malet, R. Dickson, S. MacDougall. A.

Nyburg (eds), in *Applied Arts in British Exile from 1933: Changing Visual and Material Culture, Yearbook of the Research Centre for German and Austrian Exile Studies*, Vol. 19, (2018), pp. 212–228.
21 T. Kanter, *Some Girls, Some Hats and Hitler* (London: Virago, 2012), p. 66.
22 Ibid., p. 103.
23 Ibid., p 7.
24 All information here on Ernst Dryden is from A. Lipmann, *Divinely Elegant: The World of Ernst Dryden* (London: Pavilion, 1989).
25 http://whatmenshouldsmelllike.com/2013/02/18/knize-ten/, accessed 14 August 2017.
26 U.Westphal, *Berliner Konfektion*, p. 39.
27 T. Kanter, *Some Girls*, p. 60.
28 U. Westphal, *Ehrenfried und Kohn*, *Roman* (Berlin: Lichtig Verlag, 2015).
29 I am indebted to Richard Donner, CEO of Double Two for information here on synthetics in an email 22 August 2017.
30 *Man in the White Suit*, directed by Alexander Mackendrick (1951).
31 http://www.bfi.org.uk/news-opinion/bfi-news/ealing-moment-man-white-suit, accessed 4 June 2019.
32 On Ullstein, see, for example, H. Ullstein, *The Rise and Fall of the House of Ullstein* (London: Nicholson and Watson, 1944).
33 A. Lipmann (*Divinely Elegant*), p. 94.
34 C. Ferber (ed.), *Die Dame: Ein deutsches Journal für den verwöhnten Geschmack 1912 bis 1943* (Berlin: Ullstein, 1980), p. 165.
35 N. Romer, 'Photographers, Jews and the Fashioning of Women in the Weimar Republic', in L. Greenspoon (ed.), *Fashioning Jews*, p. 93.
36 https://www.newday.com/film/ringl-and-pit, accessed 4 September 2017.
37 L. Silverman, 'Ela Zirner-Zwieback, Madame d'Ora and Vienna's New Woman' in L. Greenspoon (ed.), *Fashioning Jews*, p. 81.
38 On this see, for example, J. March, 'Women Exile Photographers', *Applied Arts in British Exile from 1933: Changing Visual and Material* Culture, Yearbook for the Research Centre for German and Austrian Exile Studies, vol. 19 (2018), pp. 49–66.
39 I. Loschek, 'Contributions of Jewish Fashion Designers in Berlin', in R. Kremer, *Broken Threads*, p. 53.
40 On the Vienna KGS see, for example, http://www.dieangewandte.at/universitaet/profil/geschichte, accessed 31 August 2017.
41 On the Wiener Werkstätte see, for example, C. Brandstätter, D. Gregori, R. Metzger (eds), *Vienna 1900 Complete* (London: Thames & Hudson, 2018).

42 See S. Kuhfuss-Wickenheiser, *Die Reimann-Schule in Berlin und London 1902–1943: Ein jüdisches Unternehmen zur Kunst- und Designausbildung internationaler Prägung bis zur Vernichtung durch das Hitlerregime* (Aachen: Shaker Medien, 2009); Yasuko Suga, *The Reimann School: A Design Diaspora* (London: Artmonsky Arts, 2014).
43 Y. Suga, *The Reimann School*, pp. 72–75.
44 S. Kuhfuss Wickenheiser, *Die Reimann Schule*, pp. 112–119.
45 Ibid., pp. 112–119.
46 Ibid., pp. 51–52.

CHAPTER 2

The Nazi Destruction of Germany's Clothing Industry

The Weimar Republic, a time when fashion flourished, a time of excitement and style, lasted for fourteen years but it would take only about five years for the National Socialists to destroy the *Konfektion* companies, many of which had been trading since the late nineteenth century. But, however machine-like the Nazi state was, its story is also full of contradictions, failures and inconsistencies and this is certainly true of its attempts to steal *Konfektion* from its Jewish owners and to force Germans to wear 'Aryan' clothes, whatever that meant. Their aim was to create a new Germanic clothing industry, free of the taint of Jewish or French influence, but at the same time to keep up the vital export trade in clothing so as to bring in very necessary funds to feed the greedy Nazi machinery, focused as it was on re-arming and preparing to expand the Third Reich.

Nazis Come to Power, 1933

Although anyone who read *Mein Kampf,* Adolf Hitler's master plan, could see that Jews were always going to be a target as they were blamed for all of Germany's ills, nevertheless, in January 1933 when the National Socialists took power and became Germany's government, Jews were not the very first people to be singled out as a bad influence and deprived of their jobs, effectively thrown out and forced to emigrate or go underground. The first to be persecuted included left-wing activists of all sorts: communists, trade unionists and socialists were considered by the Nazis almost as much of an anathema as were Jews. Anti-Nazi employees of the German civil service, known as *Beamte*, including university lecturers, could spread anti-Nazi messages to their students or to scholars all over the world and so must be put out of action. Many were incarcerated, either in prisons or in concentration camps. The early versions of these were not systematic extermination camps although some prisoners were murdered there. Sometimes, people who were enemies of the Nazis were imprisoned in camps as bargaining tools, so that their poor families would agree to pay or to cooperate in other ways to obtain the freedom of their relative. Other measures in the first half of 1933 should have indicated that the Nazis meant business, bad business, for example the public burning of anti-Nazi books in May.

One of the next major steps taken was the introduction in 1935 of the Nuremberg Laws which set down who was Jewish, according to Nazi ideology, and who was not. Anyone who was more than one-eighth Jewish would now be subjected to measures such as a ban on marrying or having a sexual relationship with an 'Aryan', or on employing a non-Jewish girl and so on. Religion played no role in this categorisation. The Nazis were not interested in whether Jews had converted to Christianity: their obsession with blood was what decided people's fate. These new measures came as a shock to many Germans who had no longer any attachment to Judaism or who had converted to Christianity. Such a conversion for some was part of the process of assimilation, of becoming ordinary Germans. 'Non-Aryan' was the term used to identify Jews and those of mixed origins.

The concept of 'Aryan' was based on a half-baked romantic theory that true Germans' ancestry could be traced back to an Indian tribe, whose symbol, the swastika, was adopted as their own emblem. In Germany, blue-eyed, blond specimens whose true ancestry was thought to be manifesting itself were taken as models for the master race and much effort went into breeding programmes. It was dangerous to point out that Hitler was short and dark, like Josef Goebbels, the Minister for Propaganda. 'Aryan' is shown in inverted commas, to indicate that it is a concept dreamed up by the National Socialists and not a real race.

Generally speaking, those who understood quickly what was developing and left Germany or Austria early on fared much better. They lost less of their capital and belongings and had a chance to integrate into British life before the war broke out. Two men who illustrate this are the graphic designer Hans Schleger and the journalist and publisher Hans Juda (see Chapter 5) Both Schleger and Juda experienced signal success in their chosen fields in Britain, although it was not only their early arrival but also their special skill sets and experience which worked for them.

Nazis Target *Konfektion*

The Nazis' attack on clothing businesses was based above all on their resentment at the success, both financial and otherwise, of the *Konfektionäre* and their desire to appropriate the property and the geese that laid those golden eggs. Additionally, they thought German 'Aryan' women should wear clothes fit for their race. In this there was a degree of conflating French and Jewish fashion because Nazi authorities equated both with 'whorish', unladylike and unnatural appearances. One young woman, Marietta Riederer, who was a fashion illustrator, told how she used to be shouted at by Nazi men in the tram because of her make up or because she was smoking. She was also heckled for wearing a brooch from the previous century which featured the head of a Negro man, a race hated as much as the Jews.[1] She had managed in one go to present elements of almost everything that was anathema to the Nazis: Paris fashions, 'unhealthy' living not suitable for 'Aryan' women and finally a tribute to the 'inferior' race of black people.

As well as being a hated enemy to the Nazis, the French were associated with the 'immoral' trips to Paris for the fashion shows, when Jewish *Konfektionäre* supposedly seduced pure, German girls, as well as there being other unsuitable couplings. Moreover, the Parisian or Jewish fashions were unnatural. The term *'geistiges Kokain'* (mental cocaine) was used to explain its drug-like effect. Androgyny, the style which dominated the 1920s and early 1930s, was at odds with the Germanic ideal of women dedicated to bearing children for the Führer. The basis of Nazism was of sacrificing all to the greater good of the party and obedience, completely in contrast to the cult of individualism which dominated the Weimar cultural scene.[2]

A study of the destruction of the Jewish clothing industry by the Nazis, aptly named *Broken Threads*, chronicles the series of measures taken by the Nazis against Jewish *Konfektion* with the starting point in 1933 of some 100,000 Jewish-owned companies in Germany, more than half in clothing.[3] In that same year, legislation was passed to prohibit Nazi party members from buying goods at Jewish-owned businesses.

Next, 1 April saw the state-sanctioned boycotting of Jewish businesses when SA members and others daubed Jewish shops with slogans and graffiti, handing out antisemitic flyers to customers. The SA, *Sturmabteilung*, were the Brown Shirts, the early paramilitary wing of the Nazi party until Hitler turned on them and reduced their power in 1934 to gain better control himself. Although this one-day boycott was terrifying to German Jews, it served no real purpose to the Nazi cause, as it resulted in a backlash from abroad. The Americans announced they would no longer buy German goods if this behaviour persisted. In England, Israel Sieff of Marks & Spencer acted on his word that his company would no longer buy *anything* from Germany, including machinery, supplies or clothing. Germany was desperate for income from exports and those in power realised that this was not the moment to threaten such revenue.

Over the next few years German exports continued to decline, and increasingly Jews who had emigrated abroad (for their own safety) were blamed for creating competition from, for example, the Netherlands, where they had re-established their companies and were exporting abroad and so were trading as rivals to German companies. Another fear kindled by the reaction to the April boycott was that unemployment, a spectre of the 1920s and 1930s, would reappear, meaning the destruction of large clothing businesses. So it was that no further boycotts took place for some years officially, although individual attacks, including looting, went unpunished.

In 1934 the Nazis took steps to create their own fashion and to promote the concept of 'Aryan' fashion by establishing an organisation known as ADEFA, an acronym meaning association of makers of clothing by Aryan workers. There were branches in four major cities to promote healthy German clothing but the enterprise came to very little. The successful clothes designed by Paris couturiers or the German Jewish *Konfektionäre* version of these designs were dismissed by ADEFA but, in practice, nothing ever replaced them.

What was German fashion? A series of negatives: not Jewish, not French, not 'whorish', not androgynous, and so on. This left a healthy, scrubbed, chaste look, instantly seized by the French press who ridiculed German women, portraying them as fat, coarse and wearing ridiculous, tasteless clothes. There does not seem to have been a real alternative apart from possibly *Trachten*, Alpine costume. Ironically, even the best makers of *Trachten* turned out to be Jewish.

'Aryans' and Jews

However ADEFA, which was directly answerable to the Reich's Ministry for the Economy, could and did help organise attacks on Jewish companies, now in the form of 'Aryanisation'. This process which was in essence theft, meant 'transferring' (this was the euphemism used) Jewish-owned companies into the hands of non-Jews. Usually money was paid out but it in no way represented the real value of the enterprise, and often the price paid was a laughable fraction of the value. One of the results of 'Aryanisation' was an immediate fall in the viability of the firm, largely because the majority of the opportunist purchasers had no experience in *Konfektion* and were simply hoping for quick money. This in turn had further disastrous consequences for German export.

Much of ADEFA's work could be deemed propaganda as they saw their task as ridding the trade of any taint of Jewish or French influence. The appropriated businesses were re-named, one example being the Nathan Israel department store now being called a more anonymous 'Haus im Zentrum'. In any case, German authorities could now realise their long-held dream of purging the vocabulary of the sector which itself was no longer to be called the French-sounding *Konfektion* but now instead the German *Kleidung* or *Bekleidung* (clothing). Ludicrously, even colours were Germanised. Irene Guenther recounts in her book ironically entitled *Nazi Chic: Fashioning Women in the Third Reich*, '"medium blue" became "national blue". Out of "smoke grey" emerged "Stahlhelm [steel helmet] grey". "Cuba brown" became "SA-Uniform brown", "national brown" or "Nazi brown"'. Moves hardly guaranteed to endear anyone to the collections other than the most fervent Nazi.[4]

As part of the Nazi campaign to control the *Konfektion* trade, others working in the sector such as graphic designers and illustrators were required to join the *Reichskammer für die Bildenden Künste* (the Reich Chamber for the Fine Arts). Membership of these Chambers was compulsory in order to have permission to work in the relevant sector. Needless to say, no Jews were permitted to join, so they automatically lost their livelihoods.

Judenrein: the Jews Disappear from Germany

Moves continued up to 1938 to exclude Jews from the national economy and there was even a special word to mean 'purified of Jews' or *judenrein*. ADEFA continued to enable non-Jews to plunder stores. In 1936 ADEFA expanded its remit to include weaving and leather trades. In 1938 no Jews were allowed to sell businesses without permission from the Nazis, nor were they allowed to walk in the centre of Berlin where they had worked for so long. In that same year, a law was passed meaning that Jews lost 40 per cent of the sale value of any property.

More and more laws were passed stripping Jews of any remaining wealth, so that by the time the last refugees fled to Britain in 1939, they were only allowed to bring 10 *Reichsmarks* with them, just loose change. 1938 was the year that Germany annexed Austria into the Reich so that Austrian Jews were now in mortal danger too. But the *Anschluss* in March was only the beginning of a horrendous year. In November, those Jews who had not managed to escape by then experienced what is referred to as *Kristallnacht* (an allusion to the smashed glass) but in Germany is now called the *Novemberpogrom* as a less pretty version of the attacks.

During 9 and 10 November, German rabbles, individuals and Nazi thugs smashed remaining Jewish businesses to pieces, beat up or murdered Jews, burned to the ground nearly all synagogues in the country – the destruction was unimaginable. Many Jews were rounded up and sent to concentration camps or work camps to join those who had been sent there earlier.

The great department store that was Nathan Israel of Berlin survived long after others, until 1938, although Wilfrid Israel, the grandson of the original founder and now the MD, had managed to spirit out of the country thousands of his Jewish employees. His short but admirable life is described in *A Refuge from Darkness: Wilfrid Israel and the Rescue of the Jews*, [5] as well as more recently in a film which tells the story of how Israel helped set up a kibbutz in Palestine and organised other schemes, saving possibly hundreds of thousands of desperate German Jews, more even than Schindler. [6] On 10 November 1938, the enormous store was attacked:

> The young wreckers set to work as the SS guards rounded up the Jewish staff. They smashed display cases, tore down lengths of silk from the stands and trampled clothes and materials underfoot. They went up, floor by floor, scattering the frightened employees and hurled furniture into the main stairwell from the galleries.[7]

It was the human sacrifice which disturbed Wilfrid however, and he quickly contacted the Nazi authorities to persuade them to release his employees who had been taken to the Sachsenhausen concentration camp.[8]

Magda Goebbels, wife of the Minister for Propaganda who adored clothes and frequented the top *Konfektion* shops, Jewish-owned, until the last possible moment is alleged to have said that, with the exit of the Jews from Berlin, elegance too had disappeared.[9] She was not the only person to be taken to task for having continued to frequent Jewish shops, so attached was she to the exquisite clothes.

Finally, the Nazis had done their worst: 'Through a combination of massive pressure, hateful propaganda, direct intervention, blacklists, sanctions, boycotts and firings, as well as illegal takeovers, buy-outs and liquidations, the German fashion world was *judenrein*...'[10]

What happened to the Jews expelled from their own or other businesses and who had not succeeded in emigrating? Huge numbers were gassed in death camps such as Auschwitz or Bergen-Belsen. It is important to remember, however, that many others died en route to the camps as a result of starvation, non-existent hygiene and disease, a death which was another form of murder. For some of the *Konfektionsjuden* (the clothes trade Jews), death was delayed as their special skills singled them out as suitable for work making clothes for high-ranking Nazis. One such was the wife of Höss, commander of Auschwitz, who lived in luxury and had her own Jewish prisoners to make clothes for her and her family, an arrangement which led to the setting up of a workshop in the concentration camp itself.[11] Similarly, labour camps used inmates to produce uniforms and work clothes for the Reich until they died of starvation or succumbed to typhus or other diseases.

There were few survivors of the camps, especially of those who spent a long time there, but some did manage it – one refugee milliner, Martin Kaczynski, who was imprisoned in Sachsenhausen concentration camp, managed to survive his incarceration by using an incredibly simple but effective trick. He found an abandoned window frame and picked it up. Every time there was the danger that he would be seen (and therefore singled out for labour or execution), he made sure he was seen trudging slowly but purposefully forward. Somehow, he was never challenged as everyone assumed that he was doing something he had been ordered to do. It saved his life.[12]

The experience of Austrian Jews matched that of their German counterparts albeit with less build-up over time. The National Socialist party had been outlawed in Austria preceding the *Anschluss* of March 1938, so when the German troops marched in it meant a sudden brutal attack on those Jewish businesses whose owners had not foreseen the occupation by their aggressive neighbouring country.

The *Anschluss*: Austria is Annexed into the German Reich

The milliner Trude Kanter took her readers through the horrors of the annexation of Austria by the German Army. For decades after the war, Austria declined to acknowledge its own role in the *Anschluss*, preferring to assume the role of victim whereas, in fact, the Nazi troops entering Vienna had been greeted by cheering crowds wearing swastika badges and throwing themselves willingly into the immediate persecution of Austrian Jews, for example forcing even elderly Jews to clean the streets of anti-Nazi slogans. Kanter witnessed it all: '…shocked Jews, plucked from the street at random, had to scrub off all these slogans…They kept on scrubbing long after the masters had left, but the paint could not be removed.'[13]

The physical abuse she saw was compounded by a reign of terror: 'An epidemic is rife in Austria: denunciation. The true masters of the city were now the janitors. They denounced all the tenants with whom they had had rows in the past. Particularly Jews.' She goes on to say that maids enjoyed their part in this reign too, as they had heard all their employers' conversations and could easily now betray them to the authorities or blackmail them. Austria's latent antisemitism, as she tells it, comes to a boil. Jewish stores are looted, synagogues occupied by the Gestapo. 'Aryanisation' starts up immediately: 'The owners could count themselves lucky if they didn't end up in a concentration camp or at the Viennese Hotel Metropole, now the Gestapo headquarters.'[14] One of Kanter's favourite clients, Lilli, is one who was taken to a concentration camp, but was spared the gas chambers as she was so attractive, instead forced to serve as a camp prostitute and one of the 'lucky' few.

The cruel irony of the situation was that the Nazis made it both impossible to stay in the German Reich but at the same time made it impossible to leave. A combination of luck, contacts and initiative could sometimes save lives. People from the clothing trade who feature in this story have tales to tell of their persecution and horrendous attacks with very occasional incidents of kindness, which happened to hundreds of thousands of Jews and others all over Germany and Austria-Hungary.

As the rest of the world looked on anxiously, while Britain hoped against hope that they would not be plunged into yet another war with Germany – it was only 20 years or so since the last bloodbath – Hitler occupied one country after another. After the *Anschluss* of Austria, the German-speaking area of Czechoslovakia known as the Sudetenland was next on the hit list. Jews and anti-Nazis who had fled to Prague from Austria and Germany were now next in line to be persecuted. As a result of the ill-fated Munich Agreement, Hitler's troops occupied the Sudetenland on 1 October 1938.

Among the Czechs who escaped was Jacqueline Groag, the fabled textile designer, as were the Aschers, Lida and Zika (see Textile). For the non-Jewish Pasold family, owners of the children's wear firm which made Ladybird clothes for Woolworths and who had come to England for economic reasons but still had a factory in the Sudetenland, there were also some problems. German goods were being boycotted by Jewish firms in several countries and this now included goods from the Sudetenland. Initially at least, there were few changes, provided one 'fell in line with the prescribed drill, hoisted the swastika flag on state occasions…and greeted everyone with "Heil Hitler" he had a comparatively easy life.'[15] But Pasold knew this state of affairs would not last for the now British company of wool spinners and knitters and their family. On 15 March 1939, the rest of Czechoslovakia became the next victim of German ambition, a point at which many thought the British Prime Minister Neville Chamberlain should have grasped the nettle and declared war. Certainly one reason that war was delayed was that Britain needed time to re-arm and prepare itself for what was now inevitable. Not until the fall of Poland in the September of 1939 was war finally declared.

Hungary was not occupied by Germany until 1944: its history was different although no less destructive to Jewish citizens in the final analysis. Hungarian Jews managed to survive for the most part until the very end of the war, when the notorious fascist and antisemitic Arrow Cross Party took control of the government between October 1944 and March 1945. Before Arrow Cross, Hungary was ruled by

Admiral Horthy's ultra-conservative government. Antisemitism was condoned under this regime, so that there was a *numerus clausus* scheme in place, a quota system limiting for example the number of Jewish students at Hungarian universities.

* * *

To all Jews and others attacked for political and other reasons it became more and more urgent to leave, however hard that was, however difficult to leave family, livelihoods and home behind. Leaving, though, was difficult in itself, for who would take in thousands of desperate, foreign people who could bring little with them and who might become a burden on the host country?

Notes

1. U. Westphal, *Berliner Konfektion und Mode: Die Zerstörung einer Tradition 1836–1939* (Berlin: Heinrich & Co, 2009), pp. 141–143.
2. Ibid., p. 101.
3. R. Kremer (ed.), 'Preface' in *Broken Threads: The Destruction of the Jewish Fashion Industry in Germany and Austria* (Vancouver: Berg, Vancouver Holocaust Education Centre, 2006).
4. I. Guenther, *Nazi Chic: Fashioning Women in the Third Reich* (Oxford/New York: Berg, 2004), p.148.
5. N. Shepherd, *A Refuge from Darkness: Wilfrid Israel and the Rescue of the Jews* (New York: Pantheon Books, 1984).
6. *Wilfrid Israel: The Essential Link*, Director Yonatan Nir, (2016).
7. N.Shepherd, *Wilfred Israel*, p. 143.
8. Ibid., p.144.
9. http://misslindsaylane.blogspot.co.uk/2013/07/how-nazi-party-influenced-german.html, accessed 8 January 2018.
10. I. Guenther, 'The Destruction of a Culture and in Industry', in R. Kremer (ed.), *Broken Threads*, p. 94.
11. I. Guenther, *Nazi Chic*, p. 5.
12. I am grateful to Professor Charmian Brinson for this account, and to William Kaczynski, Martin's son. They are the joint authors of *Fleeing from*

the *Führer: A Postal History of Refugees from the Nazis*, (London: The History Press, 2011).
13 T. Kanter, *Some Girls, Some Hats and Hitler* (London: Virago, 2012), p. 39.
14 Ibid., p. 44.
15 E. Pasold, *Ladybird, Ladybird: A Story of Private Enterprise* (Manchester: Manchester University Press, 1977), p. 527.

CHAPTER 3

Britain: New Home to the Refugees, Ancient Home of the Knitting Trade

Before considering how it was that thousands of refugees managed to flee from the Nazi forces to asylum in Britain, it is useful to know what sort of tradition awaited them in the textile sector. For many of them, as we will see, Britain was the most famous country, at least for woollens, perhaps in the whole world. This country has been the home of wool production for centuries: the hills and fields have been grazed by sheep and indeed were shaped by generations of sheep and their farmers. But cotton too is part of British history, for example, cotton spinning was developed in Britain. The end of the eighteenth century saw such innovations as cotton spinning using Richard Arkwright's water frame, James Hargreaves's Spinning Jenny, and Samuel Crompton's Spinning Mule (a combination of the Spinning Jenny and the Water Frame). The first main move from hand-knitting came even earlier with the invention in 1598 by Englishman William Lee of the Stocking Frame, a complex iron machine. This time-saving contraption was the cause of much coveting of course, and spies managed at last to smuggle one into France.

There it was taken up by the Huguenots, a group of people who had much in common with the twentieth-century Jewish refugees in this story: they were inventive, innovative, good businessmen and the focus of jealousy and religious hatred, not in Germany but in France where their Protestantism led to their persecution. By the seventeenth century, many Huguenots had fled to safety all over Europe including to Britain, some escaping inside wine barrels. Crucially, they managed to bring their skills and knowledge with them, as silk weavers, knitters and potters, but also as experienced businessmen and bankers. One account of the history of foreigners in Britain noted that although these French refugees were 'exhausted, scared, bereaved, ruined and broken-hearted …' they made their presence felt quickly.[1] They came at the very time, the mid-1600s, that textiles accounted for 87 per cent of England's exports, and gave the industry support, technically and commercially.² So it was thanks to the Huguenots that by the mid-nineteenth century, the new knitting frame was widely available all over Europe. ³

From that time on, there was a rivalry between British and German textile and clothing production, with 'German' including the Austro-Hungarian Empire which was largely German-speaking. The biggest increase in German clothing output came at the end of the nineteenth century, between 1880 and 1895, when the number of textile firms had gone up by 50 per cent to 3,260 and the number of those employed in the sector then stood at around 580,000, more than 70 per cent up.⁴ Where Germany really forged ahead was in the development of synthetic fibres, a new area which progressed quickly in the 1930s. Just as Germany was ahead of the game in this field, the National Socialists came to power and started to destroy their own lead. As many of the leading technologists in the field were Jewish, they were forced to leave the country. Germany's loss was Britain's gain, and not for nothing were the refugees referred to by at least one writer as 'Hitler's gift'.⁵

Accounts of those clothing and textile manufacturers who moved from Europe to Britain give the reader an interesting perspective on differences between the two cultures. One such company is the Czech knitters Pasold & Sons. This company, as has already been pointed out, was not a refugee enterprise, as the owners who were from the German-speaking Sudetenland were not Jewish and so not forced to flee their homeland. In fact, they moved to Britain in 1931 because Britain's leaving the gold standard would mean import duties on their knitted goods.⁶ After the First World War there had been a huge surge in the demand for both underwear and hosiery, with Germany and Czechoslovakia covering 85 per cent of the supply in Britain right up until just before the outbreak of the Second World War.⁷ And yet the Pasold family hated the Nazis who took over their homeland, so that family members still in Czechoslovakia refused to fly swastika flags over the remaining Pasold factory in Fleissen.⁸ The author of the company history managed to persuade a Jewish friend to leave, saving his life, and despised the Nazis' antisemitism directed against his family's local buyers, all of them Jewish. So while not refugees, they were anti-Nazi and supportive of their victims and indeed of the British war effort when war broke out.

Eric Pasold's account of establishing his firm in Britain is a fascinating combination of his long-held admiration for the British, who had after all invented the Spinning Jenny and the all-important knitting frame, and on the other hand on his arrival in Britain his bewilderment at their conservative outlook. He was astounded by the Underground in London, and the spectacular Empire Exhibition at Empire, where pride in the British Dominions and their wealth were on display. But what of the famous British textile industry, 'the most advanced and largest in the world'?[9] On several later occasions Eric Pasold encountered examples of British complacence and love of tradition which prevented their forging ahead or being flexible when change was needed; they seemed to be resting on their laurels. He noted that the English had a distaste for trade, so that upper-middle-class chaps seemed to prefer farming to industry, despite their long-standing ability to manufacture.

A closer look at British traditions shows that after centuries of restrictive clothing for women, and multiple layers of linen, cotton and wool for men, in the late nineteenth-century Britain something began to crack under the weight and strain of it all and it wasn't just the whalebone corsets. The Rational Dress Movement of 1881 was a reaction to the plight of women who were struggling to sit down, hampered as they were by their bustles, padded out with horsehair and springs. And this trend had followed the crinolines which must have been a challenge to negotiate through doorways, being only one of their many disadvantages.[10] The new movement meant looser, flowing Pre-Raphaelite-inspired dresses, harking back to the medieval shape. The long, formal trains were rejected by the art critic and writer John Ruskin who condemned them as unhygienic. Corsets, too, were suddenly suspect, although it had taken centuries to realise that compressing women's internal organs was not a Good Thing. One writer of a history of Marks & Spencer opined that throwing away corsets 'did more for emancipation than the vote'.[11] A contentious claim, but shedding the corset was more liberating than the bra-burning of the 1960s.

As the Victorian age died away in Britain, social trends shaped what people wore, as always. In particular, sporting activities for both sexes meant further emphasis on facilitating movement. Comfortable, robust tweeds, even divided skirts for the new craze of cycling, became acceptable. The female silhouette narrowed and less fabric made it easier to get in and out of motor cars when these began to be a more common feature of British life.

The interwar period in Britain was a time of great social upheaval, a time when there was a blurring of the social caste borders as well as of changes to the way clothes were made and sold. Theories abounded as to why the ideal female shape changed so radically after the chested body: perhaps it was a response to the loss of so many young boys in the killing fields? Or perhaps it was because a less obviously fertile woman was a better bet in the times of poverty that followed.[12] The new fashion in 1920s Britain was very similar to the German version in Berlin. The mid-1920s were marked by the gamine look, with short, shingled hair and skirts above the knee, until the early 1930s when they started to drop again. Women were now going out to work in greater numbers, and clothing became democratised because inexpensive clothing was needed by all. A contemporary cartoon shows middle-class girls admiring their friend's maid's outfit, remarking ruefully that obviously only one of them, either the maid or the mistress, can afford such outfits on one income.

Not just sport but a healthy appearance was now attractive; sunbathing had only recently been thought desirable, brought in by followers of Coco Chanel in the South of France. In the 1930s backless long dresses were ubiquitous, ideal for showing off the brown skin, and were held up on the body by the new rubberised fabric. The Women's League of Health and Beauty was established in 1930 in Britain, and there was a craze for their exercises. Hiking was also popular, as it was in 1930s Germany and Austria. Ironically, Tyrolean style, as we have seen, had a big fashion moment in this decade in Britain too, just before the war, with women sporting little green hats with feathers and tailored loden jackets, trimmed with braid in the Austrian style.

German and other refugees not only had to change their eating and dressing habits on arrival in Britain – shopping was different too. London had equivalents of the spectacular Nathan Israel in the form of Harrods or Selfridges, but there were few, if any, sleek, modern Schocken-like stores until the arrival of Simpson in 1931 and it did not have many imitators. However, department stores like Debenhams sold 10 per cent of all clothing rising to 15 per cent in 1939.[13] But despite this increase there was a gradual trend away from department stores which catered to middle-class clients and towards multiples like Marks & Spencer, frequented by lower-middle and working-class buyers. Lord Simon Marks had studied business practices in America and returned to improve efficiency in his own stores, although still committed to selling clothes within the five shilling price range in the 1920s.[14] Europeans had no equivalent of M & S. By 1936, two-thirds of their turnover was accounted for by textile. *Prêt à porter* was now the way people shopped, and the decline of individual seamstresses began. Radio and popular magazines meant that consumers had access to the taste of others and could see what was fashionable or elegant. [15]

Great British Woollen Traditions: Pringle and John Smedley

It is possible to trace the development in the shapes of clothes and in the shift to different actual garments through the archives and company histories of Britain's centuries-old knitwear firms, in particular Pringle of Scotland and John Smedley of Matlock, although there are of course others too, many of whom do not keep historical records. Pringle was established in the eighteenth century in Hawick on the Scottish borders, a sheep-farming area for several centuries.[16]

The wool was washed, spun and knitted into socks and stockings for the local market initially, but the Pringle family were forward thinking and open to innovation, no doubt a factor in the company's longevity. During the nineteenth century Pringle perfected the technique of producing knitted undergarments for which there was great demand in the chilly border country. The author of the house history recounted a key moment in the development, as the bust of ladies' combinations had always posed a technical challenge: the greater width of the bosom meant that the garment had to be cut during production, to allow an extra piece of fabric to be inserted and the three pieces were then stitched together. But there lay the rub, literally. The stitched seams stood proud from the garment and chafed the wearers' skin. Until, that is, Pringle created the seamless gore, a way of fashioning ladies' vests or combinations the whole way up without cutting or inserting. This process could be applied to the next generation of knitwear which was outerwear. Again, it was sportswear which was key in the progress of knitwear; in Pringle's case it came in the form of bathing suits.

After the First World War, Pringle geared itself up to face competition from Austria, France and Italy. Although the house history does not specify, it seems likely that these Continental knitted garments were jumpers worn by skiers in the Alps shared by those countries. This sport necessitated flexible, warm clothing that let the body breathe, not something available from British knitwear producers. A typical outfit for the woman skier of 1926 comprised a 'long, thigh-length woollen pullover', with trousers tucked into thick socks, and of course hat and gloves. [17]

Pringle's chiefs had witnessed the trend for new, lighter knitted clothes worn in America and Europe for sports or country pursuits. By 1920 the company, now in its second century of trading, could apply their newly-acquired technical expertise and specially designed machinery to the huge changes and challenges that the 1920s brought. Next, ever innovative, Pringle started to add rubber thread to their cashmere knitwear, allowing for a better fit.

While in Europe their fine sporty sweaters were treated as seriously as up-market clothing; in Britain, 'woollies' or jumpers were seen still as sensible, warm garments worn in the country, not the town, and with pearls of course. Blouses were different, as they could have a style. So it was that Pringle cautiously started on a different tack, to compete with the Europeans. In 1930 they had engaged Miss Elizabeth

Pringle (presumably a relative) as a 'designer and stylist' for six months in their London office. But then they decided to make a more serious commitment to design.

Meanwhile, further south, just outside Matlock in a cluster of eighteenth-century mill buildings surrounded by the green hills of Derbyshire, where it has been since 1784, is the thriving company of John Smedley Ltd.[18] Today the mill looks the part, its history can be read on the weathered brickwork and the uneven buildings astride a stream which used to power the machinery in the eighteenth-century mill and which still provides the soft water so necessary for the washing of the merino wool used.

Nowadays the fine wool sweaters, such as Pringle's, are worn by young and old alike, men and women, working people and celebrities of all sorts. Its knitwear developed over the decades just as it did at Pringle; the twinset becoming a particular favourite in the 1950s. This cardigan and sweater combination was subverted by Vivienne Westwood in the 1980s when the Derbyshire-born designer chose to have John Smedley produce a twinset bearing her own logo embroidered on the front. Nowadays, the company which has produced garments for prestigious labels like Comme des Garçons, produces very fine merino wool sweaters to customers all over the world, including Queen Elizabeth II, who showed her approval by granting them the Royal Warrant of Appointment in 2013.

But to go back to its origins: John Smedley was one of the first cotton spinners of the Industrial Revolution, giving it the claim to be the oldest factory in the world.[19] From cotton, the company quickly diversified into knitting and spinning as well; there was a healthy demand for socks and stockings. Accounts of Britain's best known and oldest luxury brands tell the story of generations of Smedleys, such as the nineteenth-century John Smedley who became obsessed with the spa movement, establishing his own in nearby Matlock Bath and compelling his workers to undergo various forms of dripping wet treatment to cure their ills.[20]

In the 1920s John Smedley introduced Sea Island cotton for the manufacturing of handkerchiefs and underwear, a particularly fine type popular for example with the trend-setting Duke of Windsor. In the 'Roaring Twenties' new shapes in women's clothing meant a change in the shape of underwear too, and tubular chemises were produced by John Smedley which would not show under shift dresses. The 1930s saw the introduction of sportswear: polo shirts for men and knitwear for both sexes. As the history of Pringle shows, knitted fabric, long used for comfortable hosiery and underwear became in the twentieth century an important element of outerwear: sweaters, sleeveless jumpers and cardigans all caught on as fashionable clothing both for sportsmen and women and for people who liked the flexibility and flattering lines of woollen garments. But whereas socks and vests just needed engineering, outer garments needed to have a shape; they needed designing. So John Smedley set out in 1938 in search of a designer.

From the directors' log book we read the account of Mr Nieper's trip to the Continent in search of such a person. David Ronald Nieper (known as Ron Nieper here in the company) came as Spinning Manager in the late 1920s, rising to Company Director. He was naturalised in 1925, having been born in Germany in 1902. So Nieper was German, but not an émigré himself. His son incidentally, is David Nieper, whose successful company has been making British knitwear and ladies wear since the 1960s. And finally, recorded on 26 March 1938, success at last – Nieper recruited the longed-for designer (see Klothilde Ehrenfest).

Knitwear continues in the present day to be associated with British tradition and quality, and rightly so. However, most people probably do not realise that there was also a time in its history when the British gratefully accepted that European knitwear was more technically advanced and more stylish than British 'woollies' and that the designers involved gave us this gift, just as Britain gave them asylum.

Possible Destinations for Jewish Refugees? USA and Palestine

While Germans had slowly been leaving their homeland, leaving behind their businesses and worst of all, family members too old or unwilling to come, in 1938 the trickle became a deluge, as Austrian Jews now also under vicious attack had to run for their lives. Our Austrian milliner, Trude Kanter, didn't think of Britain first, as she recounts in her memoir. While she was desperate to leave Vienna immediately, her fiancé Walter thought of his family and his beloved apartment. And where to go?

America was the destination for those who had family there, and was it not the refuge for the persecuted, as set out on the pedestal of the Statue of Liberty?

> Give me your tired, your poor,
> Your huddled masses yearning to breathe free,
> The wretched refuse of your teeming shore.
> Send these, the homeless, tempest-tossed, to me:
> I lift my lamp beside the golden door.[21]

However, the reality was less poetic, as Trude finds out. To limit numbers, the United States, always a country of immigration, had a quota system in place. But the American government did not relax the quota in the face of the new and desperate situation of the 1930s and the door was closed to many Germans and Austrians. After the war considerable numbers of refugees who survived the war in British asylum then emigrated further to the United States, while others found that they liked British life and had settled, never to leave again.

The nineteenth century in Europe had seen the birth of Zionism, a movement founded by the Austrian Theodor Herzl, just one who had come to the conclusion that the Jews would never be welcome anywhere and needed to find their own country. So when antisemitism in Germany escalated in the 1930s, many Jews who considered Palestine the Jewish homeland travelled there to start a new life and settle in that under-developed country. It was not only a rough and challenging life there for the largely middle-class European Jews, but they also fell foul of the Arab occupants of that land, who also felt it was their own homeland. After 1936, refuge in Palestine was much more difficult in the face of so much opposition. Many other countries were considered for refuge, including Madagascar and in China,

Shanghai, which remained open to the refugees, so that a community did manage to settle there for a time.

Britain had and still has always taken in refugees, a process which is regulated by the Aliens Acts. The Act of 1919 stipulated that no aliens can land in Britain if they cannot support themselves and their dependants. Nor could they deprive a British worker of his or her employment. Here, it is vital to bear in mind that the very time when the refugees arrived coincided with a time of terrible unemployment: the 'Hungry Thirties' were so called because so many were jobless and without any means of support in those days before the welfare state with its unemployment and other benefits. One Labour Party newspaper, *The Daily Herald,* had the 1939 figure for the unemployed at around 1,800,000 (out of a total population of around 46,000,000), although they calculated that there was a further 200,000 unregistered.[22] This was due to a number of factors, including the great crash of 1929 in America and crucially, the general decline in traditional industries such as coal and steel, especially in the North (see Trading Estates).

As far as refuge in Britain was concerned, the picture was a rather mixed one: on the whole only those refugees were allowed in who could contribute to the economy or to British academic or professional life. Not a completely disinterested effort, it could be said. For example, in 1938 domestic visas were introduced whereby women (and some men) could enter the country to work as housekeepers or gardeners. This led to the strange phenomenon of housekeepers who back home in Vienna had their own help and could hardly boil an egg, let alone deal with the mysteries of British plumbing and British cuisine.[23] Among these 'domestics' there were stories of sympathy and kindness, contrasting with others of snobbery and a complete lack of understanding of what the new domestic help had recently been through.

Kindertransports

Anglo-Jewry was not always as welcoming as could be expected: while Jewish charities certainly put up funds to help their desperate fellow

Jews escape to Britain saving thousands of lives, there were often big differences between the often sophisticated Jews from Berlin and Vienna and those, for example in London's East End whose families had come from Eastern Europe, many fleeing the Russian pogroms at the turn of the nineteenth century. The German and Austrian Jews who came to Britain tended to be middle-class and assimilated, which is to say either not religious or adhering to a liberal form of Judaism, although there were also those from Orthodox communities. This difference resulted in occasional culture clashes and there were stories of German children arriving at orthodox homes of poor Jews in East London wearing expensive clothes, expecting hot baths and not even aware that they were breaking the Sabbath. There were, inevitably, also accounts of Jewish children being sent to Christian homes where their Jewish heritage was not respected, whether out of ignorance or intent. Some of these children arrived on *Kindertransports.*

Kindertransports were the mercy trains loaded with children from the occupied countries in mortal danger. Their organisation had been triggered by the *Kristallnacht* events in Germany and Austria.[24] Public revulsion in Britain put pressure on the British government to take humanitarian measures. A parliamentary debate was followed by a Home Office decision to waive the visa requirement and to allow children to enter the country with just one identity document. The British Jewish community promised to bear the costs of any children who needed it although £500,000 was raised from public donations. A combination of public and private enterprises, Jewish and non-Jewish, including the huge efforts made by the stockbroker Sir Nicholas Winton, resulted in around 10,000 children from Czechoslovakia, Germany and Austria finding refuge in this country. The Quakers helped here, as they did in several of the refugee initiatives, by taking in children themselves and helping organise these operations.

With the benefit of hindsight and knowledge of the Holocaust that was to come, people nowadays might find it unimaginable that there was general opposition to the influx of refugees. The headlines of newspapers in the 1930s spoke of them 'flooding in', railing against their taking British jobs and so forth. In fact, the influx had been very slow, for in the years from 1933 to 1937 there had been on average only 2,000 arrivals per year. Their champions were thin on the ground. Apart from the constantly vigilant Quakers, the *Manchester Guardian* and the *News Chronicle* were alone among newspapers supporting their immigration. Two MPs in particular called for help for them – Josiah Wedgwood and Eleanor Rathbone. It was Rathbone who on 23 May 1938 in the *Manchester Guardian* asked the government that if they felt themselves too weak to be courageous, at least to show themselves merciful. Harold Macmillan, later to be Prime Minister, also bucked the trend of cold disinterest by opening his own house to forty Czech refugees. It wasn't really until after war had broken out that there was more public sympathy for the Continental refugees, although there were many families who took in children from the transports.

Who could have forgotten the sight of so many little children arriving at Liverpool Street Station on the boat trains from Harwich, tired, frightened and confused? In many cases they spoke no English. Generally, the children were looked after adequately on their arrival, although some fell victim to abuse, just as British evacuated children did. Some of the 'Kinder', as they are called, were lucky enough to have their parents follow them to safety in Britain, while others never saw their families again.

British life has been enriched by the 'Kinder', only two examples being Dame 'Steve' Shirley, IT entrepreneur and philanthropist, who arrived here as a tiny child and the Labour MP Alf Dubs another. Perhaps they realised that having been given a chance of life while so many of their friends perished, they should grasp all the opportunities life offered them. However, for most 'Kinder' the trauma of separation and loss was never forgotten.

As far as adults were concerned, generally it was possible to enter the country if these aliens had desirable skills, the all-important work permits were not handed out routinely before the war broke out, at which point all the rules started to change. It turned out, however, that there were other, less well-known but ingenious methods of bringing refugees into this country that had surprising results to say the least. Here is the story of one such method.

The Great Northern Trading Estates Miracle

How so many German, Austrian, Hungarian and other refugees ended up in the North West and North East of England along with Mr Max Steiner (see Francis Steiner and Tick-a-Tee Children's Wear) is explained in a magnificent PhD thesis from 1978 which told the story behind the Steiner's firm and many others besides.[25] It was essentially the story of a marriage made in heaven: bringing refugee industrialists to the depressed North East and North West of England, saving the refugees from certain death and creating literally hundreds of thousands of jobs.

Cumbria and Tyneside had been places where coal, iron and steel had provided jobs but were now in decline as raw materials were running out and, as already mentioned, because the stock market crash of 1929 had undermined many companies. Another factor was that Britain had left the Gold Standard which resulted in a reduction in international trade, causing exports to drop. In Maryport in Cumbria, an important place in this study, unemployment stood at 60 per cent in 1934. The men had to do what they have always done in such times and left in search of work. Between 1930 and 1934 some 150,000 men had left the North West and North East, referred to in this study as 'refugees in their own land'. It was not only poverty that caused problems in those days when there was not the unemployment benefit that the state pays today, but there was the terrible depression caused by having no prospects of work, nothing to hope for and the sense of purposelessness. Inevitably there were suicides, and a rise in alcoholism and crime.

Questions were raised in the House and Ramsay MacDonald's government recognised the special situation in the North. Commissioners were appointed to find solutions. Men such as Jack Adams, Secretary of the Cumberland Development Council (later Lord Adams) and Frank Anderson MP also got to work. Some of them went to those countries where Jewish businesses were threatened, to discuss their move to Britain. Some of those visited had obviously been spectacularly successful in their own country, as one commissioner told of having the door opened to him by a uniformed servant in Berlin. (One can only imagine what these successful Continental entrepreneurs' first impressions of depressed Cumbria must have been, once they got there.)

In order to apply to come over to Britain, interested businessmen had to fill in a questionnaire. Perhaps one of the most fascinating aspects of the whole initiative is that the Home Office had no power to make conditions for the immigrants – that is, they were not allowed to stipulate that the beleaguered Jewish industrialists must move to the North. There is nothing in writing, but it is thought that the message was given out that an application to move to the Home Counties would probably not be accepted.

Meanwhile, at home, the first moves were made in 1934 to clear ground and build factories financed by the government, an absolute first in British history, and referred to as a 'novel and unorthodox' move. The pace was cracking and within one year factories were up and ready to be occupied and infrastructure had been improved. All they needed were occupants. Other projects supplying factories on demand were also set up.

It was a complete sleight of hand. But it worked, or something did and by December 1938 there were 15,000 people working for such firms. The majority of the settlers were Hungarian and Czech, with the others from Germany and Austria, mostly engaged in lighter industries, chemicals, and textiles and clothing. Only a few weeks later the number was 25,000 employees. In fact the new workers were largely local women, a ratio of two to one of women to men, but at least there were family breadwinners now. By 1947 there were about 1,000 firms there employing a quarter of a million people! It is difficult to see at this point how anyone could have questioned the wisdom of providing refuge to so many desperate Germans and Austro-Hungarians.

When they first arrived, many of the refugees spoke no English, many had little capital (it had been confiscated by the Nazis before their departure citing tax bills or as fines for fleeing the Reich), they had little knowledge of British markets or working practices and yet they threw themselves into the challenge. They had to exercise discretion before leaving their homeland too, because if the Nazis had suspected that they would be removing an enterprise which supplied the export market and brought home currency, the Nazi authorities could have made it impossible for them to leave.

At least some in Britain recognised their contribution, noting their 'brains, capital and machinery'. In the press, the refugees were referred to as 'Germans' or 'Foreigners', not 'Jewish refugees' which, it was feared, would possibly have had an inflammatory effect. Incredible though it may seem, after the war, some sections of the press ran campaigns calling for the expulsion of this 'alien menace' in order to secure jobs for returning servicemen.

The refugee companies produced a wide range of goods, not all of them textile-based. To name just one typical of these light industries, there was Hornflowa who manufactured buttons and other horn-based products. Their in-house scientist invented a new system of filling horn buttons with synthetics, thereby making them cheaper.

Then there was Tyne Textile who made casuals and sportswear. In 1976 they made the clothes for the British Olympic team in Montreal. They also kitted out a British Everest expedition team in the 1970s. The most unexpected is perhaps Lestawear who made tartan kilts! And they were successful in exporting them too, over 50 per cent went abroad. On the home market they sold to Harrods and other upmarket department stores. Did their customers know that their sporrans were made by the Germans, Messrs Lesser, Kaufmann and Stark?

The irony of the British fearing that taking in the refugees would mean job losses is underlined in Loebl's thesis. In his words: 'The number of new jobs created by refugees in their own ventures is several times greater than that of the total number of refugees admitted.'[26] Eventually, the Northern England refugee industrialists' achievements were recognised. By the 1970s, founders or their family members had clocked up two knighthoods, one CBE, one OBE and two MBEs, mostly for their services to export.

The new arrivals in Britain contributed different skills and knowledge to the industry. Apart from technology and design, they are credited with introducing standardisation in sizing. One account refers to the influx of Viennese and Berlin tailors who were responsible for a 'revolution in sizing in the mid-1930s. Clothes previously sized only as maids or matrons or later as SW, W, WX were now widely available in sizes 10–16. This benefited the manufacture with economy in laying out patterns and allowed women to buy better fitting clothes off the peg for themselves and others.' [27] Things were changing for the better.

* * *

By the outbreak of the war on 3 September 1939, Britain had taken in some 80,000 German-speaking refugees, around 90 per cent of them Jewish. Their lives were safe from the Nazis terror, but what now? Would Britain be invaded by their persecutors? What would the refugees' role be now – would they be able to fight for their host country or treated as the enemy? They would find out very soon.

Notes

1. R. Winder, *Bloody Foreigners: The Story of Immigration to Britain* (Little, Brown, London: 2004), p. 64.
2. Ibid.
3. https://www.bpb.de/apuz/198384/wirtschaftsmacht-modeindustrie-alles-bleibt-anders?p=all, accessed 21 February 2018.
4. Ibid.
5. For example, J. Medawar, D. Pyke, *Hitler's Gift: The True Story of the Scientists Expelled by the Nazi Regime* (New York City: Arcade Publishing, 2001).
6. On this see, for example, http://www.telegraph.co.uk/finance/commodities/11330611/How-the-Bank-of-England-abandoned-the-gold-standard.html, accessed 21 February 2018.
7. S. Chapman, *Hosiery and Knitwear: Four Centuries of Small-Scale Industry in Britain c.1589–2000.* (Pasold Studies in Textile History, number 12.) (New York: Oxford University Press, 2002), pp. xxiv, 328, p.178.
8. E. Pasold, *Ladybird, Ladybird*, p. 478.
9. Ibid., p. 79.
10. J. Laver, *Costume and Fashion* (London: Thames & Hudson, World of Art, 1974), pp. 177–179.

11 G. Rees, *St Michael: History of Marks and Spencer* (London: Weidenfeld & Nicolson, 1969), p.100.
12 A. Mansfield, P. Cunningham, *Handbook of English Costume in the Twentieth Century* (London: Faber & Faber, 1973), p. 100.
13 C. Horwood, *Keeping Up Appearances: Fashion and Class Between the Wars* (Stroud: Sutton Publishing, 2005), p. 11.
14 Ibid., p. 138.
15 Ibid., p. 137.
16 Information here from H. Barty-King, *Pringle of Scotland: The Hawick Knitwear Story* (Fakenham: J J G Publishing, 2006).
17 A. Mansfield, *Handbook of English Costume*, p. 123.
18 I am indebted to John Smedley's archivist, Jane Middleton-Smith for this section on John Smedley's history.
19 Information from this section is from S. Crompton, *Best of British: The Stories behind Britain's Iconic Brands* (Munich, London, New York: Prestel: 2015), p. 43.
20 Information in this section is from C. Cox, *Luxury Fashion: A Global History of Heritage Brands* (London: Bloomsbury, 2013), pp. 38–41.
21 Poem by Emma Lazarus, https://www.goodreads.com/quotes/4386-give-me-your-tired-your-poor-your-huddled-masses-yearning, accessed 3 September 2017.
22 R. Kee, *The World We Left Behind: A Chronicle of the Year 1939* (London: Weidenfeld, 1993), p. 9.
23 On this see for example L. Segal, *Other People's Houses* (New York: Fawcett Crest, 1958).
24 A. Grenville 'The Kindertransports: An Introduction', in A. Hammel, B. Lewkovicz (eds), *The Kindertransport to Britain 1938/39: New Perspectives, Yearbook of the Research Centre for German and Austrian Exile*, vol. 13 (2012), pp.1–14.
25 All information here on the Trading Estates from Herbert Loebl, *Government-financed factories and the establishment of industries by refugees in the special area of the North of England 1937–1961*, Durham theses, Durham University, 1978.
26 H. Loebl, p. 9.
27 A. Kershen (ed.), *Off the Peg: The Story of the Women's Wholesale Clothing Industry 1880 to the 1960s* (The Jewish Museum London, 1988), p. 34.

CHAPTER 4

War!

'...and consequently, this country is at war with Germany'. When Chamberlain's words from his radio broadcast faded away on 3 September 1939, while the British reacted with sad resignation, the German refugees in Britain must have felt a dreadful tug to their heartstrings. On the one hand, at last their country of refuge was going to stand up to Hitler, recognising the terrible threat that he represented to world peace. On the other, there would be bloodshed, not only in Britain but in their homeland where most still had family and friends. And the enemy was now Germany, not only the Germany of the Nazis but also the country of Goethe, Beethoven and Dresden Cathedral. Now British bombs were to destroy German and Austrian churches, palaces, houses, museums. Many refugees experienced conflicted feelings.[1]

Refugees into Enemy Aliens

More immediately, their status changed overnight. In the first few months of the war there had been tribunals to categorise the aliens according to how friendly they were to the British government. After all, some Germans in Britain were pro-Nazi, as were not a few locals: one only has to think of Oswald Mosely and the British Union of Fascists or Diana and Unity Mitford, both fans of the Führer. The aliens were divided into three groups after the tribunals according to how loyal they were thought to be to the Reich: Category A was suspect, B was undecided and C was clearly pro-British. But now that war had been declared, the German and Austrian refugees were 'enemy aliens' and had new restrictions imposed on them, such as not being permitted to approach coastal areas, or own a radio or a bike. [2]

Much worse was to come: by 1940 Britain was in mortal danger. The Netherlands, Belgium, France and Norway had been invaded and 'fifth columnists' were suspected, that is to say insiders who were

German sympathisers. Could the refugees be among these? Churchill thought so and orders were given to 'collar the lot'. So it was that thousands of men, and some women and children, were shipped off mostly to the Isle of Man to internment camps where they stayed on average for several months.[3] This was another mixed experience for the refugees – on the one hand they were being locked up in a camp and for all they knew this might be yet another concentration camp, similar to the ones some had spent time in back home. How long would they be imprisoned for? Nobody could tell them. And getting letters to and from family was hard and slow. For some it was too terrifying as, if the enemy invaded, they would be easy targets for torture and execution. There were suicides.

On the other hand, they were fed (porridge and herrings, not rationed), no bombs dropped on the Isle of Man and those who could, such as the artists and musicians, worked. Being for the most part middle-class German Jews, they soon organised themselves into unofficial universities, with lectures on a wide range of academic subjects. There were concerts and lectures and some members of one successful ensemble, the Amadeus Quartet, met in the camp. Those internees with businesses were understandably worried – who would run them now?

One route out of internment was to join the Pioneer Corps, the only part of the Army that would take these unnaturalised male enemy aliens. It was a non-combatant corps so that the work involved was often hard physical tasks such as ditch digging, for which many refugees, not a few of whom were professionals and academics, were unsuited. Most of the refugees were keen to take up arms against the Nazi forces who were murdering their compatriots, but it was some years until the British government trusted these refugees enough to let them join the armed forces.

There were other ways in which the refugees could do their bit for the war effort without taking up arms: they could use their German language skills to listen in to enemy broadcasts, for example, and report back to the British forces to help them plan. Bletchley Park, a large estate near Milton Keynes was the headquarters where teams of code breakers, including Alan Turing, spent long hours trying to decipher the output of the German Enigma and other coding machines. The second stage of the code breaking was to translate the German message into English for use. Just one of the refugees who worked on the code breaking (and loved it) was Rolf Noskwith (see Chapter 6).

Rationing, Making Do and Mending

The war had of course enormous implications for the clothing and textile industries and indeed for the civilian population who needed to be clothed, not only throughout the bombing raids when many of their private belongings would be destroyed, but also as uniformed personnel in the Forces or workers in munitions and other wartime industry factories. The two main problems posed were that men were being called up or were volunteering to fight, leaving companies undermanned. Added to this was the challenge of supplies, now that the enemy was torpedoing Allied ships crossing the Atlantic with all sorts of goods. Suddenly there was a great need to conserve materials, combined with an effort to produce more on the home front rather than relying on imports from the dominions, as Britain had become used to doing.

Rationing was an efficient way of making the best and fairest use of available clothing. The rationing of clothing began on 1 June 1941 and continued until 15 March 1949. Initially, every adult received sixty-six coupons (eighteen coupons bought a woman's coat, to give an idea of their value)[4], but the number was reduced to forty as the war drew on.

'Make do and mend' went up the cry! It was time to reuse clothes that no longer fitted, to patch and darn, with little hope of getting enough wool to knit new socks. Although some felt the lack of new clothes keenly, others embraced the spirit of fairness that the scheme was conceived in. As one welfare worker remarked: 'Most of my refugee friends have had no new clothes since they emigrated two or three years ago, and they have still managed to look nice...'[5] Who has not heard of the slogan 'make do and mend'? A 'Mrs Sew and Sew' was the

British government figure invented to feature on posters and encourage and assist women in turning old coats into costumes for themselves, bedspreads and curtains were cut up to make clothes for the family and nothing went to waste.

However, this was not the whole picture: the few, as is so often the case, managed to buck the system and look glamorous. The playing field, or here perhaps the catwalk, is rarely level. Officers who could afford it had their uniforms tailored in Savile Row, and there were silk-lined gas mask cases, or expensive jewellery made from their sweethearts' regimental emblems.[6]

The majority though wore the same clothes over and over during the war and rarely complained. After all, there were other priorities for the duration. And there was some comfort: hats were not rationed, so those who could afford them made full use of their power to make a drab outfit glamorous, and women were credited with becoming 'experts in the art of "primping", adding snippets of lace or feathers, or furnishing trimmings or artificial flowers to hats, dresses and suit lapels…'[7] With its gaze steadily on supply, the government also stepped in to create a scheme that would prevent waste. Just as books were now printed right into the margins on flimsy cheap paper, so clothes too were to be made with a minimum of waste material and the Utility scheme was born.

The wartime government's aim was to share out the limited supplies of clothing (and everything else of course) as fairly as possible. Freeing up factories, however, was just as important, and rationalisation of production was a priority. To this end, members of the organisation known as IncSoc, the Incorporated Society of London Fashion Designers, including Hardy Amies, and Norman Hartnell who designed for the Royal family were all asked to design a capsule wardrobe. These clothes had to conform to the rigorous restrictions regarding the amount of fabric and trimmings permissible per garment. Luckily, Edward Molyneux for one, newly returned from Paris because of the outbreak of the war, laughed when he heard of these restrictions, saying that he had been making 'Utility' clothes for years, in the sense that simplicity was his byline.[8] When the Utility garments hit the shops in 1941, people were generally impressed. Good news for the customers was of course translated into good news for the producers of Utility, and those refugee manufacturers who got orders for such clothes were assured a market for the duration.

Paris and Couture during the War

What happened to Paris, the world centre of couture once war broke out, the source of design for high-end clothes for both Germany and Britain in the 1930s? Bettina Ballard tells the story best because she was the American editor at French *Vogue* until September 1939, returning to Paris postwar to re-establish communications between French couture and *Vogue*. She sums up the Rococo glamour of the 1939 season just before the war broke out (few imagined what the disastrous consequences for France would be), describing a costume ball, the best one of the season, for which the host had transformed the salon of his mansion into a forest. He had invited the guests to come as satyrs or birds and they threw themselves into their roles enthusiastically. Much like Marie Antoinette on the eve of the French Revolution, the Paris fashion crowd partied on, and even when a fire broke out it was a glamorous one:

> There was a near disaster when Chanel, costumed as a tree fern, dared Schiaparelli, as the queen of the ants in black tights with long, waving antennae, to dance with her and with purposeful innocence, steered her into the candelabra where Schiaparelli's antennae took fire. The fire was put out – and so was Schiaparelli – by delighted guests squirting them with soda water.[9]

When France was taken with little effort by the Germans in 1940, the Nazi occupiers had plans for couture: they wanted to transfer the production of couture, all seventy houses, to Berlin or Vienna. Somehow Lucien Lelong, president of the Chambre Syndicale de la Haute Couture, managed to persuade the Germans that this was not possible as much of the work was outsourced, to provincial embroiderers for example.

So it was that couture sat out the war in Paris. But many of the British couturiers who had trained in Paris, such as Edward Molyneux, returned to London for the war.

British *Vogue* itself, like many other publications, could have been halted by paper rationing. However, as we learn from the obituary of a German refugee who jointly with John Parsons became the *Vogue* art director, Alex Kroll, it prevailed (see Chapter 6, 'The Fabulous Kroll Dynasty'). Kroll had formed a friendship with the magazine's editor, Audrey Withers, and they weathered the war together:

> It was a challenging role for all as Withers never knew month by month if there would be enough paper stock for her magazine to survive (it had been allowed to continue as vital to home-front morale). Fortunately for *Vogue*, the photographer Norman Parkinson had avoided war service and thrived under Kroll's and Parson's direction, while Cecil Beaton submitted regular reports from around the world. [10]

Bureaucracy

Apart from changing production over to Utility, there were big adjustments to make for all industries. Through Pasold's account of their company history we can understand how the war was experienced by textile manufacturers in general.[11] Pasolds had cannily stocked up before war broke out, having seen the disaster caused by the German occupation of their native Sudetenland. Eric Pasold noted that in the first twelve months of the war, two million tons of British and Allied merchant ships had been sunk meaning instant shortages.

On the one hand, there was huge demand for goods and Pasolds were fortunate enough to be exporting 25 per cent of their knitted goods to Central America and elsewhere, bringing in important currency for Britain. They were also commissioned by the government to make basic children's clothes, now in short supply, plus underwear for the ATS, the Auxiliary Territorial Service, which was the women's branch of the British Army. But on the other hand, the problems were legion: staff were called up or volunteered as everywhere. Despite the fact that Pasolds had a unique selling point (they recycled waste textiles, shredded and combined it with cotton, halving the amount of fabric they needed), they struggled to explain this to the authorities.

The problem was that often, with civil servants being called to deal with important affairs of state, lower ranking officials were moved in to deal with industries of which they had absolutely no idea. Not only were these officials reluctant to let Pasolds build a condenser plant to prepare the waste for spinning, but they threatened to requisition the lovely modern factory that Pasolds had recently built and turn it into a factory for producing aeroplanes. Eric and his brothers clenched their teeth as the civil servants walked around with their clipboards, measuring up as they went. Finally, they pronounced their verdict – the factory door was one foot too narrow to allow a plane to pass through. Pasold nodded solemnly, not pointing out to the official, as he could have done, that any carpenter and bricklayer could have solved that problem in a matter of hours.

However, like many immigrants in Britain at this time, Pasolds were impressed by the British calm reaction to the war: they did what needed to be done with a minimum of fuss. Staff helped them to paint their huge glass factory black to disguise it from German bombers above. They all had to act as 'spotters' on the roof at night to watch for enemy planes and later as firewatchers, to warn of incendiary bomb fires spreading. Once the Battle of Britain started in 1940, the bomb damage in London, other major cities and industrial areas was catastrophic. On a visit following one night-time raid to their London office, Pasold found that all that remained of the building was their brass nameplate.

Although the company was secure in terms of orders, the problem of premises continued. The government officials had realised that in wartime it made no sense to have several different firms competing with each other, each with their own factory. So it was that the Concentration of Industry scheme came into being. Companies should choose a partner from their own sector, then agree to share plant and premises. Jantzen swimwear was chosen by Pasold who likened the attempt to share staff and the factory to get on together to people forced to share a flat against their will, not easy but happening all over Britain to save power and space.

When the Utility scheme, known officially as CC41 (Civilian Clothing 1941), was introduced in 1941, manufacturers were told that they had to use at least two-thirds of their capacity for the production of Utility merchandise. Pasolds were ready to start making clothes for the scheme immediately but were initially told that what they produced, children's underwear and warm dressing gowns (vital for those bomb shelter dashes on cold nights), were not to be included in the Utility scheme. In those days, it seems it was possible to lift the phone and speak to the relevant civil servant, and Pasold had made sure he knew everyone with any influence. Eventually, he persuaded them to include his products in the scheme and worked flat out till the end of the war.

Unlike his British competitors, he experienced the end of the war from a different point of view. He returned briefly to Czechoslovakia where his original factory had been taken over by the Nazis. They had retreated as the Russian Army advanced and now the Russians themselves would commandeer any plant left and take it back home with them. So Pasold was given an army uniform and was flown to Germany from where he made his way back home to Czechoslovakia to see what was left of the original factory. He was lucky, and the business was restored to him and his family; although others were not so lucky. Many thousands of refugees lost their businesses under the Nazis in Germany, only to hear after the war that that part of the country was now under a Communist regime of East Germany and had been taken over by the State. Often then there was virtually no compensation, but a bitter victory.

* * *

Like Pasolds, many companies turned their production over to wartime needs. The lucky few won orders to provide army underwear, such as John Smedley and Pringle, although it meant laying off regular staff, for instance the Austrian knitwear designer at John Smedley, Klothilde

Ehrenfest. For more than one refugee manufacturer, being chosen to produce such garments was the very making of their company only relatively recently established in Britain.

Notes

1. Eva Neurath was one. On her, see *Recollections, Eva Neurath 1908–1999* (London: Thames & Hudson, 2016).
2. Czech refugees were treated differently as they were not enemy aliens.
3. On the internment see, for example, F. Lafitte, *The Internment of Aliens* (Harmondsworth: Penguin Books, 1940).
4. J. Gardiner, *Wartime Britain 1939–1945* (London: Hodder Headline, 2004), p. 568.
5. Ibid., p. 569.
6. N. Taylor, 'Frontline Fancy Goods', in *Selvedge: The Fabric of your Life*, Jan/Feb 2010, pp. 49–50.
7. J. Gardiner, *Wartime Britain*, p. 572.
8. P. Nicol, *Sucking Eggs: What Your Wartime Granny Could Teach You about Diet, Thrift and Going Green* (London: Random House, 2015), p.150.
9. B. Ballard, *In my Fashion* (London: Secker & Warburg, 1960), p. 143.
10. *The Times*, 27 June 2008, Obituary of Alex Kroll.
11. E. Pasold, *Ladybird, Ladybird: A Story of Private Enterprise* (Manchester: Manchester University Press, 1977), pp. 532–612.

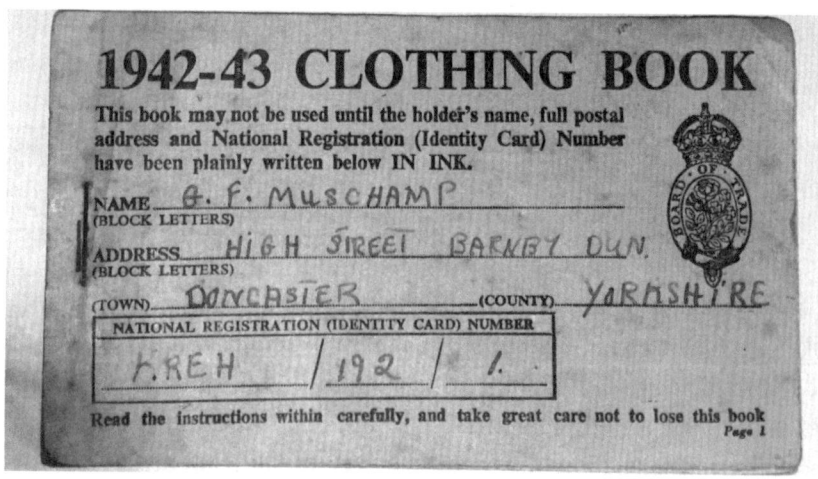

CHAPTER 5

Showing Off

VE Day, 8 May 1945, as we know from the Pathé newsreels, was celebrated in a frenzy of dancing with friends and strangers, kissing and more, drinking, laughing and much weeping. This last because it was also a time to remember the dreadful loss of so many military personnel and civilians. For the refugees the end of the war did not mean immediate news of what had happened to their families in the homeland who had not emigrated. Often it would be years after the concentration camps were liberated that they heard the worst. Not a few of the refugees now carried out what had been their original plan and emigrated on further to the United States or Palestine as travel over the sea was now possible again.

Britain, and some parts more than others, lay in rack and ruin. There were bombed-out buildings, rubble, people wearing the same threadbare clothes they had worn for years; they themselves were often thin and exhausted. What a sight they presented to the likes of Bettina Ballard who had been American Editor of French *Vogue* up until the war. After serving in the Red Cross in North Africa during the hostilities, she eventually returned to Paris to set up communications between French *Vogue* and the couture industry in Paris. Just after VJ Day, however, she went to England to write a story on postwar Britain.

Apart from the deprivation, what struck her was that the British sense of fair play had survived: all the Brits were in it together and there were no privileges for those who had contacts. 'After three months of Paris where every Frenchman availed himself of whatever he could get in that time of austerity', she wrote:

> I wasn't prepared for a country where people frowned on privileges, where rationing was accepted by all classes, where integrity, fair play – all the qualities I had been taught as a child to believe in and had conveniently forgotten – were in full force.

I saw the long queue of women in the street waiting patiently for sausage…I felt the cold and damp of the British *Vogue* office that had had no heat for years, and I saw the rough red hands of the fashion staff, chapped from cold water, cold raw air, poor nourishment and bad circulation.[1]

Reconstruction was vital. For the refugees, especially those who had been able to work successfully during the war, consolidating their newly-founded businesses, often bringing new technology and design to Britain, it was time to look to the future and plan for the new era. It would be a Britain fit for the returning servicemen and their families. Of course, the cost of war had been phenomenal and rebuilding it literally and figuratively would be costly. Now, more than ever, Britain needed to manufacture goods for the domestic and the export markets.

Refugees at 'Britain Can Make It', 1946

Wartime production had been streamlined and rationalised; could the nation capitalise on this experience and modernise? In some ways this would unfortunately not be the case: industrial relations would ironically be better in defeated Germany, thanks to new regulations imposed upon them by the Allied victors. Nevertheless, Britain could and did make use of the abilities of the German refugees whose strengths lay in design, technology and display. One fact alone bears this out: the disproportionate representation of refugees at the two postwar showcase events for British goods, 'Britain Can Make It' of 1946 and The Festival of Britain in 1951.

The 1946 show was rudely called by the general populace 'Britain Can't Have It', a reference to the rationing and shortages which dragged on disappointingly long after the war ended. The focus of the show was trade: it was time to get British products out into the marketplace both at home and abroad. Of the thirty-nine designers whose portraits appear on the University of Brighton website about the exhibition, six are refugees. An early issue of *The Ambassador* (on this journal see below) of 1946 covered the event under their 'Stop Press' rubric as follows:

> The 'Britain Can Make it' Exhibition, which opens in September, will include new designs in consumer goods from over fifty British industries. All goods on show will either be in full production by that time or will be ready for production shortly afterwards.[…] Completely new designs and techniques for the textile industry will be seen. In addition to men's wear and women's wear of every description, clothing and toys for children of all ages will be extensively shown…[2]

The war was won and things could surely only improve, albeit very slowly, with rationing still in place. New houses were being built to replace the bomb-damaged homes and even the pre-fabricated bungalows ('prefabs') were better than much pre-war housing: many lasted for years longer than their intended use.

Festival of Britain, 1951

In the official *Guide,* The Festival of Britain, which was intended to mark the centenary of the 1851 Great Exhibition, was described somewhat defensively as 'neither a museum of British culture nor a trade show of British wares' but it did include both those elements. It was a nationwide celebration of all things British, also described by Herbert Morrison as 'a pat on the back' for the British[3] and a chance to showcase the latest British goods for export and for the domestic market. Certainly the *Guide*, with its striking logo by the Anglo-Jewish designer Abram Games, was packed with advertisements for everything from nylon stockings to civil engineering companies.

Nominated Artistic Director of the South Bank in 2005, Jude Kelly noted in her opening speech in her new role that of the artists whose work featured at the Festival of Britain, 57 per cent were refugees.[4] However, it should also be pointed out, as Daniel Snowman does in his comprehensive book about the refugees from Nazism, that the Festival authorities were not always aware that they had chosen 'foreigners' for these various roles. Misha Black, a Jewish refugee from Russia, was one of the three main architects of the Festival. Among attractions on the South Bank site was architecture by Peter Moro, born in Heidelberg in 1911, who helped design the Festival Hall, furnishing fabrics by Tibor Reich and a project of designs all inspired by crystallography based on discoveries by the German refugee chemist Max Perutz. Mrs Gisela Perutz, yet another refugee, proudly modelled a dress made from fabric bearing the printed motifs of horse methaemoglobin.[5]

The New Window Display

Along with the refugees' technological prowess and their design ability came their innovative approach to display. In order to compete on the international market, Britain had to learn how to market her goods. Shops themselves had evolved, albeit in England with only a few modern examples in the inter-war period.[6] In London, the two most salient examples of modernist shop buildings were Simpson of Piccadilly and Peter Jones in Sloane Square, both completed in 1936. The author of a book on display noted that Simpson was marked by 'its strong horizontal bands of windows, its wide open floor space, its immense light fitting filling the stairwell', and that, moreover, its interior was designed by none other than László Moholy-Nagy of Bauhaus fame. The new store which was to sell men's wear was about to 'astonish Piccadilly shoppers'. Nor was the sleek building which housed Peter Jones without a refugee reference, for its architect, William Crabtree, was influenced by the émigré architect Erich Mendelsohn who had designed the beautiful Schocken stores in Germany before his emigration.[7]

However, where the German newcomers really made their mark was in window display. In Britain, up until the First World War, shop windows were used as sort of dumping grounds for goods, more store than display. In the above-mentioned book on display, there is a photograph of an early Jaeger shop front amply illustrating this point, proudly announcing 'Pure Jaeger wool' but filled with folded shirts and blouses without any regard for arrangement. The larger stores like Harrods and the American Selfridges featured wide shop windows, but nobody seemed to know how to fill them. The only idea that they had was foliage. And so every garment displayed was accompanied by a vase of flowers, a sprig of blossom or a brave branch or two. The new trade journal *Display* wasn't much help either, with such pallid advice as 'If you can't be original aim for neatness and dignity'.[8] The author of a book on the Reimann School (see Chapter 1) pointed out that the British had been ashamed of their poor attempts at display in exhibitions too, notably at the Paris International Exhibition of 1937.[9]

It was time for some Continental style and modernity. At the turn of the century Germany had recognised the need to modernise their displaying of products in stores. They grasped the nettle and in 1910 founded a specialist trade school which was integrated into the Reimann school in 1912 with a total of a hundred students enrolling that year. The underlying ethos of the department was true to the Werkbund's commitment to raise the quality of mass production. (The Werkbund was a body dedicated to embracing design for the Machine Age in both Germany and Austria.) The students were imbued with a sense of their responsibility to develop good taste in the consumer and ultimately to act as a consultant to the stores.[10]

British shopkeepers in the first decade or so of the twentieth century would perhaps have been amazed to hear that the German school was teaching their display students subjects such as Perspective, the Study of Style, Colour Science and Spatial Design. Their tutors were, as always, practitioners with their own studios. The artistic side was important, with the new movement of *Neue Sachlichkeit* (New Objectivity) also being adopted when it became fashionable for window displays. What was almost most impressive was that each student had their own study plan to suit their own talents and the setting of goals were individually catered for. It was no wonder that Berlin by the mid-1920s was known as the city with the best shop window displays in the world. Not only this, but it was said at least once in 1929 that the best art exhibition in Berlin was actually the shop windows. Reimann students came from America, Japan and other countries to take home this best practice.

Export or Die! *The Ambassador* Magazine and Hans and Elsbeth Juda

If you were invited to a certain address in South Kensington in the first decade of the 2000s, you could be forgiven for thinking you had strayed into Weimar Berlin. There was white Bauhaus-style furniture, German china and fabulous art on the walls. For this was the home of Elsbeth Juda, then in her nineties.[11] She had been born in 1911 in Germany and lived until 2014 in London. Elsbeth née Goldstein had come with her husband Hans Juda to London as early as 1933, after Hans had witnessed a row with a Nazi brownshirt and was summoned to appear in court.[12] Luckily, a friend had warned them that as Jews their best option was to leave Berlin as soon as possible. Hans was a journalist on the *Berliner Tageblatt* where as a financial editor he oversaw the textile industry. This was possibly when the first spark of his passion for textiles was felt, one which led both to his own minor design career (for Heal's he designed several prints in the 1960s[13]) and crucially to his founding and running of *The Ambassador* magazine, to which he gave the subtitle *The British Export Journal for Textiles and Fashions*.

This trade journal had had the more prosaic title *International Textiles* under its originator, the German Hans Katz. Katz had previously worked for the publisher of *Der Konfektionär*, the trade journal for the *Konfektion* sector and was also a patron of the Bauhaus. He was therefore well placed to work on a textile journal but in 1933 was forced to flee to Amsterdam where he founded *International Textiles*. His great coup was to hire László Moholy-Nagy, former Bauhaus photography teacher, as his art director, setting the tone for the modern, attractive journal. Hans Juda contacted Katz from London offering to set up a London office, and promising that, in the event of Holland's being occupied by Germany, the publication of the journal would continue from London.

This is, of course, exactly what did happen in 1940 and Hans Juda took over. But he was not alone: Elsbeth took lessons in photography in London from Moholy-Nagy's ex-wife Lucia, herself a former Bauhaus teacher, and became an outstanding photographer in her own right both as a freelancer and for the journal.[14] Elsbeth found a job at a photographic studio in Soho and learned the technical side of developing prints in a darkroom, as well as the art of retouching. She chose a short working name, 'Jay', just as ringl, pit and other female photographers back in pre-war Germany and Austria had done. Meanwhile, László Moholy-Nagy continued as art director in London, ensuring that *International Textiles* looked ultra-modern and attractive, unlike most trade journals of the time.

Juda was helped enormously by the fact that during the war Britain needed to export goods and also to create positive propaganda about British industry. This is why the Ministry of Information which was responsible for propaganda supported the journal throughout the war, crucially guaranteeing it supplies of paper which was rationed and otherwise hard to obtain. Not one issue was missed in six years and the journal was exported to the free world via Portugal.

However, it was after the war that Hans Juda decided to re-launch the magazine as *The Ambassador*. The first few issues inevitably contain references to wartime, and the gradual return to normal life, with advertisements promising goods that are available 'again' and there are advertisements for Utility tweeds. There is a letter printed in full from Sir Stafford Cripps, Chancellor of the Exchequer, promising that the country would expand with 'all speed and vigour our overseas trade', once the population of Britain had been decently clothed again. Apart from the huge number of British advertisers, there are serious editorials and pages of reports on the state of the economy in different countries. Furthermore, there are specialist articles on textile all over the world. What is striking is the colour photography at a time when colour was still a novelty. 1946 saw issues with a feature on the artist John Piper, the Royal Ballet and the start of a regular feature on British crafts as a reflection of the Judas' commitment to supporting British cultural life. Inevitably, some refugee companies made an appearance, notably an advertisement from Hornflowa, one of the Trading estate companies in Cumbria, and others from Sekers, Ettinger and Ascher.

Complementing Elsbeth Juda's creative photography in the magazine (see below) was the stunning design, the layout, typography and some of the covers. This was thanks to 'Ett', that is to say Trude Ettinger, a Czech refugee who wore black turtle necks, smoked like a chimney and whose talent made a major contribution to the appeal of the magazine. It signalled that this was a state of the art publication so that surely what was featured within the pages would be similarly up to date?

Ett had had a good teacher – Ernst Dryden (see Chapter 1). Dryden's biographer explained how the famed poster artist had left Berlin and opened a teaching studio at Trattnerhof in Vienna after the First World War, a turning point in his life following the breakdown of his marriage. Trude Ettinger, who had apparently married at nineteen, ran away to Vienna to become a designer under Dryden. 'She turned up disguised in grown-up clothes, gloves, high heels, veil and enormous hat at Ernst Dryden's door.'[15] Acceptance would mean career, glamour, modelling and drawing, just what she craved. Dryden looked her up and down and drew the veil back from her face. He said: 'Don't try and look older than you are. Go and draw some people from real life.' She must have done it well because she was accepted, the only woman among a class of men which included the famous film-maker Fritz Lang. Ett is identified in the Dryden biography as the designer and illustrator who made her name on *The Ambassador*.

Refugee Photographers at Vogue

Is there fashion without *Vogue*? Nowadays of course, there are Chinese and Russian editions of the magazine among others but it was originally American, founded by Arthur Turnure in 1892. The American, Mr Condé Montrose Nast, took over in 1905 and started publication in other countries, notably Great Britain in 1916. The launch of British *Vogue* (known by *Vogue* staff as *Brogue*) was an indirect result of paper rationing during the First World War and was followed not long after by

French *Vogue* (inevitably nicknamed *Frogue* and then *Frog*).[16] The character of the magazine has of course changed over the years, but the British edition soon after it was established became a source not just of fashion news but of excellent writing on many subjects. Authors included Aldous Huxley, who being short-sighted unfortunately sat on a new hat in the *Vogue* office.[17]

Vogue continued to appear throughout the Second World War and was considered a great morale booster, as well as providing useful tips as to how to remain stylish while dealing with the challenge of clothes rationing and general deprivation. *Vogue* even took part in reporting the war. In 1944, the American model and photographer Lee Miller persuaded the Editor to send her to France to produce an article on wartime nursing; Miller then followed the Allied advance through Europe, reporting on the Liberation of Paris and sending a story from a newly-liberated concentration camp.

By the 1920s photography was seen more and more in magazines and taking over from drawn illustration, a trend which had been born with the great Berlin journal, *Die Berliner Illustrirte*. It seems that a German photographer was the very first to use the medium:

The first fashion magazines, *Harper's Bazaar* and *Vogue* – both founded in the late 1800s – were initially illustrated by hand. It was not until Condé Nast hired Baron Adolph de Meyer (German, 1868–1946) in 1913 to shoot portraits of models, actresses, and aristocrats for *Vogue* that photographs began to be used in fashion editorials […] With the help of photography, rising couturiers in the 1920s and 1930s, such as Chanel, Schiaparelli, Balenciaga and Lanvin, each became known for their distinctive styles. Paris was the centre of the fashion world at this time, and photographers such as Horst P. Horst, Man Ray, Cecil Beaton, Edward Steichen, George Hoyningen-Huene, and Erwin Blumenfeld flocked there.[18]

Steichen's German-sounding name is deceptive: he was actually American. And Horst P. Horst who changed his name to the shorter 'Horst' had been born in Germany in 1906, actually as Horst Bohrmann, changing his surname to disassociate himself from the Nazi Martin Bormann, Hitler's right-hand man. Horst was not a refugee but was one

Showing Off

of many Germans leading the way in Europe and America in fashion photography.

Photography was after all a modern medium and brought an edginess to fashion. Central Europeans had developed lighter, better cameras so improving photography, making it their own. Just one example was the Bauhaus lecturer László Moholy-Nagy who applied the German art movement of *Neue Sachlichkeit* to his photography. This is why many of his shots show oblique, diagonal views, a novel and striking way of showing a building. Often his photographs include urban features such as metal struts, or shadows cast by modern buildings.

Refugee Graphic Designers in Fashion

Trude Ettinger of *The Ambassador* fame was not the only refugee designer at work on fashion publications. Graphic design, like photography, was an area in which German and other refugees excelled. They were in a sense ahead of the game in terms of both their training and cultural experience. And in this field of expression they were not hampered if they had less than perfect English. Their graphic work could speak for itself and it did. During the war, talented designers took up work in the ministries and other government offices, something they could do while British men and women were away fighting.

F. H. K. Henrion does not sound particularly German, but in fact his real name was Heinrich Fritz Kohn.[19] Born in 1914 in Nuremberg into a Jewish family, he was sent to France by his parents in 1933 to get away from Nazi Germany and it was there that he embarked on his long and illustrious design career. His first training was as an apprentice for the textile company Fred Levi (which also employed the artist Sonia Delaunay), where he was taught to churn out up to four designs a day, commercial experience he valued all his working life. Thereafter he attended the Paul Colin school of art, specialising in posters which was to become his preferred albeit not his only medium, but one which came into its own during the Second World War when propaganda posters had a significant role to play.

Next, Henrion went off to work in Palestine, where luckily a Crown Agent for the Colonies spotted his posters and offered him work on a citrus fruit campaign in Britain, the reason why he emigrated in 1936. Just before the war Henrion, who had been dubbed 'eclectic' by Colin, living up to this reputation amply, began to contribute work to British *Vogue*, for example a series of illustrations about the blackout in London. His impact can be inferred from a letter the then *Vogue* Editor wrote to him on learning that he was leaving:

> I do hope this will not be the case as during the last year, you have got to know our requirements in the illustrative field and if you were no longer available, we should find it difficult to replace you.[20]

The reason he was leaving in fact was to replace McKnight Kauffer, the American designer who had been creating the covers for *Harper's Bazaar* but was now returning to the States. Henrion duly designed the covers for the wartime issues, only to be told in a telegram from Randolph Hearst that his services were no longer required. Perhaps the magnate was thinking ahead to the new postwar period and simply wanted a completely new image.

After the war Henrion's work was sought after on many fronts: his versatility and style had caught on. Only one of his many advertising commissions which reached him via Crawfords (one of the first advertising agencies which had also employed fellow émigré Hans Schleger), was for the clothing company Harella. The now defunct company's story is related on a website:

> The firm was founded by tailor's apprentice Lew Harris who in 1919 returned to England from the USA and set up a small clothing manufacturing business in London which began trading under the name 'L. Harris (Harella) Limited'.[...] The operation moved to Halifax in the 1940s and grew to be a huge exporter of fashions across the world.[21]

What is striking about the advertisements is the strong reference to Surrealism, the twentieth century artistic movement that explored the workings of the mind especially in dreams, often picturing the irrational. Surrealism is probably most associated with Salvador Dali. Modern art movements were sources of influence on commercial art, not only advertisements as in the case of Harella but in *Vogue* illustrations too.[22] The drawings often reflected the style 'du jour', whether Expressionist or indeed Surrealist. In a book on this fashion illustration (published by Alex Kroll) the author notes in the mid-1930s 'a certain disembodied quality in the imagery, a sense of dislocation'.[23]

Henrion's prolonged stay in Paris combined with his fluency in French led to his familiarity with the new movement of Surrealism. In Henrion's Harella advertisement, the banner on the left of the model pronounces 'It's a dream.' A woman wearing a tailored Harella costume is 'dislocated' as she stands isolated in a somewhat lunar landscape holding onto two plants, both twice her size.

The second advertisement shows Henrion's familiarity with photomontage, a medium using cut-out photographs superimposed onto other photos or graphic work. This medium had been popularised by the political artist John Heartfield (1891–1968) whose original name was Helmut Herzfeld. German-born Herzfeld had changed his name in protest against anti-British feeling after the First World War and as a fervent anti-Nazi fled first to Prague and then in 1938 to London where he managed to eke out a living designing book covers for Penguin and other publishers. Henrion admitted that he was inspired by Heartfield: 'As Heartfield had borrowed montage from Rodchenko, so in turn Henrion borrowed from Heartfield.'[24] In the Henrion Harella advertisement, the photographic images were subsequently hand coloured and montaged with old engravings and a painted background.[25]

Hans Schleger, the graphic designer who signed himself 'Zero' had a stellar career in Britain, arriving after he had worked for Crawfords in New York on Madison Avenue.[26] While he is best known for his posters for Shell and his wartime admonishments to the British public to eat vegetables, to be careful in the blackout and to dig for victory, he produced modern, beautiful brochures and posters for several clothing companies. His archive is held in the Victoria & Albert Museum where his huge output is both catalogued and described. One commission was for Forsyth of Regent Street, a high-end gentleman's outfitter, with the advertisements for the company to appear in a newspaper at an unspecified date in the 1930s.[27]

The archivist has noted that the campaign 'was innovative in that Schleger's decision to leave empty spaces within the small space available meant that that they stood out from the surrounding editorial matter.' Another striking advertisement is for Marjorie Castle, an American clothes shop, to appear in *Vogue* in 1934.[28] This time Schleger has used a plain, typographical approach with the words on the diagonal à la *Neue Sachlichkeit* a sure way to arrest the eye on a page of horizontal type. 1937 saw an advertisement for Teddy Tinling, a Mayfair fashion designer who specialised in tennis wear. Like Henrion, Schleger alluded in his commercial work to art movements of the time: 'The surrealist imagery for his advertisement (a disjointed hand sewing) evokes luxurious fabric made up by hand to suit each individual.'[29]

It was perhaps inevitable that Schleger should also produce work for his fellow émigrés, the Judas, in *The Ambassador*. The opportunity arose when ICI wanted to showcase their new synthetic fabric, Terylene, around 1953. The archivist noted Schleger's approach: 'The brief was to stress the essential qualities of Terylene [...] The designs for this series were based on the photophysical harmonic traces of Professor Gysi, a well-known Swiss scientist whose photographs Schleger used. The advent of a new material demanded a more abstract approach visually, while at the same time linking it to practicalities.'[30] Schleger himself was a devotee of English tweeds, preferring the tradition look of an Englishman and would have had little time for synthetic shirts himself, yet he rose to the challenge providing a thoroughly modern image which hints at chemistry but also simplicity.

* * *

So refugees not only produced clothing of all sorts for the British before, during and after the war, but also helped them create a more modern and attractive way to market and display their clothes and other goods, making use of newer technology and European art movements in their efforts. Once again, the British would have little idea of who the people were who helped shape the look of what they read and saw in the fashion world. And often they did not know where they had come from nor why.

This was the back story to the immigration of around 80,000 Germans, Austrians, Czechs, Hungarians and others. Around 90 per cent were Jewish, whether they saw themselves as Jews or not, whether they were practising or not. Some of them had come to Britain for study or work in the early 1930s but found themselves surprised by political events and unable ever to return home, some of them would never see their homeland nor their families again.

The majority, however, came after 1933 and, generally speaking, the later they came the more desperate and stripped of their belongings they were. Of those engaged in textile and clothes production some were interned in 1940, while others again were allowed to get on with making the clothes so desperately needed by citizens and military personnel alike. And the refugees were for the most part keen to do their bit for Britain, whether they were allowed to fight or not.

Although the refugees had much in common with each other, from their linguistic and cultural heritage and loss of their homeland, their stories are inevitably all different, full of twists and turns, unplanned paths taken and unexpected successes.

Between them, they had us covered, literally from head to toe. The Lobbenbergs' Silhouette Little Xs kept us in shape, Kangol crowned our heads with warm, soft berets, Ettinger's wallets kept our money safe and Lord Kagan's Gannex raincoats kept us dry. Here follow some of their stories; possibly more will come to light in the future.

Notes

1   B. Ballard, *In my Fashion*, (London: Secker & Warburg, 1960), p. 211.
2   *The Ambassador, the British Export Journal for Textiles and Fashion*, no. 6, 1946, p.108.

3 *Festival of Britain Official Guide*, p. 8.
4 https://www.standard.co.uk/lifestyle/summer-on-the-south-bank-6394873.html, accessed 15 October 2017.
5 On this see, for example, L. Jackson, *From Atoms to Patterns: Crystal Structure Designs from the 1951 Festival of Britain: The Story of the Festival Pattern Group* (London: Richard Dennis Publications in association with Wellcome Collection, 2008).
6 R. Artmonsky, *Showing Off: Fifty Years of London Store Publicity and Display* (London: Artmonsky Arts, 2013).
7 Ibid., pp. 20–23.
8 Ibid., p. 35.
9 Y. Suga, *The Reimann School: A Design Diaspora* (London: Artmonsky Arts, 2013), p. 46.
10 This section on the Berlin Reimann is from S. Kuhfuss-Wickenheiser, *Die Reimann Schule in Berlin und London 1002–1903: Ein jüdisches Unternehmen zur Kunst- und Designausbildung internationaler Prägung bis zur Vernichtung durch das Hitlerregime* (Aachen: Shaker Media, 2009), pp. 221–244.
11 In an interview with Elsbeth Juda by the author in July, 2005.
12 Information on *The Ambassador* here from C. Breward and C. Wilcox (eds), *The Ambassador Magazine: Promoting Post-war British Textiles and Fashion* (London: V & A Publishing, 2012).
13 For example, 'Vortex' for Heal's.
14 Jay's work was celebrated in more than one exhibition, for example at the London Jewish Museum, 'Elsbeth Juda: Grit and Glamour', March-July, 2018.
15 A. Lipmann, *Divinely Elegant*, p. 61.
16 For an amusing account of this period in *Vogue*'s history, see E. Woolman Chase, I. Chase, *Always in Vogue* (London: Victor Gollancz Ltd, 1954), pp 129–139.
17 Ibid., p. 131.
18 https://news.artnet.com/market/a-brief-history-of-fashion-photography-32620, accessed 3 Aug 2017.
19 Information here on Henrion from R. Artmonsky, B. Webb, *F. H. K. Henrion Design* (Woodbridge: Antique Collectors Club, 2011).
20 Ibid., p. 19.
21 http://www.examiner.co.uk/news/west-yorkshire-news/calderdale-writer-jean-illingworth-sparks-10460973, accessed 6 November 2017.

22 On this see W. Packer, *Fashion Drawing in Vogue* (London:Thames & Hudson, 1983).
23 Ibid. p.103.
24 https://www.dora.dmu.ac.uk/handle/2086/6063, accessed 7 November 2017.
25 R. Artmonsky, *F. H. K. Henrion Design*, p. 53.
26 On Hans Schleger, see P. Schleger, *Zero: Hans Schleger: A Life of Design* (London: Lund Humphries, 2001); also a film by R. Sternberg (Director), A. Nyburg, *Refuge Britain: Stories of Émigré Designers* (2017).
27 AAD/2008/11/3/187.
28 AAD/2008/11/3/174.
29 AAD/2008/11/3/192.
30 AAD/2008/11/3630.

CHAPTER 6

Refugee Stories

Hats off to Otto Lucas: Gay, Glamorous and German

The door to the Belgravia apartment opens slowly to reveal a tall but frail elderly man, the Norwegian Rolf Andersen. Behind him, antique furniture burnished in the light of low gilded table lamps and the walls adorned with old paintings. On a Rococo chest sits a model of a house, some six inches wide, an Elizabethan half-timbered mansion. It is a scale model of Hush Heath Manor near Marden in Kent, the one-time country home of Otto Lucas, milliner extraordinaire whose New Bond Street business allegedly produced 55,000 hats in its last years of trading and whose hats were said to be worn by Wallis Simpson, Duchess of Windsor. Now one can find his hats in museums such as the Victoria & Albert in London, or the Museum of London, but Otto Lucas died in an air crash under slightly mysterious circumstances in 1971, and with him apparently died all traces of the person himself. There are no letters and no diaries to tell his story.[1]

And yet, in the Belgravia flat, sits Mr Rolf Andersen who was Lucas' partner from around 1960 until Lucas' untimely death, helping to reconstruct Lucas' life.[2] Explaining that Lucas was unwilling to talk about painful early memories, he nevertheless manages to piece together a narrative. Otto Lucas was born in Mülheim an der Ruhr on 9 July 1903 to a Jewish horse dealer and his wife. Here Andersen remembered being told that in the Nazi period the Swedish philanthropist Raoul Wallenberg had tried to save the Lucas parents' lives by removing them to Holland, but further attempts had failed and the couple were murdered in a death camp.[3] Little wonder Lucas was loth to speak of the past. It seems too that Lucas had had a wife and daughter but had lost contact with them, as he had with his sister who had managed to escape to Britain.

The story fast forwards from Lucas' birth to Paris, where he trained to be a milliner. However, no records have come to light of his training there but his familiarity with Paris and his fluent French would be of constant use to him professionally for the rest of his life. Next his name appears in the Berlin Jewish Address Book of 1931 (Jews were registered separately, as were their births, deaths and marriages in Germany and Austria), and it is thought that he worked in some capacity in millinery in that city.

But the next sighting of him is in London in 1932, preceding the Nazi takeover, which meant, of course, that he could not return to Germany. His company, Otto Lucas Hats, is registered in that same year. Here, Andersen helps fill in the details, for he thinks that it was the Jewish businessmen and philanthropist Sir Louis Stirling, of His Master's Voice fame, who helped fund the milliner's new business.

In any case, the workshop, showroom and shop were established at 87–91 New Bond Street (the building no longer exists). It obviously was an immediate success, judging by the profit and the clientele. There were some forty staff working away behind the scenes making the hats. By happy chance there is a Pathé film, *Heady Stuff* (1958) which shows an Otto Lucas hat being made for the film. We see Lucas putting together the hat on the seated model, then the hat being assembled in the workshop before finally being displayed in the shop window. Who comes along and spies it there? The 'It' model girl, Barbara Goalen, the 1950s equivalent of Kate Moss, who then strides out of the shop sporting the wide-brimmed creation.[4]

However, only a few years after the business was established war broke out. The paper trail reveals that Otto Lucas was interned on the Isle of Man, then released on 9 September 1940 after four months. No details of his internment are known, other than a brief note in the *Association of Jewish Refugees Journal* to the effect that Lucas was the spokesman for inmates in Kitchener Camp, where refugees were often held before being sent on to the Isle of Man. Otto Lucas Hats by then would have been generating revenue and providing employment. If Lucas had only got round to naturalisation before the war he would have been spared this disruption to his business. As it was, however, he received his British passport in April 1961.

Another voice can be added to the story as an Austrian milliner, Susie Hopkins (née Kommenda) worked for Lucas for a year or so and remembers how he operated.[5] She explained that in 1966, having trained in Austria, she went to Paris having been offered the chance of working as a *stagière* (intern) at Jean Patou. Adding practical work experience in fashion to her college art and design education was the perfect foundation for her career. It didn't take long for her to be promoted to become a millinery design assistant. Otto Lucas used to come to Paris regularly to buy the latest new model hats, which he copied and produced for the English market in his workrooms at New Bond Street. Respected as well as feared, Monsieur Lucas was a very important and influential foreign client. He was welcomed but also dreaded because of his unannounced visits, his impatience and sharp criticism. Mademoiselle Paule, the high-fashion saleswoman at Jean Patou, used to get into a hysterical panic when Monsieur Lucas' visit was announced. The salon had to be prepared, the hats displayed and, most importantly, the house mannequins had to be dressed and made up ready to show the new *chapeaux* models.

On one of these short-notice visits, with no house models available, Susie Kommenda was asked to squeeze herself into a little black Patou dress, put on make-up and model the new collection. It was a series of hats inspired by the current Tutankhamun exhibition and partly designed by herself. This was Kommenda's first personal encounter with the famous Lucas who, she had heard, ran the most prestigious and successful hat business in the world.

Lucas traditionally recruited his French designers direct from Paris but Kommenda was recommended by La Maison Patou and of course, it is possible Lucas might also have remembered her modelling Egyptian-inspired hats. Waiting in Paris for her British work permit, whilst already on the company's pay roll and receiving an 'amazing' salary, Kommenda was called one morning and told to catch a plane to London that very afternoon. Speaking very little English, she arrived anxiously at Heathrow Airport on a grey and rainy evening on 1 November 1967. She was met by Otto Lucas' chauffeur-driven Rolls Royce. By chance, it is possible to read Lucas' original advertisement for this chauffeur which gives the reader an inkling of the lifestyle which Lucas quickly earned for himself.

The Rolls Royce picked her up for work early the following morning. Otto Lucas presented her to the workroom and to her ten *filles*, all excellent milliners and far more experienced than herself. And so designing hats started immediately, in full view and under the sideways glances of the girls, who didn't have much confidence in this new, young designer wanting to make her mark. During the following nerve-racking weeks, the chauffeur carried on driving the young Austrian to and from work, which might sound glamorous, but was purely a way of gaining more working time and more new designs until the collection of about fifty hats was produced on 15 November. In her interview Susie Hopkins thought back to her former boss:

> Otto Lucas was a hard taskmaster, impatient, ill-tempered, often very hurtful and rude, chain smoking and unpleasantly coughing, but he had vision, elegant taste and a perfect sense of style.

Otto Lucas (courtesy of Rolf Andersen)

Being consulted by *Vogue* and listened to by all the important London buyers, he was a fashion and style leader, not only in the hat world, but overall.

Otto Lucas Ltd was a wholesale company, despite having private clients too. Although he was a milliner, he didn't design the hats for his own company, instead going to Paris as often as every three to four weeks for inspiration. His favourite port of call there was Mme Paulette:

> She was the last of the *grandes modistes* (great milliners) of the Parisian school…she was part of an era sadly in decline during the 1970s. At the height of her career Paulette had reigned over a much admired hat salon, with workrooms of 125 milliners and 8 *vendeuses mondaines*, society ladies with personal relations to important clients.[6]

Back in New Bond Street, Lucas worked up his collections from sketches. The hats produced under his direction were elegant, sometimes simple. In Susie Hopkins' house, the author watched one woman transformed before her eyes as she lifted onto her head a soft, red velvet Otto Lucas hat, reminiscent of the *Laughing Cavalier*'s, untrimmed except for a band of red silk ribbon round the crown. It became clear in that moment what hats could do for a wearer in the days when they were worn routinely and unselfconsciously: they brought presence and style to any outfit.

Susie's time with Lucas was short but helped her up the ladder of millinery success as it did for other milliners too. Surely the pinnacle of her career there was when *British Vogue* featured a fur hat designed by her for Lucas on the cover.[7]

The Museum of London has a website dedicated to the concept that London is and always has been a global city, displaying objects as diverse as the skeleton of a Roman girl, a medieval Jewish lamp from 1200 and a pocket watch made by Huguenot refugees, c. 1720. Object number 11 is a spectacular hat by Otto Lucas described as follows: 'This coral red velvet pillar box has a small shaped rim, in the style of a nineteenth century riding hat. The black net veil has tiny tufts of soft black 'fur' dotted throughout and this can be worn either up, on the black wings and velvet decoration, or down, covering the face.'[8]

Otto Lucas pillar box hat (courtesy of Museum of London)

Ettinger pouch (courtesy of Robert Ettinger)

Mentioned also in the caption to the Lucas hat is a point about his export sales: 'His creations were not only popular in England, but also in France and America. It doubtless helped his hat sales that headgear (other than that made of scarves) was coupon-free during World War II.' Lucas made huge sales in New York. Andersen remembered accompanying him on trips there, where they went to SAKS store, their best customer. Australia too was quick to recognise the quality of the Lucas hats and his visits were covered in the Australian press, for example on 14 July 1954 in the *Sydney Morning Herald*. Having pointed out that Lucas had the exclusive rights with the David Jones store, the journalist noted: 'The man who leaves such an elegant mark on his work is a big name and a highly respected personality amongst the world's leading milliners…America, to which he sends large quantities of his model hats, is visited by him several times a year.

It seems that Lucas was a major player in the postwar export drive, generating income for the British economy, working together with his friends Hans and Elsbeth Juda, editors of *The Ambassador* (see Chapter 5). In 1953, he supplied all the hats for a fashion show in St Moritz organised by *The Ambassador* to showcase designs by Norman Hartnell, Digby Morton and Victor Stiebel, the movers and shakers of the postwar British fashion scene and members of IncSoc. In London, Lucas was the go-to milliner for hats for Fortnum & Mason and Harrods. He supplied the hats for the fifth London Fashion Week; in short, he was among the most successful milliners in the world in his day.

It is obvious that his income was impressive and he led a life of luxury. Always an Anglophile according to his partner, Lucas had his suits tailor-made by Benson, Berry & Whitely. These he wore as he enjoyed English life to the full. In the early 1960s he bought Hush Heath Manor in Kent with its vast grounds and a celebrated garden. He threw himself into re-designing the garden, a project which was featured in *House and Garden* and *Country Life*. The grounds were used also for fashion photo shoots. Jean Shrimpton, the model who was *Vogue*'s face of the 1960s, appears in photographs taken at Hush Heath. Lucas' partner, Rolf Andersen, can be seen at the model's side; he remembers that they needed a male figure in shot.

While the couple lived in their elegant Montpelier Square house during the week with their two unclipped black and white standard poodles Olga and her son Whisky, weekends were spent at Hush Heath where the couple entertained. There was music, especially opera, poetry and endless champagne, Lucas' favourite drink. Susie Hopkins recalls wistfully the glamour of it all. And yet, Lucas had arrived in the early 1930s in Britain with a double disadvantage: he was Jewish in a time of barely disguised antisemitism, often a form of snobbery. and he was gay at a time that homosexual acts were illegal. When asked whether either of these potential problems had ever stood in Lucas' way, Andersen thought not. It was obviously possible for the authorities to look away when they chose to. And they chose to live and let live when it came to two outstandingly successful, openly gay, Jewish refugees: Hans Schneider of Marks & Spencer and Otto Lucas.

However, while studio portraits of Lucas show him as a serious, wealthy businessman exuding natural authority, he also had a different side to him, the side that was a member of Soho's famous and sometimes notorious Colony Room Club.[9] Not only a member, Lucas was the best friend of the owner, Muriel Belcher, a 'handsome Jewish dyke' according to one regular and one who never wore a hat.[10] Her sexuality made the club attractive to London's gay community, the painter Francis Bacon being only one, but there was a varied clientele of artists and people in the rag trade, including the great Jean Muir, musicians and journalists, the more outrageous the better. The novelist Julian Barnes realised during his only visit to the club that Francis Bacon's paintings could have been based on scenes from the club rather than on some external inferno.[11] The parties were legendary and anything went in those days before the 1960s.

Lucas certainly lived like a lion and, had he been conscious for those last few seconds of his life, he could have had little cause for regret. Salzburg was a regular destination for Lucas who went regularly to the *Festspiele* for the music. He and Andersen had been planning to buy an apartment there for summer holidays, and then there was the hat business as there was everywhere. On 2 October 1971 Lucas was on his way to Salzburg to buy tickets for the *Festspiele* and to look at property, sitting in BEA Flight 706, sipping his second half bottle of champagne as was his wont. The plane went down over Aarsele in Belgium; no one survived.

Was it a random fault? Perhaps not, for Andersen recounted that a friend of the couple's, Peter Coats, an editor on *House & Garden,* had been on the same aircraft while on a trip from Ireland just two days before but that the flight had been cancelled before take-off because of a bomb scare. These were the days of IRA activity and such scares had to be taken seriously. Could a bomb have been missed in the search and exploded on its way to Salzburg?

There was a service for Lucas at Golders Green crematorium, the last resting place for many German Jewish refugees. Andersen kept on

Hush Heath for some years, occasionally renting it out, notably to the actor David Hemmings of *Blow Up* fame who mentions the house in his memoirs.

Now the house belongs to the vineyard owner Richard Balfour-Lynn and the grounds are covered with pinot noir vines – how Lucas would have enjoyed that sight! The head gardener who kept the grounds for Balfour-Lynn's father, the previous owner, had also worked for Lucas and told of the days when Lucas would arrive for the weekend at the Tudor gatehouse to be dropped there so that he could stride up the immense driveway to his beautiful house.[12]

It is perhaps better that Lucas didn't survive to witness the decline of hat-wearing although, astute businessman that he was, he may well have divined its beginnings. However, his millinery legacy survived him for decades because two men who trained with him and worked for him went on to glory: Frederick Fox and Philip Somerville. They were also the executors of his will. Both milliners designed hats for Queen Elizabeth II, as well as for other members of the Royal family and acknowledged their debt to the master of millinery, Otto Lucas.

One day, perhaps his name will be as well known as the celebrities who wore his gorgeous hats. Until then, we can only marvel at these Otto Lucas hats in their museum vitrines.

Ettinger: Bags of Style

If you go to the Gentlemen's Accessories department at Fortnum & Mason in London's Piccadilly, you will enter the hushed world of carpeted luxury. The air is scented with the finest wood and leather. The sales personnel, wearing their morning suits to the manner born, are omnipresent but discretion itself.

In one antique vitrine are displayed, as if they were sapphires or emeralds, exquisite wallets and small cases stitched, as if by Beatrix Potter mice, ten stitches to the inch. These leather goods are by Ettinger, a company created by Gerhard Ettinger, as he was then in 1934. 'Oh yes, I remember Mr Ettinger,' said Mr Stanley Grant who joined Fortnum's decades ago, having run his own leatherware company for years, 'He was a real gentleman.'[13]+

One of the greatest success stories among the refugee entrepreneurs, Gerard Ettinger, as he was to become, is certainly one of the most glamorous figures. His obituary is studded with words like 'Marlene Dietrich', 'multi-lingual' and 'skiing until the money ran out'. But his origins were somewhat more prosaic.[14]

He was born in 1909 in Posen then in Prussia (but which is now Poznan, part of Poland) where his father owned a military tailoring shop, not the only successful émigré to come from this background.[15] As his son Robert remarked decades later, the family had both business and craft in their blood and the step from cutting and sewing suits to making leatherware is a relatively small one. Also typical of the experience of many Germans of this generation was that after the First World War, when Posen was handed over to Poland, his family had to leave for Berlin, rather than choosing to become Polish and start life anew. Gerhard's first job was with a locomotive company, not something he enjoyed but, after moving to another company in the same sector he was sent to Rome and things started to look up. In fact, he left that company in order to stay on in Rome, and soon got wind of a German film production looking for Italian-speaking staff and he was taken on.

This was his first experience of how speaking one or more foreign languages can lead to employment. Indeed, many European Jews were familiar with the idea of speaking more than one language, as a people who were often on the move, and who had to communicate across borders – a tradition dating back to the Middle Ages when Jewish sellers of cloth walked across countries (see Chapter 1). It is also clear from accounts by others who knew him that he had a natural gift for charming people, another essential attribute for success in the world of retail.

He was kept on with the film company when they returned to Berlin, moving up to becoming a producer on films such as *Zigeuner der Nacht* (1932) many of which starred Felix Bressart and Marlene Dietrich, both of whom were later to flee Nazi Germany for the freedom of Hollywood. 1933 arrived and the inevitable consequences for the Jewish Gerhard Ettinger. Ever resourceful, he used his now considerable knowledge of the film world to contribute actor profiles to a film lexicon, moving yet again, to Paris this time, to finish the project. It was from Paris that he moved to London, hoping to find contributions for the book and taking English lessons from the actor Hubert Gregg, whose tuition led to Ettinger's cut-glass accent.

He now was at ease in three foreign languages and impressed those who met him with his confidence. Although his British documents clearly state that he was not allowed to carry out work, 'paid or unpaid', he was then offered an opportunity which enabled him to capitalise on his ability to move within different spheres: the chance to represent several German leather goods and other accessory companies in Britain. It was probably around this time that Mr Ettinger adopted an English look: a bowler hat became his trademark and what could be more English? In keeping with his smart appearance and his BBC vowels, Ettinger set up in Regent Street from where he sold German luxury wares to Harrods, Asprey and Fortnum & Mason. This was the first version of G Ettinger Ltd, est. 1934.

When war broke out in September 1939, Ettinger did as other Germans and Austrians in Britain did and applied to join the armed forces. His great nephew Pablo who is researching Gerhard's life reflected:

I am fairly sure he started out in the Pioneer Corps and was a dispatch rider in Devon. And that was a typical job given to them I believe. Somewhere I found out he ended up in Belgium towards the end of the war transmitting propaganda into Germany. Oh and I have just remembered that after the war he was invited to join MI6 but he declined and as a small detail, in his Pioneer Corps detachment was a certain Robert Maxwell.

Typically of that generation, he said little about his wartime activities and records are at best patchy, but it is thought that at first he was a despatch rider in Devon, moving on later in the war to fly gliders to Belgium, dropping off either material or people to help the Allied war effort. Pioneer Corps activity was for the most part heavy, dirty work, while the refugees would far rather have been actively fighting the Nazi troops, an option not open to them until around 1942. But at least Ettinger seems to have been able to do his bit.

For many, the postwar period was drab, depressing and austere: the Allies had won the war but devastation was all around, rationing was severe, and a life of deprivation and shortages stretched ahead. However, bowler-hatted Gerry Ettinger was not part of this image: at the end of the war he joined a film company that had been commissioned to rebuild the German film industry, now de-Nazified and looking to the future. The project was based in Schloss Warenholz, a castle which had been used by the Hitler Youth. In later years, Robert Ettinger met a Canadian woman whose father, also German, had worked on the Warenholz project too, but he too had never told his family, like Ettinger keeping all his wartime activities a complete secret. It seems it was not only the former code-breaking employees at Bletchley Park who kept 'schtum' about their activities for decades after.

No dried egg, no scrimping and saving for him as once this work came to an end 'Ettinger spent a year skiing and socialising in Gstaad until his money ran out'.[16] Back in London, though, his future looked less certain. But strolling through the West End one day at a loose end, he was spotted by Mr Asprey, he of the jewellery and luxury accessories firm founded in the eighteenth century. 'Come here Ettinger! What are you doing? Come into my office.'[17] It is a good thing he did, because the encounter resulted in a new business venture. For while the demand for goods was high, materials were difficult to find. Mr Ettinger was the chap who could find them in Europe where he knew the people and spoke by now four languages.

This was the rebirth of G. Ettinger Ltd, now a maker of leather goods rather than a retailer of other brands. The refugee company had to have a British director in those days and one was duly appointed. Some of the products were made in London or in Walsall, home of the English leather industry for centuries, while other leather was sourced from the Continent. Ettinger travelled around provincial cities as well as London, always by train according to his son, even when flying became cheaper. He continued to represent other British luxury brands abroad, unfazed by the prospect of 'foreign', unlike his more insular peers.

Gerry Ettinger (right) at a press launch (courtesy of Robert Ettinger)

The company went from strength to strength, although still a 'niche' product for those in the know. In the 1960s Ettinger bought up a luggage-making company called Prestwick: leather suitcases were no longer selling well. Realising that export was the future and so well fitted for it, Ettinger started to market his leather wares in Japan, learning Japanese for that purpose. This was a very new market then, with few Western goods sold there.

Gerry Ettinger had now settled down, marrying a Viennese woman whose mother was Jewish. Her family had stayed on in Vienna, refusing to believe that they could come to any harm under Nazi rule, having lived in Vienna for eight generations. The Ettingers had two children. It took the next generation in the form of Robert Ettinger, Gerry's elder son who took over in 1990 (Gerry having continued to work into his nineties) to spread the word and strengthen export to the Far East. Robert had been sent by his father to Frankfurt am Main to learn both the trade and the German language. Unlike many other refugees who could not ever imagine returning to Germany even for a visit, this open-mindedness was a sign of Ettinger senior's deep-rooted attachment to his European heritage which could not be wiped out by mere Nazis.

The Ettinger brand has a cult following in Japan and Korea. The only Ettinger store is in Tokyo, where Anglophile aficionados pore over the elegant card cases, leather-clad flasks, cases and wallets. They love the fact that the leather is made in a factory in Walsall, specialising in leather since 1890, and in an online film *A Celebration of Craft*, Robert Ettinger describes the long, narrow building with natural daylight as being a perfect workshop. We see the cutting, assembling and fine tuning of an Ettinger piece, the lining in a deep velvety purple, for the Sterling range features the colours of British bank notes. Robert Ettinger points out that the wallets are like English City suits: darker and conservative on the outside with a flash of vivid colour on the inside, which reveals a different feature of the Englishman, his flamboyant side. This colourful lining is also a popular feature of, for example, Paul Smith's jackets. Against the bright lining, the Royal Coat of Arms can be seen, as Ettinger was awarded a Royal Warrant to HRH the Prince of

Wales in 1996. The prestige afforded by this symbol of approval has enabled Ettinger to export successfully all over the world.

In a sense, Robert Ettinger is continuing what his father started: constantly adapting, looking further afield than others, embracing the challenge of trading in a foreign environment, learning the rules of engagement and making a success of it. Ettinger seems to be a perfect marriage of English traditional quality combined with European cosmopolitan flair.

The Little Refugee Kangaroo: Kangol

In clothing, the greatest success story of the Trading Estates project (see Chapter 3) is Kangol, who made berets and other hats and still do. The little kangaroo who identifies berets as Kangol is the result of putting two and two together and getting five. For Kangol, according to family member Nadine Meisner, comes from K from silK, Ang from ANGora and OL from woOL and has nothing to do with Australian marsupials. Another version has the 'K' from Knitting, as suggested in the crossed knitting needle logo, but in any case, it was the Americans asking where they could get those 'kangaroo hats' that decided the company on their kangaroo logo, adopted in 1983. And the 1980s was a boom time for Kangol, though only one of many for this refugee hat company. Because Kangol berets, like denim jeans, like Doc Marten boots, are democratic, universal wear, sported by intellectuals, actors, the cool as well as the simply chilly.

Jakob Henryk Spreiregen came from France to Britain in around 1914, no doubt alarmed by the outbreak of the First World War.[18] Spreiregen had been born into a Jewish family in Warsaw in 1893 but his family had moved to France because of the uncertain political situation, the first of several moves.[19] It was in France that Spreiregen first saw dark blue Basque berets, worn by French Alpine soldiers. These early berets were made by felting wool: pounding wetted wool so that it could be shaped and would also at least be showerproof if not rainproof. Having changed his name to Jacques, Spreiregen fought on the British side in the First World War and was awarded British nationality as a result. This must have made his move to London easier when Spreiregen, alarmed by the Nazi takeover in neighbouring Germany, took this prescient step. His London company imported and exported silk, angora wool and also berets, eventually becoming Kangol in 1936.

In the interwar period, the beret enjoyed a brief moment of popularity when sported by the Duke of Windsor. In Paris Schiaparelli had designed a beret among her more outrageous hats, which had then been adopted by Marlene Dietrich and Greta Garbo, style icons of their day. Berets were in.

Finding that he could not import enough berets from France to fulfil his orders, Spreiregen decided to manufacture his own. Nigel Watson, author of a study of the company takes up the story:

> Berets then as now were made using a knitting process rather than the feltmaking process more commonly used for hats. Spun woollen yarn was delivered on conical rolls of thread known as cops, which had been wound onto a spindle. The yarn was rewound onto cones for use on the beret machines which turned the yarn into knitted U-shapes. These woollen shapes were machine-seamed down the middle, using an invisible sewing process known as linking. The small hole left at the top was crocheted together by hand, leaving a small length of yarn to become the beret's tip. The knitted woollen hoods were scoured in soap and water and pounded by wooden hammers into soft, pliable felt before being dyed in open paddle vats. The damp, dyed berets were stretched over special flat wooden doughnut-shaped forms to create their size and shape. After being dried by hot air…the berets were placed in a teaser, which, acting like a wire brush, raised the berets' nap. Finally, to create a smooth surface, the berets were sheared using a machine with rotating blades working on the same principle as many lawnmowers.[20]

John Jackson Adams, a local politician and driving force behind the West Cumberland industrial Development Council, invited Spreiregen to set up his new enterprise in Cleator Mill (see Chapter 3). Following Spreiregen's acceptance of the offer, he was able to start work at his new factory, helped in this by the arrival of his nephew Joseph Meisner, who came over from France in 1938 to work with his uncle. Meisner and Spreiregen became a lifelong team.

An impression of life from a worker's point of view at Kangol in the late 1930s is provided by a former employee in an interview held with her in 2005.[21] She worked as a linker, a job described above: 'I am

Kath Ford and started my working career in 1938. A firm called "Kangol Wear" had recently come over from France to manufacture berets in the premises of the old linen mill in Cleator. It was in its very early stages and there were only four people working there.' She explains that they were familiarised with the looms by a French lady and her mechanic husband who could speak no English but that 'by concentration and observation, we conquered the language barrier and I learned my trade.' She was proud to have learned to be a 'linker', which was fine work. She moved on to train up other workers.

'The factory,' she said, 'was owned by a Mr Sperrigan [sic] who was a French Jew and his nephew, Mr Meisner, helped him run the firm. We always knew when Mr Meisner was around because we could smell his aftershave which was something new and unusual in Cleator, so we were forewarned of his arrival and seldom got caught out!' Continental sophistication in the form of aftershave had reached Cumbria. The French lady referred to was either the technician brought over by Spreiregen or else his wife, and all early employees recall the language barrier of the first years.

But evidently the experience was positive all round, as Watson summarised: 'Jacques Spreiregen never for a moment regretted coming to Cleator. He fell in love with the Cumbrian fells and had the highest regard for his workers. He always claimed that he could have found none more eager to learn or more conscientious in their work.' Pointing out that the workers were no doubt grateful for the work in those straitened times, Watson is nevertheless short of the mark regarding the poor wages, as Mrs Ford remarked: 'I have many happy memories of working there for the princely sum of ten shillings [50p!] per week until we went on to piece work when we could earn as much as three or four pounds a week', finally concluding 'I stayed at Kangol for four years until I was twenty years old when, in 1942, I was conscripted to work in munitions, but I still stay in touch with the girls I worked with at Kangol and we meet now and again to exchange memories of sixty-seven years ago.' Spreiregen cared for his workforce in other ways too, paying for one girl's treatment for tuberculosis in those days before the National Health Service.

Initially there was healthy demand for the Kangol berets both made in Cleator and imported, but the outbreak of war in September 1939 brought instant restrictions. In 1939 when Britain declared war, Meisner went over to fight for the French Army. Kangol was one of many who embedded their British company on the strength of their wartime success. 1942 brought a welcome change of fortune for Spreiregen for there was now a surge in demand for berets for the armed forces and for Air Raid Wardens, among other services. Watson picks up the story again: 'Thanks to the natural attributes of wool and the practicality of its design, the Kangol beret was soon selected as the non-dress fatigue hat for all uniformed men and women...' The most famous wearer was

Kangol wool Monty beret (courtesy of Sean Leon)

Field Marshal Montgomery, known as Monty, hardly ever seen without his, a habit which resulted in most other officers taking up this form of headwear too.

One of the several reasons for its suitability was the fact that it made a poor target for snipers. Now demand was huge, and production was aided by a government 'Essential Works Order'. This meant the maximum realisation of the plant's capacity, a feat which was achieved by another refugee, Gustav Huber, who was brought out of internment on the Isle of Man for this purpose. The military is still one of Kangol's biggest clients, with berets also supplied to the United Nations soldiers as well as to the British forces.

Demand continued after the war, though much reduced. However, Kangol were keen to be part of the postwar export drive and Kangol agencies were established in India, Pakistan and the Americas. By 1952 Kangols were sold in forty-nine countries. In 1948 a 'feather in the Kangol beret' was identified at the London Olympic Games where all the British team members wore a Kangol they had been presented with by the company and their smart appearance was commented on.[22]

A second factory (known as 'the Fez', because of an early plan to manufacture fezzes for export to the Middle East) was opened in nearby Frizington after the war to produce berets which were finished at Cleator, making a total workforce of about 300 workers. For this reason Spreiregen decided to design his own machines, like the clothing giant Pasold, and had them made in Leicester, 200 in all. The machinery fine-tuned by Gustav Huber, with his 'many technical improvements', worked well and business boomed. By the end of 1952 Kangol was floated on the London Stock Exchange.

The 1950s were a time of expansion and diversification, bucking the trend for the hat industry as a whole which was in decline after the war, hats no longer being routinely worn. They bought up an existing hat firm hard hit by this decline, W. Carrick and Co, and also acquired a Yorkshire yarn spinner to supply their own wool, thus making Kangol a completely vertically integrated and efficient business. But the boom years did not last and Kangol started to diversify into safety helmets and seat belts. Determined not to return to the pre-war doldrums

Spreiregen, no longer young but feisty, inventive and forward-thinking, had some time ago engaged a new designer called Eileen Greig. By 1955 there were four times as many Kangol models available with peaks, for children, and even a furry 'Kangora'.

It was not just the designs which were new but the technology too: the introduction of thermo-forming, a process which made the beret keep its shape if sat on, or worse. The process was overseen by Gustav Hubner. By then, yet another refugee had joined Kangol, this time a Hungarian, George Dan, fluent in several languages. But it was a Polish refugee, Walter Wolfram, who as Export Sales Manager tripled sales within only months. Later George Dan took over this role. By the 1960s Kangol, always creative, were using their own patented equipment to carry out this process. An American press cutting of the time summed it up the effect neatly:

> The Basque beret, its price is reasonable, it always looks smart. Squash it in your pocket – it comes out fresh and uncrushed. Perch it at any angle you please – It stays there. Decorate it with a feather or a brooch – It will go with your best outfit. Snug and warm for winter – not too hot for summer...[23]

The litany of its qualities continued.

George Dan, like Spreiregen and Meisner, was fluent in several languages and took on the task of exporting Kangols all over the world, trebling sales within only months. Once again, having had to adapt to a new country and culture stood them in good stead, giving them the confidence to travel and communicate with foreign businessmen, something which their British counterparts often felt was alien and difficult. Japan proved a great untapped market. Watson takes up the story: 'Continued success resulted in the company winning the first of three Queen's Awards to Industry for Export Achievement in 1966.'

By 1968, as Watson pointed out, the export sales were worth £1.9 million, or 70 per cent of their total sales. The Swinging Sixties were of course about more than sales figures and Kangol obtained the sole right to make and distribute hats which featured the Beatles.

Eileen Greig designed a range of Beatle caps and berets and a press event to publicise them. Mary Quant too, the celebrated 1960s style-maker. was commissioned to design a Kangol beret in 1966 as was Pierre Cardin. But none of these ventures into fashion made much impact on sales. The biggest marketing failure, though, came in the form of the golfer Arnold Palmer because although Kangol acquired the rights to use the name, the campaign was poor and crucially Palmer was hardly ever seen sporting a Kangol. Celebrity promotion would, however, bring spectacular results later.

By 1956 Jo Meisner had for some time already been Joint MD with his uncle who remained active until at least 1962, the date for his formal retirement being unclear. They could look proudly at their three Queen's Awards for export and take the credit for being major employers too: 1,250 employees in that year, having grown from 35 in 1938. But the wholesale system was costing large amounts of money and so it was that Kangol, ever changing, moved over to a retail-only system. From 1976, Kangol reps went all over the UK selling the brand to stores.

By the late 1980s the company was selling around five million hats a year, not bad for a company which had started in Cleator with Mrs Ford and three others. Meanwhile, in the USA, Kangol started to make hats for the American market, different models from what the Brits bought and wore, manufactured by local industry, not Kangol, The greatest coup here was the success of their hats with the African-American community who had always had their own style preferences. Suddenly, Kangols were being worn by young and old, each in their own way. Also, hats for the warmer American climate included the new Vent-Air, ideal for summer. Strangely, though, it was a furry 'furgora' bucket hat which was adopted by the rapper L. L. Cool, and overnight, the brand became cool. DJs, musicians such as Boy George and Goldie and actors made Kangols their own. Samuel L. Jackson sported his '504' throughout the entire length of the film *Jackie Brown* directed by Quentin Tarantino.

Back in the UK Graham Smith became the Head of Design, an RCA graduate who had trained first as a milliner with Lanvin in Paris. He had sold his own designs to Fortnum & Mason. Diana, Princess of Wales appeared in a Kangol and the brand went up-market.

Gradually, the company moved across to the United States so that today sadly nothing remains of the Cleator site but the memories. There are, however, two rather pleasing links, as Sean Leon, Global Marketing Director based in New York City explained:

> Bollman Hat Co., America's Oldest Hat manufacturer turning 150 years old next year, recently invested in bringing the original Kangol knitting machines from China (moved from Frizington in the 1990s) to Adamstown Pennsylvania.[24]

So the original machines that are at least 100 years old are still making Kangol hats. These are the single-bed knitting machines which create a dome shape that is open at the back and are still linked together in the traditional way, leaving a small hole at the top which is hand sewn together. And yet more continuity is assured by the presence of Head of Design, Nic Harris, who has clocked up some twenty years at Kangol, first at Frizington, then London and now in New York, not the only Kangol Brit, she explained, to have emigrated there. 'The brand is ever evolving, creating understated styles which are trend-led without being ostentatious.' While, she adds crucially, 'staying true to its heritage'.[25] By heritage, Nic explained that she meant the combination of old and new: using the traditional machines which were custom built and create beautiful quality but have limited functionality, while at the same time creating contemporary Kangol designs. Asked whether she had been aware that she was working for a company with foreign origins, Nic reflected that so many workers had been with the Cumbrian company for generations that all the stories about the past had come to light eventually.

Nic laughed when she thought back to her first days in Cleator: she couldn't understand the local Cumbrian dialect, coming as she did from Lancashire! Cleator, like neighbouring Whitehaven, was on the edge of the country – nobody was going anywhere from there. Like Mrs Kath Ford faced with the French mechanic, Nic couldn't communicate. However, she also remarked that textile factories the world over are places where women, foreign or local, learn to communicate without language, because of the noise as well as any language barrier, just like the weaving rooms of Lancashire where women learned to lip-read in the past because of the deafening sound of machinery. In any case, given that they earned piece rates, they are not keen to stop working to chat.

The mainline collection reflects Kangol's continuing commitment to its heritage. In 2018 the brand celebrated its eightieth anniversary in the hat-making business. There have been recent collaborations with Marc Jacobs, Comme des Garçons and Stussy. The Kangol story is one of stamina, hard graft and flexibility as well as of vision; one played out by two refugees from Nazism, determined to survive.

Joseph Meisner (right) with two French engineers installing the knitting machines in Frizington, 7 April 1938 (*The Whitehaven News*)

Making Sparks at Marks: Hans Schneider brings Dior to the Masses

The Sieff family, who together with the Marks made Marks & Spencer what it was, were convinced Zionists. They were also committed when it came to it to giving a helping hand to the refugees from Nazism when they could.[26] There is no doubt though, that the company benefited from this help too, as refugees from a textile background in Germany or elsewhere brought with them technical, business and design innovation. Just one such was Dr Eric Kann, who had been employed in Chemnitz by the Schocken company 'to start a laboratory for merchandise quality testing and standards development'.[27] His obituary refers to the 'rising tide of antisemitism' in Germany which forced him to leave, implying his Jewishness rather than spelling it out. 'In 1935,' it continued, 'the late Lord Marks appointed him to build up a laboratory which could give impartial advice to the textile industry as a whole, and thus was involved in that important part of the Marks & Spencer selling slogan: "quality tested"'.

Another was Erich Heim, a refugee from Vienna who eventually became Head of the Colour and Print department at M & S. He brought with him a PhD in Physics and Chemistry but also a passion for art. After completing his studies, he tried to find a career which would enable him to combine science with design. He ended up in Prague, spending eleven years in a textile company. It was there that he received an invitation from M & S, a company which he said was known in Europe as it was in Britain. He was now stateless like other Austrian Jews since Austria had been annexed into the German Reich in 1938. Even worse, he spoke hardly any English and apparently there was much miming at M & S when he first arrived. Nevertheless, in the *Sparks* article about him, Heim paid tribute to the members of the Board and to his colleagues who had helped him through the challenging early days enabling him to lay the foundations of the Colour and Print Department. Erich Heim was the one who put on the first of many exhibitions of cloth and clothes at Michael House. The stories of Kann and Heim illustrate how M & S was improved by embracing science as well as Continental design.

But the author of a study of the refugees at M & S warned against seeing the employment of the refugees as only positive: less well-known, younger refugees, she maintained, were sometimes resented by the British workforce at the company. They could also 'encounter in their careers restrictions and delays that reflected their special status for some considerable time after they joined the company'.[28] She concluded, however, that those who were allowed to thrive at the company amply repaid the trust put in them.

In 1949 Marks & Spencer took on Mr Hans Schneider (1910–1995), small, dapper and full of Viennese wit as their Head of Design, a move they must soon after have blessed their cotton socks (and knickers) for. The many stories in the company magazine *Sparks* tell of his triumphs. It was Schneider who was instrumental in improving the quality of design following years of Utility clothing. In 1949 Schneider had taken on a team of eight designers but by 1967 not only had he upped that figure to seventy but he had taken M & S into couture. Moreover, he brought glamour and publicity to the previously somewhat wholesome and conventional clothing from this company.[29]

Who was this charming and influential Austrian? A regular feature in *Sparks* was the 'Who's Who in the Business' and in March 1952 it covered Hans Wolfgang Schneider, at least as far as the basic details are concerned. What it did not say, of course, was that he was both gay and Jewish and it hardly touched on his contribution to the arts, as one would expect from a house journal. The only nominally fictionalised account of Schneider's life by the novelist Julian Barnes gives a little more detail of the hardship he experienced before emigration.

He had started his career working for a jersey and knitwear company in Vienna where he had a good grounding in organising skills, then moving on to learn machine knitting. It was in 1934 that he left Austria for Leicester where he 'specialised in the production of continental-type jumpers and dress collections'. His reasons for leaving are not given but 1934 was the year that Austro-Fascists destroyed the social democrat regime of Vienna, violently attacking people and buildings. And of course, it could simply be that he saw a work opportunity and took it.

But as a Jew he could not return to Austria after 1938, as he would have been deported and murdered. The *Sparks* account notes that Mr Schneider was in the Army between 1939 and 1941, almost certainly not the case: he wasn't naturalised until 1947 and later admitted to his friend Neil MacGregor (former Director of the British Museum) that he had in fact been interned on the Isle of Man. He then had a spell working for John Lewis, advising them on their manufacture of army clothing and of women's wear, after which he became their Fashion Buyer for a short time.

Schneider's career at Marks & Spencer was marked by the end of Utility clothing and clothes rationing. He knew Norman Hartnell and other members of IncSoc, and was seen in photographs with them, a mark of the respect with which M & S design was held in the 1950s and 1960s. It was Schneider who attended the Paris collections regularly, adapting and simplifying the shapes so that they could be produced less expensively but with no loss in style:

> A blouse in a small shop may catch the eye of the ever watchful Mr. Schneider, the collar may have something special, the sleeves are new, perhaps the embroidery could be adapted[...]A nightdress with the new rounded neckline will soon be reaching stores – It was found in a Paris shop very recently.[30]

One of the M & S archivists noted that the Design department under Schneider worked a year in advance and that every one of the designers was also a technician and fully qualified as a cutter.[31] This, she suggested, mirrored Schneider's admiration for Balenciaga. But it is Dior who features in an article in a *Times* clipping.[32] A charity fashion show, described as 'lavish', had been held at the Royal Festival Hall to benefit the British Heart Foundation in which the very best of M & S was shown off:

'PARIS INSPIRED'

The facts behind the claim, as told to Mary Welbeck

PARIS INSPIRED really does mean inspiration and ideas from Paris—Mr. Hans Schneider, head of our design, said last week. Paris is teeming with ideas from the big shops, the little shops, from "haute couture" to "confection". Of course, not everything can be copied, for M. & S. has to watch fashion trends very carefully and while not lagging too far behind, must not rush up with the "avant garde"—on the other hand as the line changes and a new silhouette emerges M. & S. must keep abreast with the times.

A blouse in a small shop in a side street may catch the ever watchful eye of Mr. Schneider, the collar may have something special, the sleeves are new, perhaps the embroidery could be adapted—a dress from one of the big houses may be just that something. A nightdress with the new rounded neckline will soon be reaching stores—it was found in a Paris shop very recently. A French lingere (that is an expert underwear cutter) is a full time member of the Design department bringing French influence right to the spot. A pocket on a skirt; a new pleat, Paris invariably leads the way.

Hand-made buttons, (used frequently in couture houses) can make all that difference to a dress, but the hand-made buttons from Paris can be translated into mass-produced M. & S. possibilities.

A child's embroidered dress found in Paris led to one of our dress manufacturers getting in a special machine from the continent to produce the same type of embroidery—and what a difference to the garment it makes.

It's ideas, ideas all the way.

Mr. Schneider at work.

'Paris inspired' article, *St Michael's News*, April 1955 (courtesy of the Marks & Spencer Company Archive)

Designer Hans Schneider is most excited about his group of his and her safari clothes and by a brilliantly striped tunic dress worn with white pants. This outfit is the St Michael adaptation of an original Christian Dior model which they bought in Paris.

Those who remember M & S in the 1960s will look back fondly on the incredible value for money, the style and the quality of the fabrics but perhaps be unaware of who was behind it.

Early on in Schneider's career, he showed himself keen to enjoy publicity for M & S. There are two accounts of the television show featuring Schneider and the M & S design process. The first is by the Departmental Manager of the Hammersmith store: 'The purpose of the T.V. Film Unit was to complete the film in the Children's Hour series "Men in Action", in which Mr H. Schneider, the M & S Fashion and Design Specialist, played a leading part.'[33] The content of the programme is explained by Floor Supervisor Mrs L. Smith in *Sparks*. She begins her account, 'We were introduced to Mr Schneider, head of the Design Department at Head Office, and before our very eyes the history of one of our Spun-Rayon Teenage Dresses from the designing room through the factory to our Stores was revealed.' A television set, still a rarity in those days, had been hired for the staff to see the programme. It made an impression on the sales staff, as Mrs Smith revealed: 'We emerged from the rest room, with even more respect for the garments that we sell. For we realise more than ever that the actual sale to the customer is but the last desirable act in the short life of a dress at the Store but maybe a joyful act in the life of a satisfied customer.'

The next appearance of Schneider on screen, in 1963, was more glamorous as this time it was a cinema screen. The event was covered in *St Michael News*, the business-orientated in-house newspaper. '"Glamour gets a Passport" is the title of the new Rank Organisation *Look at Life* feature which went out recently on the Rank West End circuit.' Evidently, the fashions featured were from IncSoc and 'the fashion department of Britain's largest chain store'. The Marks & Spencer clothes shown off in this august company would all be seen later in the year. The film was made to spotlight the 'ever-increasing impact of British fashion – both ready-made and made-to-measure – on the world's export markets.' A proud moment indeed for M & S in general, and for Hans Schneider in particular.

The Summer 1965 *Sparks* covers another design coup: M & S had taken on the internationally-known Irish designer Michael de Carlos, whose real name was Michael Donnellan (1915–1985). 'These two

'Television, the Dress Designer and Dressmaker' article, *Sparks*, April 1957 (courtesy of the Marks & Spencer Company Archive)

intense and nervous individuals,' wrote the excited reporter, referring to Schneider and Donnellan, 'sparking each other like flint on steel have ignited a brilliant new chapter in the adventure story which began with the slogan: DON'T ASK THE PRICE, IT'S A PENNY.'

After the war Donnellan had worked for Lachasse, the company which had launched the careers of Digby Morton and Hardy Amies, and had opened his own London couture house in 1953. However, it had not been easy for M & S to woo him; Schneider had tried and failed. Six years later Lord Marks himself had asked Schneider, 'Why can't our skirts look as good as my wife's?' 'Who makes your wife's suits?' asked Schneider. 'Michael of Carlos Place' came the answer. 'I approached

The Designing Department's party was reputed to be the gayest of all Head Office parties, the main theme being Paris. (L—R) Mr. B. Muldoon, Mr. L. Moran, Mr. H. Schneider, Miss M. Spottiswood, Miss B. Goulden, Mr. R. Whitecross and Mr. K. Burgess.

Hans Schneider at an office party, *Sparks*, April 1957 (courtesy of the Marks & Spencer Company Archive)

him once,' replied Schneider, 'it's your turn now'. 'This time,' recounted the reporter, 'Michael was won'. Michael brought to the team an intimate knowledge of fitting clothes to women from his private salon. Schneider and Donnellan obviously drew inspiration from each other and found their joint trips to the European shows stimulating.

Schneider's reign at M & S coincided with the Swinging Sixties. While he visited Carnaby Street to see what young people were wearing, he kept away from the popular throwaway fashion of the day, preferring to steer a more middle of the road course raising, rather than lowering, the tone.

In *Sparks*, Schneider's potted biography ends by mentioning his role as Visitor and Chairman of the Examining Board of the Royal College of Art, a role previously held by Digby Morton and Norman Hartnell. This was cited as an example of Schneider's commitment to the training of designers. But lest it be thought that Schneider yearned for the Continental glamour of the catwalk, the article ends: 'Mr Schneider considers that a boy or girl starting a career as a designer, has a much more rewarding and interesting field in working in M & S than in the narrowing world of *haute couture*.'[34]

Other photographs in *Sparks* show him at M & S parties having the time of his life in a conga line or dressed as a pierrot and in his element. The caption to one is 'The Gayest Head Office Party', meant of course in its older meaning of the word 'gay'. Schneider was gay in both senses of the word, in his private life and in his role at M & S. There can be no doubt either that he was happy to be alive.

Over Here and Underwear: Silhouette

The refugees covered every inch of the British body with their clothes, and this included underwear. But lest this topic should be thought dull, the reader should be warned: this story contains a radioactive corset, a mysterious artist walking in off the street to offer for free the perfect logo for the company and an unlikely musical. For this is the story of Silhouette (Salop).[35]

The company had its origins in Cologne in 1887 when it was founded by two Jewish businessmen, Emil Blumenau and Max Lobbenberg. The former was clever with finance and legal matters while the latter was the technical genius, responsible for construction but also having a gift for sales. Their product was the corset in an era when such garments were crucial for the creation of an hourglass figure for even quite substantial ladies.

Once again, skiing played a part in the company's history, this time when Mr Lobbenberg went to St Moritz for a skiing holiday:

> From the shape of the ski he got the idea and the name for the *Ski-Federn* or 'stays bent into the shape of skis'. These were incorporated into the back of corsets for stout women. It was then that the Ski-Korsett was born which was the main brand name trade mark.'[36]

Now heavier women would be able to associate their corsets with the healthy sporting activity of skiing and success was guaranteed. All went well and the company even weathered the First World War relatively unscathed, as did they the new trend away from structured shapes for women in the 1920s by diversifying partly into bathrobes. The sons of both partners joined the firm and the prospects were good.

But by 1930 Otto Lobbenberg was worried. He was one of the few to understand early on that if the National Socialists did manage to get into government then the Jews would be in mortal danger. After all, *Mein Kampf*, Hitler's autobiography, had been published in 1925 and his intentions towards the Jews were set out in it quite clearly. In 1930 Otto Lobbenberg set up a separate company in Paris, Manufacture de Corsets Silhouette, while Max and Hans Lobbenberg, together with Hans Blumenau, stayed on in Germany. One account has it that their elegant art deco logo was sketched by a young Montmartre artist whom they had met while he was working as a waiter.

In 1936, with great foresight, Hans Blumenau moved to London and set up another company named Corsets Silhouette Ltd. Meanwhile in Cologne, the underwear company Lobbenberg & Blumenau celebrated their fiftieth anniversary. But in 1938 the German company was forced to sell to an Aryan competitor, a Mr Wendling, as well as to pay 30,000 Marks as a fund for his non-Jewish employees left behind, a form of punishment. In December of that year the Lobbenbergs and their families moved to London sponsored by Hans Blumenau, who put up the £50 per head to guarantee that the family would not become a burden on the British state.

Corsets Silhouette Ltd had been incorporated in 1936 in Islington, London. Luckily for them slimness was fashionable in the 1930s, as was health and beauty generally. Rubber girdles helped women to look slim and the new models were perforated so that they didn't 'split, peel or crack'.[37] But the German corsetiers wanted to go one further, as the author of their house history relates:

> Silhouette became responsible for the world's first (and perhaps only) radioactive corset when, in 1937, Hans was approached by his partner Otto, from the Paris office and offered the manufacturing rights for a 'new and revolutionary' garment – the radioactive corset, 'Radiante'.

This foundation garment was advertised with claims that it was made with fabric 'impregnated with radioactive elements – uranium , thorium and radium' and was said to 'give a feeling of energy, fitness and resistance to chills'. Incredible to us now, it was an immediate

'Radiante' corset (courtesy Peter Lobbenberg)

success, with several department stores making orders.[38] Whether it made a large profit is another matter.[39]

Nothing is known of the long-term effects, if any, on the wearers. Despite this success the new company struggled to make profits and limped along until the outbreak of the war, when they were ordered to make garments for the Utility range. At last there would be a big demand for their products, but on the other hand there were supply problems and, worse, there were bombs. But before they decamped to safety yet again, a family story (possibly embellished over the years) maintains that a stranger walked in and asked for an interview with Hans Blumenau. He had created an advertisement for Silhouette in the form of a shapely woman with a gazelle on a lead, in silhouette. He asked for no payment should they accept, simply the pleasure of knowing that his design had been appreciated. The advertisement, so the story goes, was duly adopted for their letter-head, packaging and window display and the man was never seen again.

Imagining that the countryside would be less likely to be hit by German bombs, the two refugee partners decided on Shrewsbury as a suitable home for their corset making. Coventry had been another option, luckily they had rejected it, given what a strafing that city suffered during the war. They soon found a collection of buildings for storage: a disused church hall, what had been a waterworks and a former pub, all suitable for corset making. The pieces, once cut out for the garments, were wheeled in an old pram across the River Severn to be machined, a far cry from their smart factory back in Cologne. The Blumenaus and Lobbenbergs, quite different personalities, set up an unlikely 'commune' sharing a villa near the company premises. There was a brief scare when both the incumbent Blumenau and Lobbenberg were brought to the police station to be interned as enemy aliens, but it soon became clear that the employment of so many would suffer if the partners were absent and they were released.

After the war, some restitution was paid for the loss of their German business and in addition Silhouette bought up the entire stock of elasticated fabric from a source in France, an astute move which meant that they were the first postwar company to be making good foundation garments. Things were looking up at last. The London office re-opened, and the next generation of both families joined the Shrewsbury firm. In 1956, an elegant ultra-modern factory was built nearby.

But their biggest success was yet to come. Czech-born Annemarie, Hans Lobbenberg's second wife, was a designer (she had studied art in Vienna). It was probably she who had approved the design of the amazing 'Radiante' before the war. Now, after she was shown some new lightweight material, she designed a girdle with two crossover panels over the front which would flatten a heavier stomach and flatter the figure while still being relatively light to wear. 'Little X' was launched in 1956. The suppliers of the new fabric and Silhouette held their breath: after all, the company had gambled all their money on the success of Little X. But after a short wait the product took off, requiring the new factory to work flat out. In 1956 the firm's annual turnover had been £700,000 but by 1957 with the new product it reached £1.3 million.

There followed the inevitable challenges of staffing and production that major expansion brings to any firm. But Silhouette moved with the times, adding mail order to its portfolio, producing garments for an American supplier and acquiring other firms and premises in Bristol and Market Drayton. By 1970 Silhouette's turnover was up to £6,000,000 and their staff numbered around 2,000.

And there was more. Silhouette was an exemplary employer, providing sports and social facilities for their personnel. There was an in-house journal which, like most, provides a picture of life at the firm and of the people who worked there. As was common with the refugee entrepreneurs, several other German-speaking refugees were on their staff too. Peter Lobbenberg fondly remembered one: Leo Borger, the cutter. Lobbenberg recalled that when he was a small child, Mr Borger would 'lift me onto the cutting table, whip out his shears and give me an impromptu haircut'.[40] At least six other refugees were employed there at one time or another.

Girdle-wearing started to become less popular in the 1960s and the company began to produce more swimwear instead.

'Silhouette' swimwear (courtesy of Peter Lobbenberg)

After years of acquiring companies, mergers and other measures, the company was finally taken over by asset strippers and the different parts of the firm were sold off. One branch, the production of bras for mastectomy patients, was taken on by Gerry Sigler (see below), now made redundant, who ran the enterprise on a freelance basis with an ex-employee of Silhouette, Michael Donovan.

But the company had had an enormous impact on Shrewsbury, becoming part of its history as well as being a major employer. Volunteers were asked to come forward and talk about their memories of working for Silhouette, resulting in about 120 interviews. This formed the basis of a musical play, *Silhouette*, by Chris Eldon Lee, about the period when Silhouette was based in Shropshire. It was staged in Market Drayton on 13 and 14 November 2009 and at Shrewsbury's Theatre Severn from 17 to 21 November in the same year.

In the house history, we read of the 'new sales team headed by Gerry Sigler'.[41] Gerry Sigler was one more of the refugee employees. His son, Nick, added his family's story to the Silhouette's. Gerhardt Sigler was born in Prague in 1921 into a family who then moved to Chemnitz, which was the centre of the pre-war German textile industry something like Manchester or Leeds in Britain.

Under the Nazi regime their company was 'Aryanised' and the family received a pittance for that loss. A family member, Leon, who had a shirt business in England guaranteed Gerhardt and his sister when they came on one of the *Kindertransports* to the UK. Gerhardt Sigler moved straight into agricultural work in the Stratford area as he had good English but initially no other openings. In 1940 he was interned on the Isle of Man. There he made friends with Ludwig Spiro who later became the chairman of the Wiener Library (the London-based Holocaust library). On release, Sigler worked in agriculture again in the Midlands.

However, after the war in around 1945, Sigler joined the American Army as an interpreter and was based in Frankfurt am Main. It was about this time that he met his future wife, fellow German refugee Gisela Heineberg. They married in London in 1946. They spoke English at home unless they needed to communicate something private in front of their children. He rejected all things German. However, he retained his Jewish identity, becoming a member of the North London community, although not attending synagogue regularly. He later volunteered at the Wiener Library.

Sigler hosiery factory in Chemnitz (courtesy of Nick Sigler)

In 1947, Sigler joined Silhouette which had been co-founded by a cousin of his wife's mother, Hans Blumenau. He always worked in the London Head Office in Park Lane, going three times a month to the Shrewsbury factory and travelling widely with his work. Restitution for the Chemnitz company did not come until 1990. The only way to prove the size of that factory, no longer in existence, was to show the image of the building featured on the letterhead, one sample of which the family still owned. It seemed that Sigler would not be paid any German pension. Luckily, however, he remembered that he had worked for three weeks one summer in the factory before emigration and so, in the event, was entitled to a German pension.

Nick Sigler spoke of the humanitarian, philanthropic tradition which prevailed at Silhouette, possibly shaped by the founders' refugee experience. The house history by Nigel Hinton contains many testimonies to the sports and social events held for employees. Gerhardt Sigler's experience made its mark on the next generation too, with some pressure exerted on Nick not to go into agriculture but to go into a graduate career instead, since Gerhardt himself had not had that opportunity. Luckily, Nick Sigler found the perfect compromise studying agriculture at university, then pursuing a career in the labour movement. Silhouette, it seems, supported both Britons and refugees in more ways than one.

Textiles and the Refugees: Colour, Texture, Pattern

While Britain could look back on centuries of wool production and since the Industrial Revolution on cotton processing, the refugees brought with them their own traditions of creating fabrics and also of decorating their surfaces with prints or woven patterns. There are structural fabric designers and surface designers, and some makers are both, such as the Hungarian-born Tibor Reich.[42]

Not a few came as young people and studied at the progressive Leeds University Textile Technology Department, thereafter able to combine British with native concepts in textile production. These included Tibor Reich, Bernat Klein and Joseph Kagan. Those who succeeded managed to weather the challenging war years, to emerge at a time when Britain was more than ready for some colour, pattern and texture and this they brought us in bucketfuls. Below is a brief introduction to the stories of eight people: one German, one Czech, a Czech couple, two Hungarians, a Serb and a Croat, all Jewish, who together changed the look of British fabrics and what we wore. At least one of these has risen again from the ashes of the refugee grandparents' companies and is trading successfully.

Elisabeth Tomalin

We are sitting in the enormous studio of Elisabeth Tomalin's famous grandson Thomas Heatherwick, designer of the Olympic cauldron for the 2012 Games, the new Routemaster buses and much, much more, all over the world. As Thomas recalled his memories of his grandmother, he made clear connections between her life and his. He remembered sleeping under the drawing bench that she herself had designed for her new job, that of Head of Printed Textiles at Marks & Spencer.[43]

But to begin at the beginning, in 1912 in Dresden.[44] Elisabeth Wallach was born into an assimilated Jewish family but moved after school briefly to Vienna in search of the artistic company she sought. Around that time she recreated herself as 'Suaja', much as the photographer Elsbeth Juda called herself 'Jay' and like many other female creatives in Germany adopted a single-word pseudonym. On her return in 1932 she enrolled at the Berlin Reimann Schule (see Chapter 1) remaining there until 1936, albeit without gaining any formal qualifications, as the school and its owners were forced to move to Britain while she was a student there. She worked as an assistant for the last period she was at the Reimann, thereby able to study without paying the school's fees. A lack of money remained a source of anxiety and difficulty for her until her marriage in 1940 and her subsequent successful career. That she learned new techniques at the Reimann such as batik is evident from the samples of her work from that time held by Heatherwick and his mother, but she studied a wide range of other applied arts subjects too, including window display and poster design. All her professional life she could draw on this training.

When the school 'emigrated' to London in 1936 (the English branch was founded in 1937 after the Berlin school had been sold under pressure from the Nazi authorities), Wallach too threw in her lot with

Thomas Heatherwick with printed scarf from Elisabeth Tomalin's archive (courtesy of Thomas Heatherwick)

Britain now that it was clear that in Germany, Jews were *unerwünscht*, 'undesirable'. But as so often, the necessary job proved elusive and in any case left-wing refugees such as Wallach were a source of suspicion at that time of appeasement. She was now desperate, as the author of perhaps the only article on her related: 'Unable to find professional employment, she was advised to purchase a return ticket to Paris and to remain illegally, gathering a portfolio whilst in black market employment.'[45] She experienced real hardship while in Paris. Little wonder, as her grandson related, she had not much sense of humour, something which she compensated for with her loving and affectionate nature. But a wonder perhaps that her creativity survived intact and that she was able to go on to love and create a family. Back in Britain she finally landed the sought-after job as a textile designer at Barlow & Co in Manchester, who manufactured printed silks until the war put an end to this luxury production.

1938 proved a better year for her: she was able to bring her immediate family over to Britain and safety and she met Miles Tomalin. He was returning from action in the Spanish Civil War and was a handsome, aristocratic journalist, convinced Communist and member of the family who had taken on the Jaeger firm (see Chapter 1). It is unfortunate that this connection didn't lead to a job for Elisabeth, as they had no textile print section.[46] Allegedly, Miles met Elisabeth at a soup kitchen at which he was volunteering and she receiving, quite possible in the circumstances. The couple married in 1940, thereby changing Elisabeth's nationality to British and sparing her internment at one stroke. And now that Barlow could no longer employ her, other wartime opportunities opened up for her with her excellent training. The newly-formed Ministry of Information Exhibition department must have thanked their lucky stars for finding Elisabeth Tomalin with her display and poster skills. Their daughter Stefany was born in 1945 to much delight.[47]

Only after the war could she return to her real love of textile design, working for another silk printing business, but there were tensions between her work, her child and her marriage. In 1949 Marks & Spencer gave her the recognition she deserved, employing her to set up a new printed textile department. Here she would be in good company as many other refugees worked here in prestigious posts including Erich Heim and Eric Kann,[48] as well as Hans Schneider, Head of Design or Illo Sommerfeld.

Part of what she brought to M & S design was modernity. In a film in which she is one of the subjects, Heatherwick said that she was the most modern woman he knew, citing a ring which she wore all her life which looked like nothing in nature but was a swirl of abstract movement. But now at M & S she had to design for literally millions of women in postwar Britain, not wealthy but able to afford a bright new headscarf or blouse to perk up their shabby suits which had seen out the war. The patterns are beautiful. Beauty, reflected Heatherwick in the film, was not a word which sat easily on the lips of Britons, not when he was a student anyway, but was taken seriously by Europeans without any connotations of sentimentality. Her colours were subtle and attractive and the patterns sold all over Britain. And yet all that remains of her career in the M & S archive is one photograph of Tomalin in the house magazine *Sparks*, leaning over her desk intent on designing.

But at least her husband made notes on her career in his diary so that we learn that in 1950 she 'set up all designs and colourways, visited printing factories in northern England and travelled to the couture shows in Paris and Milan'.[49] Her job at M & S came to an end, a reflection of the decline of the British textile industry in the face of cheaper competition from the Far East, and instead she embarked on a busy freelance career. However, in 1969, she retrained as an art therapist. She worked in Germany too in this capacity, with people struggling to make sense of the Nazi past, something which helped her as it helped them. Her dark past was obviously very much still with her, although no one could possibly have guessed this from the colourful and elegant designs she produced for M & S.

Jacqueline Groag

One who numbered among Elisabeth Tomalin's émigré friends was the glamorous, elfin and highly talented Jacqueline Groag who was born in Prague with the more prosaic name of Hilde Pick in 1903.[50] That she was so successful in Britain is probably due to two factors: firstly her art education and training and secondly, her early recognition (helped by the former) in Paris before her emigration. Her childhood was an important factor in her design career and in fact she said that she had an inner age of eight years. Childhood motifs, especially the wooden Czech dolls she loved, were a common feature in her patterns. She married very young but her first husband died, leaving her a widow at twenty. It was then that she decided to move to Vienna and train as a designer. She went straight to the best place and enrolled at the world-famous Wiener Werkstätte's school. There, she was fortunate enough to benefit from an experimental education project under Professor Franz Cižek at the Vienna Kunstgewerbeschule. Cižek's idea was to rid his students of any pre-conceived notions of art, especially with regard to copying and instead to encourage freedom of expression and to retain a childlike freshness in producing art. Music was played during classes. Blumberger, as she now was after her marriage, flourished and quickly became the star student with a natural aptitude for pattern. She was accepted onto the KGS's architecture course (without having to apply) where she specialised in 'the design of textiles, wallpapers, carpets and posters'.[51]

Her trademark was a grid pattern covered with small motifs, often inspired by Czech folk art or vernacular buildings. She was singled out at college early on, winning prizes, and was soon designing fabric in Paris for the *crème de la crème* of couture designers like Paul Poiret, Coco Chanel and Elsa Schiaparelli. She married a fellow Czech, the architect Jacques Groag (changing her whole name to chime with his) and decided, rather rashly as it turned out, to return from Vienna to Prague in 1938. When the Sudetenland too was occupied by German troops, the Groags fled to London where at least Jacqueline's work was well known and respected. The couple moved into the fashionable Isokon building in London's Hampstead where the great Bauhaus architect, Walter Gropius, himself had stayed. They quickly became part of the arty set in London, numbering many émigrés among their friends including Elisabeth Tomalin. Jacqueline was very striking with her 'large green eyes, jet black hair and delicate, almost waif-like physique'.[52] She soon received orders, mostly for her quirky furnishing fabrics. However, one dress fabric that she did design enchanted more than one British couturier. In 1946 Princess Elizabeth posed in a dress designed by the Anglo-Irish couturier Edward Molyneux, the tulip-sprinkled fabric designed by Jacqueline Groag.

Postwar Britain celebrated the new era with the Festival of Britain in 1951 and of course it was not only the British who provided the design: 'Refugee textile designers too were well represented at the Festival, in particular Jacqueline Groag', who contributed 'textiles and wallpapers, [a] three-dimensional sculptural screen for the *Living World* section of the *Dome of Discovery*'.[53] She combined elements of her Viennese training with modern themes featured at the festival, as noted in a monograph on her:

> Decorations derived from molecular imagery were rife at the Festival and in each of the screen's large elements, smaller individual components were strung and suspended to appear like free-floating molecules contained within a grid-like frame, strongly reminiscent of Josef Hoffmann's early work.[54]

Hoffmann had been the director of the Wiener Werkstätte and teacher of the Vienna KGS where Groag had trained. Her designs often followed the grid form mentioned and other British designers, such as Lucienne Day, took up the same theme in some prints. Groag's screen design was the starting point for both a wall covering for the Festival's Information Centre and later was adapted for domestic use for David Whitehead.

Her own home was featured in *House and Garden*. She had a long and successful career in Britain, designing fabrics of all kinds, although her private life was marred by the early death of her beloved Jacques.

Tibor Reich

One who is certainly associated with the concept of 'modern' is Tibor Reich, born in 1916 in Budapest into a Jewish family of textile manufacturers who produced braid and ribbons both for Hungarian traditional costumes but also for military trimmings worn by soldiers in the Austro-Hungarian army. Tibor grew up with the factory as his playground, absorbing this colour and texture. He had a comfortable childhood, enriched by travel to Paris and other cities.

His school days at an end, he was sent to university in Vienna where his first choice was to study architecture but his stern father insisted on textile studies. A rich collection of Tibor's diaries, photos, sketchbooks and notebooks chronicle the look of Vienna in the late 1920s, some modernist buildings appearing, the speed of modern transport noted, the look of the streets and people's clothes and, above all, the visual patterns seen in everyday life. However, despite its attractions, Vienna was uncomfortably antisemitic and already by 1933 Tibor and his family were evidently becoming anxious about the Nazi takeover in next-door Germany.

In a filmed interview Tibor Reich's grandson, Sam, pointed to a photograph of the Reich family, explaining that his grandfather had made a copy of it and ringed the members who had not survived the Holocaust, which he thought was about 75 per cent of them.[55] Once safely in this country, Tibor Reich created a family of four children with his wife, and was a loving and involved father despite being extremely busy professionally.

From Vienna Tibor was to move now to Leeds, where the university had a state of the art textile department which attracted international students. Here Tibor's talents as a structural designer were recognised: the young Hungarian wanted to bring textured, 'fancy' yarns usually reserved for couture to furnishing and his results won prizes. Enormously ingenious, Tibor simply invented what he needed, just one example being felt pens to design prints before such things existed (unfortunately he didn't succeed in patenting them). In England, while Tibor was enchanted with the novelty of the way of life, especially the gentlemanly, tolerant manners of the English, he was dismayed to find his surroundings rather drab. Interiors were dark, flat and old fashioned. Where was the modernist excitement of Vienna or Budapest?

Refugee Stories

'Spaceflight' by Tibor Reich, 1957, the same year as the Sputnik satellite (courtesy of Sam Reich)

Tibor saw ways to recycle fabric scraps, just one example of his inventiveness. With his home-made felt pens he produced colourful fabric designs for the home. But he also had success with fabrics for couture: he found support from the couturier Edward Molyneux, who had relocated from Paris once war broke out. Molyneux (and Digby Morton too) bought Tibor designs, just as he had bought Groag's, lending his august name to the émigrés' creations and so helping them along the path to becoming established.[56]

Tibor Reich's story is far too long and eventful to recount here in full, but he founded his own company in Warwickshire after the war and started producing fabrics with bright colours never before seen in English homes.

Tibor combined British and Hungarian traditions; literally weaving together Harris tweeds and bright or shiny colourful yarns from back home in Budapest. He invented several printing techniques, one of which involved cutting up photographs of, for example, straw, mud and stone to create a completely new pattern. These elements can be seen in his design 'Spaceflight'.

Fortunately he was able to exhibit at the Festival of Britain, which helped spread the word about his striking designs. But one of his finest moments was certainly gaining the commission to design curtain fabric for Buckingham Palace. His 'Princess' fabric was chosen by the future Queen to be a wedding gift for herself as Princess Elizabeth. To the simple white and stone-coloured yarns, Tibor had added 'a hint of aluminium yarn, a subtle highlight to the plain weave, just enough to create the illusion of a spot of water on a leaf'.[57] Still today the fabric sells well, being a 'British' classic.

Along with his friend and fellow émigré the Serbian Bernat Klein and others, Tibor made a real change to the fabrics bought and used in Britain, bringing colour, texture and modernity to the new postwar era. Far from belonging to the past, Tibor fabrics have risen again from the ashes and the company has been re-launched by Tibor's enterprising young grandson Sam, who now sells the fabric as a luxury brand to exclusive hotels and similar venues all over the world.[58]

Molyneux outfit, drawing by Eva Aldbrook (courtesy of Eva Aldbrook)

Bernat Klein printed dress (courtesy of Heriot-Watt University Heritage Service, image by Douglas McBride)

Zika and Lida Ascher

Zika Ascher was born in Prague in 1910 into a family of successful, upmarket textile company owners. His father was Jewish but his mother was not.[59] Zika and his brother set up their own fabric shop in 1933, one which had a complicated history of ownership through the Nazi and then Communist regimes in Czechoslovakia. After Zika left the country, his mother claimed (in an attempt to prove that he was not Jewish) that his brother had been fathered out of wedlock – a brave act in those days.[60] The shop was very fashionable, for example, the brothers arranged a moving window display that was otherwise spare and modern. And, possibly as a marketing gimmick – their advertisement claimed that a Monsieur X had recruited famous painters to design fabrics for them – something which would become reality later in British exile. A champion skier (Zika represented his country at Hitler's 1936 Winter Olympics in Garmisch-Partenkirchen), he was known as the 'Mad Silkman' for his recklessness on the slopes. Attractive and confident, this cosmopolitan Czech spoke French, German and English fluently, a great asset to one who would need to negotiate and socialise in Europe. He married Lida Tydlitat, from a Catholic family, in 1939 and they left for a honeymoon in Norway.[61] Lida had studied business and was similarly at ease speaking French and other languages.

While they were on honeymoon in Norway, Hitler annexed the Sudetenland and the couple discovered they could not return home. Were they prepared for this? It has been noted that they took books with them on their honeymoon. They were saved by members of the Ski Club of Great Britain, who supplied letters of recommendation for the English border authorities. They entered Newcastle Upon Tyne by the skin of their teeth, said Zika's son, Peter, 'with a few hundred pounds and Lida's jewellery hidden in a sock'. After moving to London they rented a tiny top-floor flat off the Marylebone Road, bought a stout wooden table and slept under it every night as the bombs fell over London. By 1942 the energetic young couple had established premises at Regent Street, but of course war was raging and Zika joined the Czech army in Britain. In 1943 he was invalided out. Lida, who had no design background, began producing patterns in diminutive florals and lines of mock calligraphy.[62] The British couturier Edward Molyneux quickly realised the appeal of their fabric designs and bought most of Lida's first collection of Modernist designs and continued to support the couple.[63] Later, Princess Elizabeth and her sister wore Molyneux dresses in Ascher silk on their South African tour. Decades later still, Elizabeth, now Queen, came to Lida's studio in person to buy clothes, as did Wallis Simpson. Some of the fabric printing for the Aschers was carried out by fellow Czech exiles, the Socher company.[64]

In 1944 the Aschers came up with the idea of producing scarves designed by artists. Scarves were ideal garments during the war, for not only did they protect the hair from wind and dirt but were affordable and could ring the changes when women had to wear the same clothes for a long period of time while they collected ration coupons for a new item of clothing. And they could be combined to make a skirt or top. They commissioned artists such as Henry Moore and Feliks Topolski to design squares. 1946 saw Ascher prints featured at the V & A's 'Britain Can Make It' exhibition. After the war Zika went to Paris where he phoned French artists including Matisse and persuaded them to design 'squares' as they called their scarves. In 1947, thirty-seven of their squares were exhibited at the Lefevre Gallery in London to much critical acclaim.

In 1948 they became British citizens: like other refugees, they had to wait for the long backlog of applications to be cleared before it was their turn. They had no desire to return to Prague now that there would be a Communist regime there meaning more uncertainty and possible danger to them. For their host country they had brought in export income from their scarves schemes and others. Their son, Peter, was born in 1950 and although they spoke Czech at home, they rejoiced in their English life and their beautiful house in Hampstead. Like other 'textile children', including Richard Donner (see Double Two), Peter remembers visiting the Ascher store in central London where he would slide on the chute to the storage basement, landing softly on Ascher mohair bales. Typically, too, he was taken to art galleries by his cultured parents.

Constantly open to innovation, the couple embraced the use of synthetics when they first appeared. In the early 1950s nylon was combined by the Aschers with mohair, so fashionable in that decade, to create a puffy but lightweight fabric. Perfect for a coat to be worn with a slim-fitting sheath dress, a typically 1950s silhouette. So popular was this look that the term 'Ascherised' was coined. Although used to mock the ubiquity of the fabric, it was a compliment of course. Scottish wool was combined in different ways with synthetic fibres, and some of the resulting mohair was bought by the French couture house, Lanvin Castillo and later Givenchy.

In 1987, there was a retrospective exhibition of the Aschers' work at London's V & A Museum. However, it was only in 2019 that the Museum of Decorative Art in Prague put on an exhibition of the Aschers' lives and work, recognition finally of their country's great cultural loss through exile in the 1930s. According to the chief curator, it was only now that Czechs were slowly learning about this chapter in their history, long ignored under the Communist regime.[65]

The company folded in 1980 although there were other companies owned by the Aschers. Lida, who had had TB in Britain, died in 1983 while Zika lived on until 1992, having returned at least once to the Czech Republic to ski in his old age. In his own contribution to the book published to accompany the Czech exhibition, Peter Ascher pondered on the unlikely success of his refugee parents. Zika in particular had thrown himself into one untried project after another, with barely a care for overdrafts and bills: 'Was this just sheer folly, reckless risk-taking in the extreme? Or was it perhaps a reaction to having had their lives turned upside down in 1939?'[66] Perhaps for them, as Peter said, nothing could ever be worse than that. This was why they lived life to the full. Their *joie de vivre*, their multilingual cosmopolitanism and openness to new ideas, their sense of taste developed in one of Europe's most sophisticated cities and their creative energy resulted in the production of joyous prints and weaves that were a boost to British fabrics at the very time they were needed.

Miki Sekers

Yet another refugee textile company, which like those mentioned above still trades today, is Sekers, established by Sir Nicholas Sekers (known as 'Miki') who came to Britain from Hungary in 1937. He had been trained in textile technology in Krefeld in Germany and had already experience of textile manufacture at the family's silk mill in Budapest. In Britain, together with his cousin Tomi de Gara, he set up West Cumberland Silk Mills in 1938 in a depressed non-textile area at Whitehaven. It would be another of the refugee success stories in England's North West.

When war broke out it meant changing from producing silk for clothing to manufacturing material for parachutes. Sekers made the transition from a natural fabric to a synthetic, calling on his experience in Hungary, France and Germany and thereby safeguarding supplies to make enough parachutes for the war. Eventually they wove two million yards of the synthetic parachute silk.

Once the war ended Sekers used his new fabrics for postwar fashions. The smart advertisements featured in *The Ambassador* show how attractive the garments made in these fabrics were. Soon he was selling fashion fabrics at home and abroad. That great unsung hero Capitain Molyneux (who had bought dress fabric from Jacqueline Groag and Tibor Reich) was a client, as were Christian Dior and Givenchy in Paris.[67]

Like the Aschers, he commissioned artists including Graham Sutherland to design on fabric for him. In 1962 one of Sekers' ranges was awarded the Duke of Edinburgh's Prize for Elegant Design. On these fabrics, the company's website comments that again Seker's aim was to give the biggest choice in the widest price range. This range consisted of about 100 qualities with more than two thousand colours all of which were in stock. These fabrics were an immediate success.

After the 1950s, the company decided to focus on furnishing fabrics instead of fashion and eventually relocated to Scotland. In 2018 Sekers were still trading, as their website relates, which is an incredible achievement given the problems of the 1970s for British textiles:

Sekers are currently in their eightieth year of trading and specialise in the design and supply of furnishing fabrics and wallcoverings to the international hospitality market. Servicing architects and designers involved with this industry, they are key suppliers to many famous hotel chains along with cruise ships, restaurants, bars and healthcare markets. Sekers have partners in all the key design regions globally including America, Europe, the Middle East and Asia, making it a truly international brand.

A contemporary sketch of Sekers, the man, showed him to be the cosmopolitan *Kulturmensch* (man of culture) as much as he was a successful businessman:

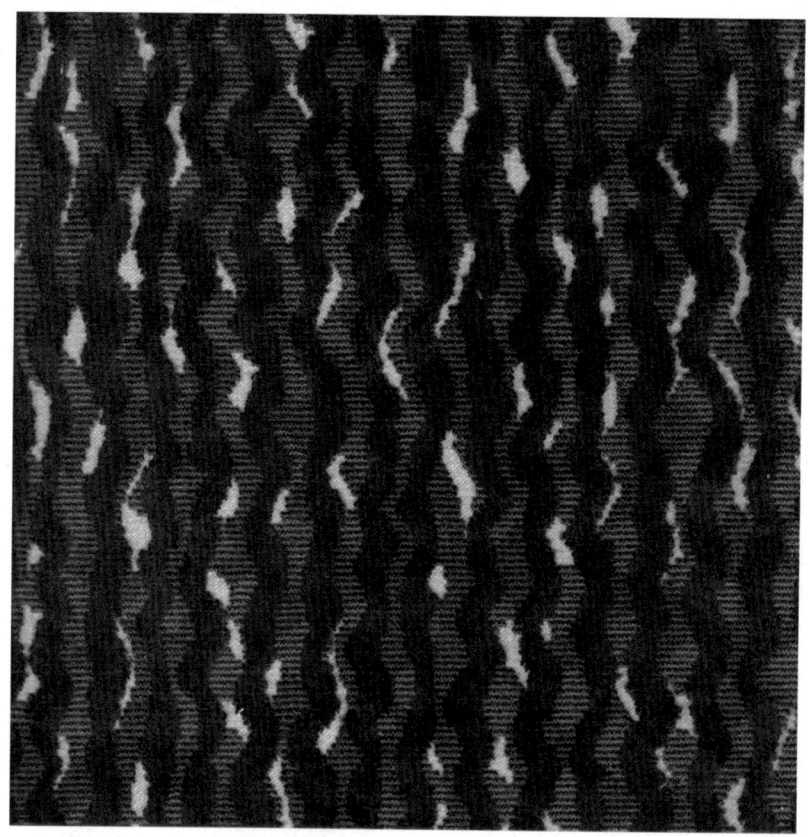

'Aldo 01', Sekers (courtesy of Sekers)

> If anyone comes to me for an interview I ask him how many languages he speaks and if he is interested in painting or music or books. If he's not, then he's not for us.' He believed that all businessmen if they are to be successful need inspiration. And one of the many outside sources of inspiration is art. Through art he believed people find fresh inspiration for themselves and the people who work under them. As it is art which brings beauty into people's lives.[68]

It should come as no surprise, then, that Sekers was one of several successful refugee entrepreneurs who also made real changes to Britain's cultural life. (See '*Kultur!* Textile Refugees in Opera, Theatre and Visual Arts'.).

Bernat Klein

The Serbian Bernat Klein (1922–2014) had such a lot in common with his Hungarian friend Tibor Reich that it is easy to see how they became friends. Like Reich, Klein was born into a family of Jewish textile manufacturers. But, rather than choosing Vienna for his studies, in 1940 he enrolled at the world-famous Bezalel Academy of Art and Design in Jerusalem. Again like Reich, he went afterwards in 1945 to Leeds University Textile Technology Department to learn more about innovative textile production. Klein too took a job at Tootals before settling in Scotland and setting up his own company, Colourcraft. After admitting he was frightened that Scotland would be very, very cold (it was) he obviously acclimatised. However, there was another problem in his country of adoption:

> The clothes he had seen in Scotland in the aftermath of war seemed to be mainly a dingy brown or green: 'And that was just the women', Klein recalled. 'At least the men had their kilts, tartan ties and trews.' Determined to make his adopted country a brighter place, he set up his own business, drawing on his flair for colour to create the exotic tweed and mohair fabrics that would become his signature.[69]

His imagination was fired by colour and he loved the challenge of translating nature into woven and later printed fabrics. He was a painter (to Tibor's photographer) and, inspired by Impressionism, created fabrics which broke colour down into its component parts. The National Museum of Scotland takes up his biography in their online account of Klein:

> Klein's first success was a rush mohair loop yarn. This was Section dyed – a hank of yarn was clamped twice – producing a two-coloured effect with grading between the two. Klein built up trade with the likes of Marks & Spencer, but in 1962 the fabrics were bought by the couture market. The first break was a check mohair tweed taken up by Chanel inspired by a rose. This proved successful, with customers including British designers Hardy Amies, Ronald Paterson and John Cavanagh, also selling extensively throughout the United States and Europe, including some pieces for the French Fashion Houses of Balenciaga, Chanel, Yves Saint Laurent, Christian Dior, Nina Ricci and Pierre Cardin. French couture described Klein's fabrics as 'fantasy'. In 1964, a honeycomb fabric was used to fill Harrods' windows.[70]

Credited with playing 'a huge part in reviving Scotland's weaving and cloth-making industries after the war',[71] his colours appealed to all buyers, both at the top and bottom ends of the market. He described his varied and creative life:

> In the mornings I would show my scarves to Woolworths and, later, mohair stoles to Marks & Spencer; then in the afternoon I would meet Yves Saint Laurent or Pierre Cardin to show my exclusive textile designs. It was a most unusual way of doing business.[72]

Building on this success, Klein established his next company. Unlike Tibor Reich, he concentrated on fashion fabrics as well as the more humble knitting yarn. His colours were a visual treat and sang out in the grey austerity Britain of the 1950s and well into the Swinging Sixties and after. He won the Design Council Award in 1968. And what of his legacy? His archive today is displayed at the National Museum of Scotland and at Heriot-Watt University where it continues to inspire young Scottish designers who today are enjoying a particularly successful moment.

Not all the refugee textile producers and designers were well known of course, and some sadly never made it. The V & A Museum holds the archive of a Bertha Sander (1901–1990) who had trained at the prestigious Vienna KGS and also had a thriving company in Vienna selling her wallpaper, furnishing fabrics and furniture designs. When, as a Jew, she fled to Britain in 1936, she too was denied a work permit initially and although she survived the war and was allowed to work at menial jobs she never re-established her textile career.[73]

One of the most tragic cases is Otti Berger (1898–1944) who had trained at the Bauhaus and had her own textile company in Berlin. Although she did get work in Britain where she had come to escape the Nazi persecution of Jews, her work permit was not renewed and she had to return to her native Croatia from where she was deported to Auschwitz and killed. [74]

This is a dreadful reminder of what may well have happened to the refugees had they not managed to enter Britain in time. As it was, those who came to safety and set up textile companies gave back so much to their host country.

Otto Weisz at Pringle and the Twinset

On 5 April 1934, the *Hawick Express* published a classified advertisement from a Mr Otto Weisz, an Austrian who having apprenticed at the world famous Viennese knitwear company, Bernhard Altmann, had come to Britain to improve his English and learn about natural fibres, wool in particular. His mother had advised her son, born 29 January 1908, to come to Britain, home of the wool trade rather than to go to America. At first he spent some time in Northern Ireland and was now looking for work as a 'Designer', a concept not known in the grey stone Scottish border town which had for centuries been the home to wool mills and knitting companies. In fact, Weisz had to advertise his services twice before anyone responded.

Finally, Pringle of Scotland (see Chapter 3) invited him for an interview, or rather Mr Robert Pringle, the MD did, but Weisz's quest was not yet fulfilled.[75] The story goes that when in January 1934 he arrived at Hawick Station, Weisz, puzzled to find no taxi rank, was asked on his inquiry whether he had booked one? Apparently, he had imagined that Hawick was an enormous industrial metropolis, much like Manchester, because he knew that so many knitted garments were produced there and it had such a respected reputation even in his native Vienna.

Hawick would become his home for the next thirty years, although his original plan had been to stay for only eighteen months. The *Anschluss* and then the war intervened, making it impossible for this Austrian Jew to return home. Eventually, he was able to bring over his mother and his brother to Scotland, to marry and have a family and make a home among the muted heather tones of the countryside, as did another émigré, the textile designer and manufacturer, Bernat Klein, based only a short distance away in Selkirk.

On Weisz's arrival at Pringle, his interview did not go well. Robert Pringle showed him a Pringle sweater, still a relative novelty for the company which had been producing knitted hosiery and underwear since the 1800s, which was plain and square in shape. 'Can you improve on this?' he was asked. 'Certainly I can' was the answer, in heavily accented English and too cocksure for the conservative Scottish businessman who retorted 'We don't need an Austrian here!' With this Weisz was curtly dismissed. But Mr Oddy, the Sales Director, said: 'Like hell we don't!' He knew that Pringle needed an experienced designer's services for the new outerwear and rushed after him, telling him to wait in the Crown Hotel. There Oddy persuaded Weisz to stay, promising 'I'll get you, stick to your guns.'[76] Oddy got his way and Weisz was at Pringle to stay.

The Directors' Minutes Book records Weisz's stellar career, albeit reported in the subdued tones of Pringle's management's non-sensational style. But before his development from Designer to Company Director is revealed, the story of his most famous concept should be told. Did Otto Weisz invent the twinset?

The light but warm cashmere or lambswool jumper, short-sleeved or long-sleeved, worn with a matching round or V-necked cardigan in the same weight and the same stitch, with a row of small buttons down the front? Associated with beauties like the ballerina Margot Fonteyn or the actress Sophia Loren, the twinset was worn more prosaically by the grammar school teachers of the author of the present study – a different colour for each day of the week, always combined with a string of pearls and a slim tweed skirt, a uniform that met with approval all over the country at that time. Americans, particularly co-eds, had started to wear matching sweaters and knitted jackets in the 1920s. It was not unusual, by the time that Otto Weisz arrived, for women to match their jumpers and cardigans. Local knitwear companies referred to these then as 'double sets' and the garments were also available individually as cardigans or jumpers. Weisz was convinced that their potential had not yet been realised but how to market them? One day, strolling along Hawick High Road, he saw some twins in their pushchair and the name 'Twinset' formed in his mind.[77]

The rest is fashion history, and Pringle twinsets sold well enough even to please the dour Mr Robert Pringle. Nowadays, twinsets are again part of the collections of for example Prada, the Italian fashion house which mixes vintage and contemporary pieces in an unconventional, eclectic style.

Anne Crawford – Twinset (courtesy of Pringle of Scotland)

Weisz, one reads in the Directors' logbook, was a convincing salesman too, albeit in a language not his own. And what is more, he was entrepreneurial and adventurous, for he had offered to go to South America to sell knitwear, braving German torpedoes and submarine-infested waters to sell woollen jumpers to the chilly and Anglophile Argentinians. The directors, probably by now out of their comfort zones but trusting in the exotic powers of their new employee, agreed that if

Weisz could get a permit to travel then they would approve his trip, stipulating, however, that he was to insist on cash payments for any orders.

They also noted Weisz's own modest remark that foreigners may not welcome another foreigner selling Scottish goods. But these fears were unfounded. At this time of the war, Britain was desperate to keep exporting goods, such was the cost of warfare and the loss of traditional sources of export revenue, given the danger of the seas. By July 1941 the Minutes show that Weisz had clocked up £3,000-worth of orders from his trip to Chile and Argentina and in August the Directors 'expressed their great approval of his journey', awarding him a £100 bonus, no mean sum for a man on £900 per annum. Weisz had shown

Vintage Pringle advertisement (courtesy of Pringle of Scotland)

that he was open to opportunities and comfortable out of the Anglo-Saxon world, where his Pringle employers were less at ease.

Regular reports followed in the Minutes of Weisz's sales trips abroad, although most of these were made after the end of the war. Weisz had applied for naturalisation in August 1938, swearing his oath

John Smedley, contemporary advertisement (courtesy of John Smedley)

of allegiance on 18 August of that year.[78] Bizarrely, *another* Otto Weisz appears in the National Archive records, also born in Vienna but with a different date of birth: 28 March 1903, *also* a knitwear designer but living in Northern Ireland (as had Pringle's Weisz) and working for Etam, another company with a refugee history. One wonders if this is a coincidence, or whether the authorities are guilty of having got their knitters in a twist, this being one and the same man?

Otto Weisz's British passport meant that while he would not be interned on the Isle of Man like thousands of German and Austrian refugees in Britain but on the other hand, he would be liable for military service. The Minutes record his unsuccessful attempts to obtain a commission, his application to the Air Force, the Navy (not the obvious choice for a man from landlocked Austria) and finally, in August 1942, we read that Weisz has been signed up by the Army. Although there is no record of his service, it is thought that he worked in Britain in Intelligence, because he continues to be present at most of the Directors' meetings. His native language, German, would of course, have been extremely useful to the Armed Forces in that capacity. Finally, in March 1945, efforts to release Weisz from his service were rewarded with the news that he would be free one month after the end of hostilities.

The author of a history of Pringle noted that Weisz's service gave him a chance to test out Pringle's wartime production military underwear.[79] This included submariners' long johns, a wonderful feat of woollen engineering being both fabulously thick and warm and thoughtfully soft, as one specimen held in the Hawick Museum archive shows. But that Weisz really wore anything similar seems unlikely given the nature of his actual service. One result of Weisz's successful activities in sales and design was that Pringle now dared to take on another Austrian. In December 1943 the Board notes that they received an application from one Eugen Klappholz, and decide to take him on as an assistant designer to help Weisz but to work independently as well.

The following year, responding to a suggestion by Weisz, Pringle took on an underwear designer on a part-time basis, Mrs Klappholz.

The Klappholz couple also did well: the suggestion was made in October 1944 to put them in charge of a 'skirt and blouse factory' in London where apparently there would be more suitable labour available. Whether this took place is not clear, but evidently this Austrian couple were a success, as by March 1945 Mr Klappholz is designing on his own while Weisz was busy with his responsibility for all clients in America and Europe. Mrs Klappholz rose to the rank of Head Forewoman at that time, too.

Weisz's familiarity with Continental customs and etiquette were an asset to Pringle and he was able to advise them to alter their approach more than once. On 18 September 1948, reporting back on his trips to France, Switzerland and Italy, he headed one section 'Relationship with Continental Customers', and noted: 'I saw one or two letters written by our organisation to Continental customers and I would just like to add that we ought to try to be a little "more personal" in our correspondence with Continental customers. Some of our letters read extremely cold and "matter-of-fact" and nothing else.' He suggests that Pringle make an effort to 'speak' to the customers. 'They would appreciate it and think a lot of Pringle for it.' Not flowery, but the letters should show a little flattery, something which the Continental customer would be used to. One can only imagine the flinty Pringle directors trying to conjure up the right amount of flattery.

He also expressed himself forcibly when he thought it necessary. For example, in June 1947, returning from a trip to the United States, he had been struck by how different the female customers were from their British counterparts in that they were a sophisticated lot, far more demanding and changeable in their tastes. Weisz fulminated 'We must keep up! We will be left behind!' One can imagine that his manner made Weisz objectionable to some of his conservative fellow directors, and yet he obviously had a sense of humour too. In January 1946 he reports on a questionable new agent for Pringle in Switzerland who promises wonderful results. 'I hae ma doots,' writes Weisz laconically.

By 1947 Weisz was earning a handsome £2,000 a year and obviously worth every penny. Pringle also advanced him the money to buy a house locally. As early as 1936 Weisz had been invited to join the

Board, becoming a Director after only two years. His reports from his selling trips to postwar Paris are great reading. No shrinking violet, Weisz holds tirades against the corruption he encounters in Paris, having of course experienced the communal deprivation of British wartime himself. In one report of August 1946, after pointing out that Pringle cashmere jumpers were in 'tremendous' demand, Weisz lamented that France was in a grave situation, but that anything was available on the black market. 'If the authorities were to imprison people dealing in the black market I feel convinced they would put the whole population of Paris, or France, behind bars.' 'Prices', he noted, were simply fantastic, 'so that a Buyer in a department told me that he could sell a Cashmere Set quite easily, and without any trouble at all, for £40 or £45.' Evidently he disliked the famous Dior 'New Look', referring to the term itself as 'hackneyed' and implying the style was too common to be special.

On marketing, he attributed the fame of the Pringle brand to advertising placed in '*I. T.*, *Vogue Export* or *Tatler*.' The '*I T.*' referred to here is *International Textiles,* soon to be re-launched as *The Ambassador*, the spectacularly successful textile and fashion journal dedicated to the export of British goods and created, designed and illustrated by two multi-talented German refugees Hans and Elsbeth Juda (see Chapter 5).

It may be hard to believe now, but in those days even the concept of 'knitwear' was not established, and in early records one can find it as 'knit wear' or even 'KnitWear'. But names were important ('Twinset' had proved that), as was the representation of names, as Ernst Dryden had shown in Vienna with his handsome lettering. Here Weisz followed in the footsteps of his fellow countryman for it was he who designed the 'Pringle of Scotland' logo. The actual name and presentation have varied over the years, with 'Pringle of Hawick' appearing briefly, but the one in use at the present time was designed by Weisz. Apparently, Weisz also designed the Bernhard Altmann label while he was an apprentice there.

The Altmann story is one which became entwined with Weisz's own but the plot was worthy of a Hollywood film, literally, in the form of *The Woman in Gold*,[80] a film which tells the story of Maria Altmann.

She was Adele Bloch-Bauer's niece, her aunt was a wealthy Jewish patron of the arts who served as the model for some of Klimt's best-known paintings.[81] In 1937, Maria married Fritz Altmann. Not long after their Paris honeymoon, the *Anschluss* of 1938 incorporated Austria into Nazi Germany. Under the Nazis, Fritz was arrested in Austria and held hostage in Dachau concentration camp to force his brother Bernhard Altmann, by then safely in England, to transfer his successful Bernhard Altmann textile factory into German hands. Fritz was released and the couple fled for their lives. They made a harrowing escape, leaving behind their home, loved ones and property, including jewellery that later found its way into the collection of Hermann Göring. Many of their friends and relatives were either killed by the Nazis or committed suicide. Travelling by way of Liverpool, they reached the United States and settled there. Shortly after Maria arrived in Los Angeles, Bernhard Altmann mailed her a cashmere jumper – something unknown then in the United States – accompanied by the note: 'See what you can do with this.' Maria took the sweater to Kerr's Department Store in Beverly Hills and attracted a multitude of buyers in California and across the United States for Bernhard Altmann's cashmere sweaters. Maria became the face of cashmere in California and eventually started her own clothing business.[82] Weisz wrote up his meeting with Bernhard Altmann 'who was my chief some twenty years ago' around 1950, during which the two men discussed supplies of cashmere to Altmann's two factories in Vienna and Texas. Nowadays, Pringle makes cashmere sweaters for the New York store Altmann's.

Never does Otto Weisz allude to the Nazi period or the *Anschluss*, obviously having decided that it was best not to dwell on the past but to focus instead on his very satisfying present and promising future. Nor does he express any doubts about returning to his homeland, despite its murderous recent history. In the *Pringle Bulletin* Weisz writes an account of the new Pringle store established recently in his native Vienna near the smart Imperial Hofburg area, in which he describes the beauty of the surrounding countryside and names the city as a 'very important centre for the textile and knitwear industry'. In 1948 he had also been asked to look for an Assistant Designer in

Vienna, obviously Pringle now thought that Vienna was the best possible source of talent.

Weisz understood what was in a name, here again treading in the footsteps of Ernst Dryden, and wrote in 1947 following a trip to the USA that 'Pringle is a sound which echoes quality and repute' and that generally, 'Scottish' merchandise sold better than if it was marketed as 'British'. Moreover, he was instrumental in creating the reputation of the brand. Not only did he sound the Pringle trumpet abroad but, on one occasion, recorded an address in German in the Pringle factory for a radio programme for BBC Europe. *The Cashmere Story* film was made during his time at Pringle too.

One factory visit during Weisz's time at Pringle stands out. The Royal Princesses Elizabeth and Margaret, long-standing wearers of Pringle jumpers especially during their perhaps under-heated stays at the Scottish Balmoral Castle, visited the works in 1952 and were presented with gifts of Pringle jumpers. In the photograph displayed in the *Pringle Bulletin*, Otto Weisz is standing a yard or so away from Princess Elizabeth, smiling slightly. What was he thinking? Perhaps he was blessing the day he put his advertisement in the *Hawick Express*, but somehow one can't help feeling that had that not done the trick, then Mr Weisz would have found another avenue for his drive and talent.

Not all newspaper reports involving Weisz were quite so glamorous: the *Dundee Courier* of 3 September 1936, not long after Weisz's arrival in Britain, ran an article entitled 'Cow Carried 15 Yards' as follows: 'Otto Weisz (28), dress designer [sic] of 50 Weensland Road Hawick, was fined £2, with 15s costs, at Berwick yesterday, when found guilty of driving without due care and attention at Panama Cottage, Cornhill-on-Tweed.' Evidently, Weisz had not yet mastered the art of driving on the left and in any case, had not experienced cattle, Highland or otherwise, wandering along the streets of his native Vienna.

As well as helping to establish Pringle as an international brand, creating their new designed knitwear and marketing it successfully, Weisz also saw to the continuity of design by recruiting the next generation of designers.[83] His first appointment was Stuart Beaty in around 1950. Weisz had approached not a local apprentice or employee from a rival knitwear mill but the prestigious Glasgow School of Art. In fact, Beaty was a sculptor by training, and although delighted to take up his post at Pringle, first left for Mexico where he had already committed himself to a year's study leave. In post at Pringle and trained by Weisz, he proved to be a talented designer. He also sculpted Weisz's head, and that of fellow director Oddy. This art school source of designers continued as Pringle practice as it consistently provided designers who were more flexible and innovative than people who only had experience of making knitwear.

Weisz's vibrant, sometimes outspoken personality resulted in clashes, and apparently led to his quitting Pringle, not in clouds of glory, as befitted him, but with hardly a mention. He retired in 1967 to live in the Channel Isles. It seems that he had a falling out with the holding company Dawsons, but no details are known. His retirement is noted factually and without a word of thanks or recognition for his outstanding contribution to Pringle's success.

Pringle is still trading today, although the garments are no longer produced in Hawick but in Hong Kong, made out of wool from Australia or cashmere from China. Designers like Vivienne Westwood have chosen Pringle to make their knitted clothes, as have Glasgow-born Jonathan Saunders and many others. Much like Burberry or John Smedley, Pringle became a popular label with young people in the 1990s, worn by wealthy football players among others, sometimes with the label displayed proudly as the sweater was worn draped over the shoulders. Associated with many sports, especially golf, Pringle sweaters are often worn by Ryder Cup players.

Otto Weisz even featured in the BBC TV series *The Clothes Show* in an episode filmed near Burgh Island and dedicated to the twinset and its origins. Caryn Franklin, the presenter, looked at contenders for the title of originator of the sweater and cardigan combination, considering Coco Chanel. But no, hers were usually three-piece outfits. Jean Patou was dismissed also before moving to Scotland and Pringle. There, an elderly Weisz, speaking with a Scottish accent underpinned by a Viennese one, recounted how he had come across the idea after seeing some twins.

It had made Pringle's fortune, he said, although, no, he himself was not a millionaire as a consequence. Huge numbers of companies had followed suit making their own versions, but he considered this more a case of flattery than plagiarism. He finished by predicting that the twinset would always be worn and would never be out of fashion. He was certainly right on that score so far. Nowadays the Pringle label is internationally recognised and as glamorous and prestigious as it was in the 1930s, thanks in no small part to Otto Weisz.

Mr Berdach, Mr Churchill and the Bow Ties

This is a story of inspired making do and having a go, combined with a pinch of Jewish *chutzpah*.[84] A story with a very happy ending but with a sorry beginning. It starts with the birth of Walter Berdach on 22 May 1904 in Vienna, to a father who would go on to serve in the Austro-Hungarian Army during the First World War, like many of his Jewish friends. Blinded by a shell, on his return from military service Mr Berdach senior took over a small tobacconist's shop which he ran with his wife.

By the time Walter came along money was short and Walter didn't attend the local Gymnasium (grammar school) but was sent out to work at seventeen, finding sales jobs of various kinds. At twenty-one he married Ella Sussmann and became a traveller in cloth, selling piece goods throughout the former Austria, after the break-up of the Empire, and made a real go of it. A son, Freddie, was born on 24 October 1930, and a daughter, who sadly died in childhood. The family lived in the now famous Karl Marx Hof, a workers' apartment block that was symbolic of Red Vienna, the socialist municipal utopia that was set up in 1923. That regime came to an end in 1934, defeated by Austro-Fascists.

Worse was to come. In March 1938 the German army marched into Vienna to integrate it into the German Reich, but there was little need for an army as the Viennese received them with open arms for the most part. But the Jewish population who had watched their German co-religionists from 1933 on with mounting horror had to get out and fast, those, that is, who were not immediately seized, beaten up and worse.

The Berdachs were told to vacate their flat within two weeks, and opted for escape to Switzerland. But having reached Bregenz, Walter was told by the local Gauleiter to return to Vienna. In a moment of inspiration Walter explained that he thought it was the German wish to get rid of Jews, and all he wanted was to leave and go to Switzerland. The Gauleiter suggested meeting again at eight that evening at the railway station. He said 'I will be hidden and you will wait outside the barrier until one minute before departure to Zurich. When I give you the signal, you will board the train.' The whistle went, Walter received the signal and he ran to board the train.

On arrival in Zurich, he went straight to the synagogue and was told to report immediately to the police, so as to qualify as a refugee. The following day he was sitting in the synagogue office with several other refugees, wondering what to do next. A well-dressed man walked in and asked a few of the young men there whether they had any idea of cataloguing books. There was complete silence. Eventually, Walter put his hand up and was taken on by the man. He explained that he had no idea how to catalogue books, but felt sure that he could learn fast. At least he earned a wage in this way and was able to find accommodation. He wrote to England and was able to get the visa required for his family members provided his wife went into domestic service. Ella and son Freddie arrived in England on 20 December 1938, safe but with only a sewing machine and radio with them. They had sent a container of their furniture out via Hamburg, but the rest of the contents were stolen en route.

Walter finally arrived from Switzerland in August 1939, and immediately joined the British army in 1940, the Pioneer Corps, the diggers of ditches and movers of equipment which was the only military option open to refugees then. And yet the German and Austrian refugees would have been so useful to the war effort, with their deep hatred of the Nazis and their German language skills! But those were early days and the British did not yet fully understand their position, and had much more pressing issues.

Walter was injured in France and returned to Britain on a hospital ship before being honourably discharged for his wounds in Taunton, Somerset. It was the first time in three years that the Berdachs had been together. Missing the music, theatre and cafés of Vienna, they moved to Hampstead where many of their countrymen had settled and started up cafés. Here they could moan in private to each other about the food, the weather and the (lack of) heating, for they would *never* be heard complaining, in public anyway, about the magnificent country which had saved their lives and was now fighting for survival.

Walter became a waiter at the Dorchester Hotel for the duration (the staff were away in the forces) and was offered British citizenship in 1946. But what now? Surely there was something he could do for this fine country of heroes? Heroes like Mr Churchill, who had kept them all going during the war? Then it came to him: why didn't British men wear bow ties like Churchill did? His fellow Austrians and German men often sported bow ties.[85] He would teach the British to! Mrs Berdach was a skilled seamstress and she had brought her sewing machine out of Austria so Walter decided that he would make use of this skill. He went out to buy a 'tie-yourself' bow tie and got Mrs Berdach to take it apart and make a pattern of it.

But the next step would be easier said than done for these were days of rationing and shortages of fabric and everything else. You needed coupons to buy material for ties and they had none spare. So he wrote to the Board of Trade and to a number of other government departments, but no one would give him the means to start a business. He was walking disconsolately down Mile End Road when he saw sacks of blackout materials now surplus to requirements. He looked inside the sacks and found that there was some material that could be of use. He purchased a sack for 'a few bob' and took it home. He and Mrs Berdach sorted out the 'sheep from the goats' to find the right material that could be sewn and turned inside out. The bow tie pattern came out; she marked it and skilfully followed the outline. It was sewn inside out, so next it was turned the right way round, ironed and put into a little box.

Being an excellent salesman, Walter took the sample to Burlington Arcade, to the most expensive menswear shop in the arcade and showed it to the owner. Lots of soldiers and officers were coming back from the war at this time and 'home coming' parties were all the rage. The owner said that if Walter could produce two dozen bows like the sample, he would buy them. The Berdach couple got down to work and the two of them made the twenty-four bows within a week. Off they went to the retailer who accepted them gleefully and asked for another six dozen. Of course at each transaction, Walter received clothing coupons, so he kept supplying this shop until he had enough coupons

'Wabena' bow ties (courtesy of Freddie Berdach)

to go to the store and get proper black satin material. With this first victory, he formed a limited company and approached other retailers in London and so the business was born. The couple both worked hard for many months until Walter Berdach decided he would get outworkers to do the machining, turning and ironing once they had received the pattern from Mrs Berdach.

The ties were cut out on the premises in Golders Green and then delivered to the outworkers seven or eight at any one time. The Company, WABENA (WA- from Walter and BE- from Berdach) had a smart trading address in the West End, in Golden Square. The ties were cut at the Wingate Trading Estate in Tottenham. The box was important, it was of clear cellophane so that the tie could be seen and bore the legend 'Made in England'. The Berdachs were proud of their achievement – Mr Churchill himself would surely love these ties!

So the 'ready-made' bow ties were produced and not only in black, but in many tasteful colours and designs. Wabena bow ties were sold at Swan & Edgar, Harrods and Selfridges, not bad for what had started as blackout cast-offs. The Berdachs were approached by Marks

Walter Berdach (courtesy of Freddie Berdach)

& Spencer but they would have had to give them over a quarter of their production and decided this was too risky a move.

Business grew until early 1950 when there was a general downturn in business and Mrs Berdach was quite perturbed, more so when she heard her husband's solution was to buy a car. She was aghast. 'How can you buy a car at this time?' she said. But Walter, determined as he always was, bought a small Austin 8 and went travelling to Coventry, Birmingham and the Midlands. He came home with bumper orders and the business kept growing.

Freddie Berdach eventually took over the business. He had had a rough start in England, because his mother had come to Britain on a domestic visa. That meant that she, like many other Viennese housewives, suddenly found herself in charge of cooking and other household tasks and became a servant overnight with few rights. And she would not have been able to have Freddie with her. So he was fostered through the Jewish Board of Guardians. Well-meaning but misguided, these pillars of the community decided that Freddie, who had to live with Christian families (there not being enough Jewish families to go round), should be moved on every three months to avoid his religion being 'contaminated', so to speak, by Christians. He missed three years of school as a consequence. However, this experience only strengthened his Jewish faith, still an important part of his life today. Unlike his parents whose faith was tested severely after the death of their daughter in childhood, Freddie Berdach was always a member of the Jewish community, finding it a source of support over his lifetime. He had religious instruction during his time in the RAF.

Instead of going to university Freddie joined the Wabena company in 1952 after his National Service in the RAF. But he was told by his father he must find his own customers. He successfully exported the ties all over the world, travelling to fifty-five countries including the Lebanon, Libya and Kuwait. The locals there loved the English look of the bow ties and the company did well. Freddie also represented other British firms while out selling, as he was the one prepared to travel. Taking risks and going the extra mile, especially regarding travelling abroad to export, is something that the refugees in this field seem to have embraced. Freddie Berdach remembers that his British competitors tended to be more complacent and stayed at home. He continued selling bows in Lancashire and Yorkshire, introducing men's ordinary ties and cuff-links to the range and in 1980 sold the business to Favourite Ties, another refugee business, as the youngsters were now not wearing ties but open-neck shirts.

Freddie Berdach's photograph album shows images of the family at home in the Karl Marx Hof, unaware of what was to come. Sparse photos follow the difficult emigration period. Eventually, we see photos of bow ties, gleaming in their cellophane wrappers. And here is Walter, beaming and sporting, of course, one of his own bow ties.

Buttoned Up: Hornflowa, Lucie Rie and Issey Miyake

Buttons were of course found on nearly all clothes until the advent of the zip. The zip fastener was actually patented in 1851 but was not developed for commercial use until 1913. So, even men's trouser fly fastenings were traditionally closed with buttons until after the war. This meant that until then, there was an enormous demand for buttons of all types both in Europe and in England.

Here are two contrasting refugee button stories: one was the manufacturer, Hornflowa, which found and exploited new techniques ideal for wartime production. The other was an artisanal story, typical in another way of wartime adapting in that it meant a change of activity. In this case it concerned a potter who switched from her artistic activity, making pots, to making a product which was in short supply in the war. The potter in question was the Viennese refugee Lucie Rie.

Hornflowa, the old button factory on the Industrial Estate, Maryport, became the second largest button factory in the UK.[86] Although not much is known about the original founders, it is clear that Max Kraus and H. Winter had first owned a button factory in Moravia, Czechoslovakia. No doubt given the threat of war from Germany, they were attracted to the Trading Estates project (see Chapter 3) and it is thought that they arrived in Cumberland in 1938.

Herbert Loebl told their story in his detailed thesis, pointing out that their arrival in Britain coincided with an increased demand for buttons, most of which had been imported until the war broke out. And it was the war which was responsible for the new demand because of the sudden need for military uniforms. The buttons should be tough and be made of easily available materials, and Hornflowa could make just such buttons. While buttons can of course be made from anything from leather to metal, Hornflowa buttons were made of 'milled hoof and horn mixed with casein', a formula which resulted in buttons which could be ironed on the garment without breaking. A chemical called

Hornflowa advertisement

urea formaldehyde could be added, successfully reducing the amount of horn and hoof needed. It was the clever Hornflowa manufacturers who realised this and gradually used less of the hard-to-come-by animal product (eventually excluding it entirely).

It was in January 1940 that the company moved into one of the new purpose-built factories in Maryport on the Solway Trading Estate. Here they diversified, realising they could also make, among other products, fertiliser from the residual hoof and horn. By 1974 their versatility and reactive talent meant that they were employing 600 people. But their success had been founded on tiny but tough buttons. These featured in advertisements in all the usual journals, especially *The Ambassador*. And they can now be found on the internet to buy, little gems in every colour and every possible shape and size, many of which may have brightened up a drab wartime outfit.[87]

A complete contrast is provided by the two button episodes in the life of the famed ceramicist, Lucie Rie, whose pots are admired by fellow ceramicist and writer Edmund de Waal for one, and collected by museums and wealthy connoisseurs all over the world. She had trained at the Vienna KGS school (see Chapter1) and was part of a particularly active arts scene which was dominated by the activities of the Wiener Werkstätte (WW) studios. One who moved in WW circles was Fritz Lampl, who had created a company called Bimini which produced delicate glass figures. He and Lucie became friends, and more, after both had moved to London in 1938, obliged to leave Austria because of their Jewish heritage.

Although Lucie had already achieved success pre-emigration, for example winning a gold medal at the 1937 Paris International Exposition, she initially struggled to gain recognition in England where a different style of studio pottery was known. And it was not long before war broke out and people had other priorities than buying pots, albeit Japanese-influenced, austerely elegant ones.

Fortunately her friend Fritz Lampl had 'sharp business acumen' and realised that fancy buttons were in short supply given the rush to make uniform buttons.[88] He set about making glass buttons in moulds from ancient coins and cameos, some of which were borrowed from the British Museum. As this process was labour intensive, it brought with it welcome employment for several German and Austrian refugee friends.

From here it was a short step to using a medium more familiar to Lucie – clay. With the help of one Rudolf Neufeld, yet another Viennese refugee, production moved to ceramic moulded buttons. Then the range expanded to include a bewildering variety of buttons of all shapes and sizes which were seized eagerly by a number of clothing manufacturers, including couture houses during the war. So it was that Lucie provided a decent income for the duration, providing a living not only for herself but for several other refugees. These buttons now can be seen in the V & A Museum, with more in the Sainsbury Arts Centre, University of East Anglia, Norwich, and are works of art in their own right.

Although Lucie Rie must have been relieved to get back to making pots once hostilities ceased, eventually becoming one of the major 'British' potters of the twentieth century,[89] it was not the end of her association with the little clothes fasteners that had been her bread and butter during the war. As her biographer relates, Lucie Rie's pots had caught the attention of the Japanese fashion designer Issey Miyake in the 1980s.

In that decade, innovative fashion looks and techniques had arrived in Europe from an unexpected source – Japan. Rei Kawakubo's Comme des Garçons label was established in Paris in the early 1980s and in Britain, designers such as Issey Miyake soon found they could sell their unconventional but wearable clothes and accessories. The Japanese brought with them a long tradition of philosophy of art and were so much more than mere business people.

It was perhaps no surprise then, that in 1984 Miyake, who had admired Rie's work in a catalogue, finally met the potter herself and a relationship of mutual admiration sprang up. Rie's biographer noted that 'he was especially fascinated by the hundreds of decorative buttons made during and following the war stored in drawers…As a fashion designer ever on the lookout for something different, Miyake saw the potential for incorporating them into his designs, and he did use them on his garments.'[90] She in turn went to see Miyake's clothes in his London showroom. As she was really tiny, she was unable to wear the clothes he gave her as gifts, but no doubt admired them as works of art.

Their collaboration eventually resulted in an exhibition in Tokyo of Rie's work, with the layout designed by Miyake. A sale of Rie's pots coinciding with the exhibition led to her ceramics fetching prices of up to £5,000, a sign of the kudos they now held. Perhaps even more significantly for Rie, critics saw her work as 'embodying aspects of Japanese aesthetic in her use of scale, colour, texture and form…'[91] Rie had probably seen her buttons until then as a necessary wartime pot boiler and a distraction from her main interest, but Miyake for one saw them as inherently beautiful and useful.

Mr Noskwith, Bletchley Park and Charnos Silky Stockings

There were some examples of really outstanding contributions to the war effort from German-speaking refugees, including those who were in the textile and clothing trades. One such was Rolf Noskwith, who died 3 January 2017 aged 97. His obituary relates his wartime experience,[92] and refers to a common reluctance on the part of British authorities to trust Germans in this country. The fact that Noskwith was employed to work as a codebreaker at Bletchley Park, however, was less surprising given that he was a German Jew whose family had emigrated to Britain shortly before Hitler came to power. This probably meant that he had British nationality early on and his allegiance was not in doubt. After being interviewed by C.P. Snow, then a civil service commissioner, and Hugh Alexander, the administrative head of the Hut 8 naval Enigma team, Noskwith arrived at Bletchley in 1941, aged twenty-two. He joined a Hut 8 team that included Joan Clarke, who at one point was engaged to Alan Turing. (It has since become public knowledge that Turing was prosecuted for his homosexuality despite his outstanding contribution to cracking German codes and to computer science in general, only to receive a posthumous apology for his appalling treatment by the British government in 2009.) Noskwith's work was about to begin, breaking the naval Enigma ciphers on a daily basis. The ability to read messages sent by German U-boats giving their locations allowed the Admiralty to re-route Allied convoys around the U-boat 'wolf packs', which had sunk large numbers of Allied ships bringing supplies and US troops across the Atlantic. Breaking those messages is estimated to have cut at least two years off the end of the war. Noskwith loved his work, as we read in another obituary:

> Under Turing's supervision, Noskwith and his fellow cryptographers and number-crunchers intercepted thousands of

high-level enemy communications every day, sometimes within an hour of transmission. So enthralling was the work, that the analyst finishing his shift would be unwilling to 'hand over the workings', as Noskwith observed in *Codebreakers: The Inside Story of Bletchley Park*. Noskwith's fluent German was an added asset to the team when assessing encrypted enemy messages.[93]

In 1946, Noskwith somewhat reluctantly left his intelligence work which he had enjoyed and returned to the family firm, Charnos. The name comes from his father's first name Chaim and is contracted into their original surname Noskowitz when it was founded in Chemnitz where the family had fled from Poland because of antisemitic attacks. They had come to Britain just before Hitler came to power, thereby helping to ensure their establishment well before they had to flee.

In 1936 they started manufacturing hosiery, a growing industry now that women were wearing shorter skirts so that their legs could be a feature. Stockings with a seam running down the back were in, and Charnos had a state of the art factory in which to make them. But of course, when war broke out, it was difficult to get supplies of silk when it was needed for parachutes among other things. Gifts of silk stockings became associated with generous American GIs or else were obtainable on the black market which flourished as a result of restricted supplies.

The story goes that near the end of the war, Chaim, now with his anglicised name, Charles Noskwith, braved the U-boats of the Atlantic to travel to the USA where he bought ten ultra-modern knitting machines to cope with the expected post-war demand. Nylon was now the main material used.

His son Rolf took over in the late 1950s in time to clad the legs of Swinging Sixties London girls in the new tights. He also branched into underwear: bras, knickers and girdles, a sector which they still dominate today with Charnos products on sale in all major British department stores.

Underwear was an area in which the refugees seemed to do well (see section on 'Over Here and Underwear: Silhouette'). But

Charnos 'Killer Figure Hourglass Control' tights (courtesy of Charnos Hosiery)

perhaps not all of them were run by ex-codebreakers. Apparently, Noskwith carried round with him in his pocket until his death a list of mistakes that he had noticed in the film *The Imitation Game*[94] about Bletchley Park days so that when asked his opinion of the film he was ready with his reply.

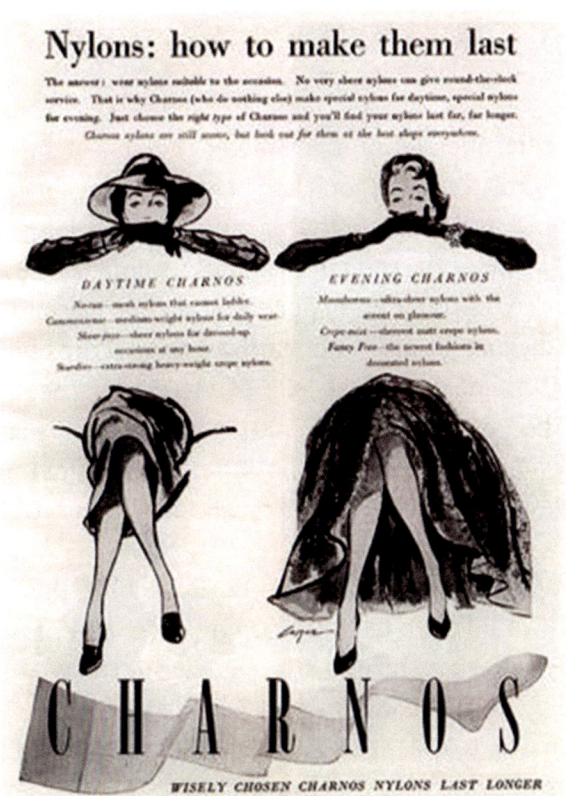

Vintage Charnos advertisement (courtesy of Charnos Hosiery)

John Smedley's Mysterious Klothilde Ehrenfest

In Derbyshire the directors of John Smedley had taken the very modern decision to recruit a designer and had been searching for one in Austria where the most fashionable knitwear came from (on John Smedley see Chapter 3). Finally, as the company Minutes recorded on 26 March 1938, there was success at last. Mr Nieper recruited one Klothilde Ehrenfest, her awkwardly foreign name appearing in the records under various spellings. 'Clothilde Ehrenfast [sic] of Vienna has been appointed Outerwear Designer at a salary of £300 per year plus travelling expenses to and from Vienna once a year. [she]...has a permit for one year after which she will have to renew it. She will take up her duties from 23 March.'[94]

As the *Anschluss* took place on 12 March 1938, this opportunity looks as if it would have been the saving of Ms Ehrenfest, although one can only infer that she was, in fact, Jewish. The next entry in the John Smedley annals is noted on 27 February 1939: 'Ehrenfast in Paris', presumably to see the spring fashion shows, to sketch and bring back to Britain, as was the practice then. The John Smedley archive is housed in several parts of the Derbyshire premises and holds the First World War helmets worn by employees then, boxes of correspondence, samples by the dozen and much else. It is presided over by a professional archivist and a team of regular volunteers. However, even with their concerted efforts, it proved impossible to find samples of Ehrenfest's work, especially as designs in those days were rarely credited. One drawing could well have been her work, as it is from 1938

Her last wages were recorded in the wage book in 1940; she was apparently 'let go' then. But why then? Surely she would want to stay in her well-paid creative job in the Derbyshire town? The reason is not hard to deduce: in 1940, John Smedley turned over its whole knitwear production to officers' underwear and there was therefore no longer a role for an outerwear designer. The other logical explanation for her sudden disappearance could have been that as an enemy alien in 1940,

BLOCK No. 27.

John Smedley design, 1938 (courtesy of John Smedley)

the year of the greatest suspicion of German-speaking residents in Britain, she could have been rounded up by the police and interned on the Isle of Man, the fate of so many of her fellow countrymen although admittedly, not so many of her countrywomen were interned. But a search of the records (these are not comprehensive) showed nobody of her name as interned, in whatever spelling. She is recorded 'At Liberty' in her National Archive Record of 10 July 1941. Far more likely then that she looked for employment again. In the *London Gazette* on 16 January 1951 she appears once more, this time as a 'Domestic Science Teacher', living in the Royal Hotel Buildings, Matlock. Her death is also recorded in the *London Gazette* as having taken place in a charitable hostel in the

Archbishopric of Vienna on 5 December 1990, describing her as 'formerly a clothes designer', with her address given as Nottingham.

It is only through the story of her relationship with her husband that one can piece together something of the woman and her life. Klothilde Angela Maria Drenning was born on 30 August 1899 in Semlin. The man who was later to be her husband, Oskar Ehrenfest, was born 13 February 1894 in Vienna into a Jewish family and was both a 'doctor and an art historian'. But Oskar's first wife was the famous textile designer Anny Schröder, one whose life is set out in a biography.[96] Anny had studied at the prestigious Vienna Kunstgewerbeschule, the arts and crafts school where the likes of Jacqueline Groag had studied, and where Oskar Kokoschka was on the teaching staff. Anny's teachers included the celebrated Professor Strnad. Anny had made her mark early and became a member of the artists' cooperative, the Hagenbund, in Austria. Her main interest was in her interpretation of classical art, which led to her being commissioned to create work for the 1936 Berlin Olympics. It is safe to assume from this prestigious commission that Anny was not Jewish. Both Hitler and Goebbels, the Propaganda Minister, were keen to promote an association between the beauty of ancient Greece and that of his athletes under National Socialism, and indeed the plan for Germania was based on classical principles also.

Anny's marriage to Oskar took place in 1918 when she was only twenty. She was apparently often away, perhaps for professional reasons and the marriage only lasted five years: in 1924 Oskar moved out.[97] Just one week later, Anny's biographer wrote, on 24 May 1924 Oskar had moved in with Klothilde Drenning and married her only a few months later on 7 August 1924. There must have been a quick divorce. Records show Oskar's presence in Vienna in 1933. The betrayal and separation left its mark on Anny, whose work continued to show her wounded feelings, as for example in her double portrait 'Doppelporträt mit Oskar Ehrenfest um 1925, Vienna'. Had Klothilde been at the KGS with Anny? It is possible, because although she is not shown in the records, there were many part-time students who would not have appeared in the main list of full-time students there.

Oskar's name appears in the National Census so certainly the Ehrenfests lived together some time in Matlock, with Klothilde earning a living for two years until her contract was terminated. It seems unlikely that the children she taught Domestic Science to were aware that their teacher had come from Vienna at a time when textile and clothes design there was enjoying a golden age. And their teacher had been the designer for one of England's best known and oldest knitwear firms in the 1930s when the sweater was a most fashionable, covetable item. Perhaps more will come to light one day about this rather mysterious character who worked for one of Britain's most famous knitwear companies.

Francis Steiner and Tick-a-Tee Children's Wear

In a village outside Banbury, Oxfordshire, there lived an elderly gentleman named Francis Steiner. He had a phenomenal memory despite his age and being physically disabled. Sitting in his wheelchair he recounted the story of his Viennese refugee uncle's firm which made children's clothes in Cumbria, a successful enterprise which had traded until the late 1970s, when so many British textile-based firms went under in the face of cheaper goods from the Far East (see 'The Great Northern Trading Estates Miracle', Chapter 3).[98] The company was called Cumberland Childwear, with the brand name 'Tick-a-Tee'. At its height, the firm employed some 300 workers.[99] Francis settled down to tell how it all began:

> My grandfather, Dr Maximillian Steiner, came to England from Vienna during the war. He received a government grant to set up in Maryport which was a depressed area. Heavy industry had declined and the initiative to find employment was headed by MP Frank Anderson and T U official Jack Adams (later Lord Adams). The deal was that if someone could create employment for at least twelve local people, then an entry visa to the UK would be granted. So the Solway Trading Estate was settled by three other refugee employers.

Maximilian (Axel) Steiner had studied law in Vienna but went to work for his father-in-law after his first marriage, manufacturing children's clothes. Then he set up his own company, Denes, with the clothes having the Registered Trade Name Haserlhosen (Little rabbits' trousers). They made jersey fabric as well. Once the Nazis came to power, he closed down the company and concentrated on opening up franchises all over Europe, which was a way of sending money abroad also. The owner of his franchise in Brno, Czechoslovakia, was Ferry

Hajek. Steiner spent six months in the USA as well as some time in Russia. Before the *Anschluss*, he divorced and remarried. His second wife, Maya, was Yugoslavian and an opera singer.

In 1938, Max Steiner was in Paris about to board the train when by chance he saw Hajek. He told Hajek that he was now a refugee, the Sudetenland in Czechoslovakia having just been occupied by Germany. The two decided to work together in Britain, taking advantage of the incentive scheme. Hajek would be in charge of sales while Steiner trained the machinists and looked after the machinery. Maya Steiner, who had no training or experience in the field, nevertheless designed the clothes and made the patterns. Axel started the business initially with two sewing machines and he ran and expanded the factory. The company's trade name was Tick-a-Tee.

Fortunately, they soon got a contract to produce children's clothes for Marks & Spencer, a regular and profitable source of revenue. During the war neither Max nor Ferry were interned, no doubt a reflection of the recognition of the importance of clothing children in wartime. The company traded from 1939 to 1987.

Francis Steiner himself came to England on a *Kindertransport* in 1938. Luckily his brother had already been accepted to read Law in London. Francis Steiner had benefited from having attended the Schottengymnasium in Vienna with its Catholic network and was able to attend such a school in Britain too. Francis was interned for some fifteen months, spending time in three different camps, including Hutchinson on the Isle of Man. He himself had a long and successful career with the Board of Trade.

Hilary Papworth, one of Max Steiner's granddaughters, added her own memories to the Cumberland Childwear story:

> Later my uncle, Frederick Stanley (born Friedrich Steiner) joined the firm after a spell in the British Army, I think he was put into Intelligence as he was German-speaking and it was at this time that he changed his name from Steiner to Stanley. Frederick, or Friedl as we knew him, was the salesman and sold a lot to the Middle East (I remember he was given a sheik outfit and a fancy

Tick-a-Tee advertisement, c. 1960s (courtesy of Francis Steiner)

watch by a Middle Eastern client). He also won a Queen's Award for Industry. He was not a skilled businessman, however, and the firm declined and was sold after his father's death in the early 70s. The Cumberland Childwear business grew and became substantial. I remember walking through the noisy machine floor of the factory on the industrial estate in Maryport. The buildings were subsequently demolished. The business must have provided considerable local employment, particularly for women machinists. I think the chief designer was called Mrs Repper and that she was Czech.[100]

Other members of the family remembered receiving boxes of Tick-a-Tee clothes, though it seems that none of these clothes survived. There are photos of children in the family wearing them though. And the advertisements are still around to show the achievements of the Steiner family.

Hans Schneider and the Arts

The Austrian émigré Hans Schneider, who made and later designed costumes for Benjamin Britten's productions, was not the only Austrian from the 'rag trade' to make his mark at Glyndebourne, the opera festival in Sussex. During the war performances at Glyndebourne were suspended, but by 1946, an exciting new chapter had begun: Benjamin Britten, fresh from his Sadlers Wells success with *Peter Grimes*, offered *The Rape of Lucretia* to Glyndebourne. John Piper, the eminent English artist, designed the sets and the costumes. And here another Austrian refugee enters the stage, or rather his costumes do, for working for Taylor and Penton Gowns of London's West End was Hans Schneider, who three years later was to become Head of Design at Marks & Spencer.

The Tate Archives hold the correspondence between Schneider and Piper[101] which both chronicles the process (and problems) of making and fitting the costumes as well as revealing the gradual blossoming of a close friendship between the men and their partners. The early letters allude to the difficulties that Schneider had in obtaining fabric as wartime shortages persisted well into the 1950s.

The later letters show that the friendship had outlived the Glyndebourne days, with at least one letter from 1956 referring to his work as Head Designer at M & S. 'I am going to Rome and Florence for the Fashion Shows.' In the last letter in this archive, dated 28 May 1962, Schneider tells Piper how he has heard that the window in Coventry [Cathedral] is 'simply wonderful' and that he is planning to go and see it next week.

Schneider's sense of humour for which the Viennese are known is present in the letters, as is his still unidiomatic and quirky English. He admits that, having met the singers, his enthusiasm for the opera was 'slightly damped by the various exteriors. Collatinus looks like the man who reads the gas meter.'

By 3 May 1946 he was writing to Piper in Wales, referring to the singer playing the principal role: 'We had Miss Joan Cross over here today and we find that owing to her outsize figure we would need 10-12 yards of wool material to drape her adequately, and she is protesting violently because of the weight of the material which tires her.' He finds a compromise: the wool is to be replaced by lighter silk which can be dyed to look like wool.

The very next day, he was writing again to tell John and Myfanwy Piper how much he missed them (they obviously spent time at each other's houses, having lunches and dinners), adding 'Life is really boring without Glyndebourne. But there is good news too: R. Bing asked me to make the costumes for *Tobias and the Angel*.'

Schneider held a party in July 1946 to celebrate the opening of the production, to which his mother, like her son and daughter saved from certain death in Vienna, was invited. On 16 July 1946 he wrote of the occasion that 'My mother was so proud of it as if I had composed the music, written the libretto, painted and designed the scenery and sung all the parts!' Schneider's dear 'Mutti', whose bosom had swelled with maternal pride figured largely in the lives of Hans and his friends, with express wishes sent to her in many letters. There is even a card addressed just to 'dear Mutti' from Kathleen Ferrier, the great contralto who became a friend through Glyndebourne. A photograph of around 1950 shows a laughing Hans with his mother and two of the singers he now knew.

By the 1950s, the relationship between the two men is purely personal rather than based on collaboration. On 8 November 1954 Schneider asks the Pipers to sell him a painting of John's: 'For years I wanted to have one of John's pictures and I would very much like to give one to Terence, as a Christmas present. You can be quite sure it would be one of our most treasured possessions.'

The Terence mentioned here is the art historian Terence Hodgkinson, of Magdalen College Oxford, Schneider's life partner whom he met in the late 1930s. They lived together for many years in Highgate, London, until Schneider's death in 1995. Terence Hodgkinson and Hans Schneider were, in the opinion of the author Julian Barnes, who knew them well and who wrote to Hodgkinson shortly after Schneider's death in 1995, the perfect couple.[102] Barnes wrote that he

Hans Schneider with 'Mutti', Anne Ayars and Kathleen Ferrier (courtesy of Magdalen College Oxford Archive)

was thinking of the last time he had had dinner with the couple and Hans had complimented him on his jacket. Thinking his memory at first 'solipsistic', he then countered saying it was 'entirely typical' of Hans: 'sharp-eyed, praising and affectionate all at once. And 'selfless, too, since he was really very frail that last time, and yet he was clocking my jacket!' Not only did Barnes and his wife love Hans, they cited Hans and Terence's relationship as the 'prime example of how it could be done, how it could be made to last, how it could be kept…how much pleasure it was possible to find in another's company.'

It is in a short story by Julian Barnes that one learns what Hans himself told the novelist in private about his background.[103] In a story about relationships, there is speculation as to whether a gay couple's feelings might have been strengthened by the illegality of their bond. Giving their names as 'H' and 'T' (obviously Hans and Terence), we read that H had come from a Jewish family in Vienna where, after the First World War, a time of great hardship, H's mother had had to give him to the poorhouse for several years. As a young man, H had met an English textile magnate who gave him a job and so helped him leave Austria in 1934. This was a year of violence and a warning of worse to come, when Austro-fascists destroyed the social democratic municipal regime that was Red Vienna.

It seems to have been the aristocratic Terence who became engaged to the magnate's daughter, unworldly and unaware of his own sexuality. But when Terence met Hans, he remembered feeling bewildered 'but sure of one thing: I was determined to marry H'. And what of the fiancée? She had felt things were somehow not as they should be, and on graciously finding another fiancé, she and the three men became firm friends. It was in this account too, that we learn of M & S's unusual, enlightened kindness. When Hans died in 1995 they paid Terence a 'widow's pension'; this in the days before civil partnerships, let alone same-sex marriages.

Julian Barnes had met the couple through his wife, Pat Kavanagh, who had apparently 'walked out' with Marcus Sieff (of M & S fame) before her marriage. She had adored Hans with whom she shared a passion for clothes: it was Hans who had helped her choose a delicate eau-de-nil silk tailored dress for her wedding, a dress that Julian Barnes still owns.

Another friend of Hans was the former Director of the British Museum, Neil MacGregor. According to Julian Barnes, MacGregor had been supported in obtaining this appointment by Terence Hodgkinson. In the Magdalen College Archives MacGregor is seen in photographs of the celebrations held for Hans's eightieth birthday party.[104] He, like Barnes, warmly remembered Hans's talent for friendship and generosity.[105] He still owns the tea set that Hans had left him, which had come from Hans' Czech grandmother.

Contradicting the M & S profile, MacGregor recalled Hans saying that he had been interned as an enemy alien during the war, and had not served in the British Army, service which would have been highly unusual, given the British government's distrust of the refugees until around 1942 when they were allowed to enlist in the combatant units.

Hodgkinson had turned to art history after reading PPE at Magdalen and serving as an officer in the Intelligence Corps during the Second World War. A tender letter to Schneider of 27 April 1943 from the Royal Masonic Hospital told of the comfort and pleasure he had received from Hans's visit to him and of his gratitude for their friendship, for in those pre-Wolfenden days that was the only way their loving relationship could be described.

How the couple met is not recorded, just referred to as in the 'late 1930s'. What is clear is that the tall, aristocratic-looking Hodgkinson whose 'English restraint' mentioned in his obituary was a contrast to Schneider's 'central European ebullience' was in no way antisemitic in the casual way that many if not most of his peers must have been.[106] His diary of 1938 records that his friend in Vienna, Mrs Lewisohn's sister-in-law and her rabbi husband had been imprisoned following Nazi reprisals for the murder of Vom Rath by Grynszpan[107]. Did he know of any non-Jews who spoke German and could intercede? Hodgkinson himself left immediately for Vienna, cancelling his other plans. When he got there, the couple had been released, but he went round all his contacts in Vienna and to the British Consulate to see what he could do to help, returning to England 'laden with errands and petitions. All the people were Jews of course, or half-Jews. Vienna was scarcely mitigated hell during those days.'[108]

Another act of kindness was cited in his obituary: '[Hodgkinson] had helped Rudolf Wittkower with translations from the German in the newly-arrived Warburg',[109] Wittkower being one of the many Jewish art historians like Ernst Gombrich who had come to London from Hamburg with the Jewish-owned Warburg, the great library of Renaissance culture.

Hodgkinson's career went from strength to strength: he became Head of the Wallace Collection and Editor of the *Burlington Magazine*. Schneider's too flourished at M & S. Their life together at 24 South End Lane, Highgate was cultured and comfortable as well as loving. An inventory drawn up for insurance purposes lists as well as the antique furniture their many paintings, including works by Sickert, the Circle of Bernini and, of course, the John Pipers that Hans gave to Terence.

Music, too, was essential to both partners: Hodgkinson played the piano and went to concerts frequently, as recorded in his meticulously-kept diaries from 1929 to 1938. One letter in the archive refers to the couple's first meeting with the composer Benjamin Britten and his life partner Peter Pears on Long Island in 1940. Long before Hans made the costumes for John Piper's designs for the opera, Britten, Pears, Schneider and Hodgkinson had been close friends, exchanging letters in which they thanked each other for dinners, Christmas presents and so on. The Aldeburgh couple were more often the ones to apologise for late answers: Britten cited wrestling to finish *Billy Budd* as what had held up his answer, whereas Pears drew a small stick figure of himself supine, to show how abject was his apology for having for so long neglected to thank their Highgate friends for a case of wine to put down. He realised it had been forty years since they met at Amityville, Long Island and added, 'A case of wine is adorable and thank you, but how much more adorable and welcome would be YOU!' Humour, affection and warmth were the keynotes of their correspondence.

Through Schneider's involvement in the Britten operas (he designed the costumes for later productions too), he and Hodgkinson became friends with several of the singers. The Magdalen archive holds photos of for example Joan Cross, obviously bearing Schneider no malice for his having weighted her down with wool for *The Rape*, as they cheerfully referred to the opera. She signed one affectionately, 'With all my love Joan'.

But there is one story chronicled in the archive which combines Hans's various talents in a quite startling and newsworthy way. Indeed, there is a look back at the story in *The Independent* of 24 July 2006 by an elderly Russian ballerina Kondratieva, who remembered the first time she had visited London on tour from Moscow: 'Hans Schneider, an executive at Marks & Spencer, invited us to his store and told us to take whatever we wanted. Here in Moscow in 1956 all the shops were empty.'

The Magdalen College archive records what might have been a diplomatic incident, had Marks & Spencer in the form of the charming Hans Schneider not stepped in to save the day. Because when the Bolshoi Ballet were first in England, several ballerinas had been arrested for shoplifting in Marks & Spencer. Presumably they had no currency and, dazzled by the goods on offer while the shops at home were bare, had succumbed to temptation. Hans Schneider of M & S, seeing a chance for publicity and for making good, offered to let the

Hans Schneider with Russian dancers, 1956 (courtesy of Magdalen College Oxford Archives)

troupe help themselves for free to anything in the store. Schneider also arranged for some of the ballerinas to have their photos taken professionally in London. Photos in the archive show Schneider helping dancers to choose clothes in the store.

Other photos followed and the grateful Russians continued to write to Schneider and sent him programmes, photos and cards. One close friendship developed with Maris Liepa. The very last item in the archive is a pack of twenty-six photographs from Terence's eightieth birthday celebrations. They show the couple, with Schneider in particular now looking thin and frail but still happy and surrounded by friends. These include Neil MacGregor, the novelist Anita Brookner with other art historians, writers and celebrities.

What a happy ending for Hans Schneider, who would certainly have been murdered had he stayed in Vienna but who instead not only found lasting love but friendship and a life of music and art, as well as his satisfying career at Marks & Spencer.

Illo, the *Kindertransportee* at M & S

It was almost inevitable that some *Kinder* should make their way into the fashion trade too. The designer in charge of swimsuit design at Marks & Spencer was the German refugee Inge-Lore (known as 'Illo') Sommerfeld (1926–2008). Her truly moving story unfolds in the archive in the Wiener Library, London, a Holocaust archive which holds just such stories. Through a series of letters, photographs and certificates, we can plot her trajectory.[110]

To set the scene, we first see her grandparents' clothing and textile shop apparently in Berlin, 'J Unruh', the name of her maternal grandfather.

Next we see dark-haired little Illo, aged around four years, with her mother's arm around her on holiday in the mountains.

We know from the Wiener Archive description that Illo was a *Kindertransportee*, one of the some 10,000 who were sent to safety in

Illo's grandfather's shop in Germany (courtesy of the Wiener Library, London)

England shortly before war broke out in either late 1938 or early 1939. Illo was only twelve. Although it is not known whether her family survived the Holocaust, there is one letter apparently from her mother which Illo kept, which must have meant more to her than anything else she owned. It is dated 27 December 1942:

> My dear *Püppchen* [little doll]
> Sometimes I wonder if we will ever see each other again. Today once again, I want to thank you from the bottom of my heart for all the joy you brought me from the first day of your life. In good conscience, I can say that you brought meaning and happiness to our lives. My darling, I couldn't spare you from losing your father so young, but that I had to send you away aged only twelve without your mother stands as a mark of dreadful guilt on the book of my life and it makes it even harder to say goodbye. I too lost my mother when I was only little and so I know only too well....

Here the letter ends in torn fragments. We can only imagine the mental state of a woman who was to make this choice: send her child alone into an uncertain future in a foreign country or let her stay at home to face almost certain death?

And yet, Illo thrived. Only four years later in 1943, we can read her Northwood College school report, featuring only As and Bs. 'She has applied herself with great keenness and has worked indefatigably. She deserves success in her examination...' Not bad for a little German girl? Perhaps the Jewish community gave her comfort and support; certainly her Confirmation certificate from the West London Synagogue of 9 January 1943 would point to this link. The next papers in the file are her certificates for typing and shorthand, English and German from a private school, a good way into various careers for girls in those days. Here is a letter from 1948 offering a post at the BBC, presumably as a secretary.[111] Now follows a gap in the timeline: did she meet someone who suggested another career path? Did she take more training? Dated 19 August 1955, a letter important enough to be saved tells her that her

Illo Sommerfeld with her mother, c. 1930 (courtesy of the Wiener Library, London)

engagement as an Assistant Designer at Marks & Spencer is confirmed from 1 September.

From a cheerful photograph in an article on the Design Department in the house journal, *St Michael's Magazine*, Autumn 1967, we see Illo, now a plump lady in her early forties and with her name changed to 'Miss Illo Summerfield', 'making the final adjustment to a two-piece swimsuit in a new trial fabric.' She also kept a cutting from the M & S *Sparks* magazine showing one of her swimsuits modelled by an M & S sales assistant, a keen swimmer herself. We glimpse her again in later life, smiling into the camera with her dachshund. She never married apparently, and died aged eighty-two in Tunbridge Wells. Was she happy? Did she ever get over the loss of her family and the train journey to an unknown country to be looked after by strangers? Of course, we can't know. But perhaps there is some comfort in seeing her clippings which must show her pride in her work. And in knowing how the M & S company cared for German refugees and understood their stories.

Launer, on the Arm of Her Majesty

At Fortnum & Mason, in the other half of the antique cabinet of leatherwear, opposite Ettinger goods, are arranged some other delicate leather wallets also bearing a royal coat of arms. 'Ah those are Launer' said Mr Grant, 'created in 1939 by another German refugee gentleman...'[112] But that, as they say, is another story.

But the first part of the Launer story is undocumented and very insubstantial. It begins with Sam Launer, who was a German-speaking Jewish businessman from Prague.[113] He is likely to have arrived in 1938 after the Sudetenland was occupied by Nazi forces, although he may have come earlier if he had family or other connections in Britain. He ran his leather goods company in London until his son Freddy, born in 1932, took it over. By the early 1980s, however, Launer was struggling financially and the company was ripe for a takeover.

Now onto the stage steps yet another German refugee in the form of Gerald Billigheimer who, with the rest of his family changed his name to Bodmer, his mother's maiden name, when they became naturalised after the war. From Würzburg near Frankfurt am Main, Billigheimer senior was born in 1892, a German Jew who had served his country as a newly-qualified doctor in the army during the First World War. This military duty only protected him until 1934 under the Nazi regime and so Ernst Billigheimer was forced to flee to Britain in 1938 with his non-Jewish wife and their three little sons.

Now aged 46, Dr Billigheimer had to start to study medicine all over again to qualify according to British standards. Medicine was one area where the refugees were not welcomed: on the whole British medics closed ranks and tried to hinder German doctors rather than help them, a shameful period in their professional history. Perhaps they feared that Austrians and Germans were more advanced in their research in some areas, and indeed they were, in psychiatry for example. When war broke out, Ernst Billigheimer was interned in Huyton Camp near Liverpool for six months.

The three boys grew up in Manchester where the German family had settled, speaking first German together; then the boys switched to English while their parents continued to speak German to them before the senior Billigheimers switched to a language known popularly as 'Emigranto', a sort of mongrel mixture of the two languages. Two of the boys excelled in science: one in Genetics and one in Physics.[114]

The third, Gerald, however, took a less travelled path and became a clarinettist at the Royal College of Music in London. Although he was employed by the Hallé Orchestra, he did not make it to first Clarinettist there and found the orchestral politics rather unpleasant. For this reason, when offered a chance in 1959 to work for a cousin of his father's, L. S. Mayer, he jumped at it. This was his first step towards a stellar career in leather goods, because the relative worked as a gift importer. Both he and fellow refugee, Sam Launer, also made handbags for Rayne, the upmarket British handbag company who had a Royal warrant. Mappin & Webb too commissioned Launer to make bags for their label.

Royal approval for one's product is keenly sought after by all makers of quality goods, but for the refugees the royal crest spelled something more: recognition, acceptance and belonging. Eventually, Queen Elizabeth II agreed to give Launer a royal warrant too. In Launer's case, the royal contact came through one of the Queen's dressers, Angela Kelly, who worked with Gerald Bodmer to make a bag the Queen would like.

Since then, Launer bags have been seen on the most important arms in the world: those of British Prime Minister Margaret Thatcher, the Duchess of Cornwall and actors and national treasures Judi Dench and Maggie Smith to name but a few. An article in *The Telegraph* had as its subject the Queen and her handbag habits: 'The Queen is said to own more than 200 Launer handbags. Her preferred styles are the Royale and the black patent Traviata (23cm x 20cm x 10cm). The bag has a longer handle to ease the process of handshaking.'[115] For the Queen, though, the Launer handbag allegedly has a strategic role:

> Her Majesty's personal bag is used as much to send secret signals to staff as it is to carry personal items. If the Queen places her

handbag on the table at dinner, it signals that she wants the event to end in the next five minutes. If she puts her bag on the floor, it shows she's not enjoying the conversation and wants to be rescued by her lady-in-waiting.[116]

When asked if this were true, Mr Bodmer blushed charmingly and declined to answer... After all, royal customers expect discretion.

The same *Telegraph* article reflects on the bag as a very symbol of Queen Elizabeth, enough to inspire more blushes from Mr Bodmer? 'And so the Queen's compact leather handbag paints a fitting portrait of our monarch. Practical, discreet and with strong family bonds – we should have known all along.'

What also makes the Launer bag distinctive is, of course, the logo which appears on the bag in cartoons of the Queen too. How did this elegant swirl come about? Gerald Bodmer explained that the Japanese clients missed a logo on the leather bags that they loved for their tradition and quality. To demonstrate how he created the brand's logo, he sketched a shape in the air, simple but like no other, and so the logo was born and registered.

In 1991, Her Majesty the Queen visited the Launer factory where the making of the bags is a source of special pride: 'Each item is handmade using traditional methods in a Grade II listed building in the Midlands, the premises have been a home for the manufacturing of leather goods since its construction in 1904.'[117]

But Launer is not only bought by royalty: it is a brand that brings in a million pounds turnover a year in the London store Selfridges alone. Gerald Bodmer is not one to dwell on his outstanding achievements; instead, aged eighty-five at the time he was interviewed, he was playing regular chamber concerts, travelling, and still steering his company. It is lucky that in this case the baton was handed from one German refugee to another who was entrepreneurial, hardworking and creative. The Hallé Orchestra's loss was the Queen's (and others') gain indeed.

Launer handbag 'Traviata Multi-cal F2' (courtesy of Launer)

The Queen visits the Launer factory (courtesy of Launer)

Double Two Collars the Shirt Market

Double Two is a company based in Wakefield and now run by Richard and John Donner, son and grandson respectively of the founder Isaak Donner.[118] Not only are they able to help tell the story of the company but the account is enriched by a lengthy recording made for the British Library in 1999 with all three Donners.[119] In his heavily-accented English, Isaak Donner, now ninety-four years old, thought back to the early days. He was born on 29 September 1904 in Belz, in those days part of Poland, into a textile manufacturing family. After the First World War Russians had attacked his hometown, and the family moved to Vienna. Not the only people among the textile émigrés to be double refugees, the Jewish Donners had to flee a second time from Vienna in 1938 when the Germans annexed Austria into the Third Reich.

Fortunately, as Mr Donner senior explained, the company had already been buying cloth from Manchester and had contacts in England. And importantly, they were able to bring something with them – an idea. The Donners had already been working on a shirt with an extra collar and cuffs. Mr Donner sought advice as to where to set up his business. He needed a good source of labour, ideally women who could sew and cut. He would be aided in his enterprise by his wife who was a stitcher, while he himself was a cutter. Wakefield in Yorkshire fitted the bill: Mr Donner mentioned a red carpet being laid out for them, metaphorically at least, for this was an area of low employment and the Donners were bringing jobs.

Frank Meyer, a suit-maker and German refugee whom Isaak Donner had not met before emigration, was able to put up £6,000 to fund the company and played a large part in Double Two's later development. When the train pulled into Wakefield station in 1939 and the clouds of steam slowly parted, the Donner family saw on the platform three men in overcoats waiting for them: the Midland Bank Manager, the Manager of the Labour Exchange and a 'business angel' brought in to facilitate the setting up of a business. Since the Donners had not much English nor experience of business life in Britain, they were allocated a translator, Dr Harry Beckhough, who later became the company's sales manager. An enlightened welcome, but then the Donners had not arrived empty-handed. They had plans, big plans.

Barely had the family set up their works in Wakefield, Yorkshire when war broke out. Donner saw his opportunity and grasped it: the blouses that girls were wearing for their work in munitions and other factories producing war machinery got filthy very quickly and few working people in those days had the money to buy multiple sets of clothing, nor could they wash, dry and iron their one cotton blouse quickly enough for work the next day. Donner's solution was to produce cheap basic tops in synthetic materials that washed easily, dried quickly and needed no ironing – perfect! They sold thousands. Assured of a source of income, the ingenious Donners started to put their next plan into action: the detached shirt collar.

The situation in Britain prior to the arrival of Double Two was that most men wore shirts with completely separate loose collars, which were very stiff and were attached with a stud. They were very uncomfortable and it was common for the collar to be washed and the shirt not to be washed to avoid wear on the shirt. During the war, British soldiers fought alongside American and Canadian troops who wore shirts where the collars were permanently attached to the shirt. The collars were soft and the shirts were comfortable. The disadvantage was the whole shirt had to be washed every time and the collars and cuffs wore out very quickly, as indeed did the body of the shirt. Then along came Double Two with a new idea which was to have the shirt with two collars, one of which was attached to the shirt via a special removable seam. The collars were soft like the American ones. The whole shirt was washed as required and then the collars wore out, which they always did first. The first collar could be removed by snipping away the remaining seam and the second collar could be inserted into a special groove which then just needed tacking down, either with a sewing machine or a few stitches by hand. The second collar was also soft and comfortable and this doubled the life of the shirt.[120]

Double Two vintage advertisement (courtesy of Richard Donner)

By 1946, they had transformed the space into a vast shirt-manufacturing facility, becoming a key player in the men's shirt market. The new product was an instant success and as the shirts had two collars and in some cases two sets of cuffs, the shirts were called Double Two shirts. The innovation became so successful that the company came to be known by the name of the shirts.[121]

In 1951 wartime patents were released for commercial use. The next innovation came about by accident, as is so often the case. Dr Rex Winfield of Calico Printers, a friend of Isaak Donner's, had been experimenting with artificial fibres when a chemical process had gone badly wrong, leaving a 'bale like steel' behind. Winfield and Donner worked on coaxing a fibre out of this substance and managed it. The next step was to bring the first reel of yarn to Double Two to see if they could weave it into shirting. This product was not very comfortable so another friend, Mr Previsa, tried it on his newly-acquired warp knitting machine. This produced a breathable fabric with excellent non-iron qualities. The first polyester, brand-named 'Terylene' shirt was born and is now proudly displayed in the Double Two premises for all to see. As Mr Richard Donner recounted, the next step was a big one for the firm: 'Dr Winfield travelled round the world with the first half dozen shirts which were of course non-iron and very quick-drying, very good for travellers. He sold licences to DuPont, Hoechst, Toray, Teijin and others.'[122]

The company grew and grew. On the company website, the Donners tell the tale of their expansion over the years:

> By the end of the 1980s a group holding company was formed called 'The Wakefield Shirt Company', owning Double Two Ltd, Wm Sugden & Sons Ltd and L J & M Refson Ltd along with a number of other smaller businesses acquired over the years.
>
> As a group of companies we were now employing over 1,500 people across six factories and selling over 3,000,000 shirts per year in over forty countries.[123]

Isaak Donner was passionate in his gratitude to Britain, turning down the offer of transferring production to Hong Kong early on, which would have been lucrative for the company. He was committed to employing local people, not just to making profit. Happily the story continues today, as the website relates:

> In 1995, Richard Donner's son, John Donner, joined, his father and grandfather in the third generation family business. Isaak Donner died in 2000 but to this day Richard and John continue to run the company, making Double Two one of the very few original family-run branded clothing companies in the world.

Since joining the business, John Donner has been instrumental in driving new brands to bring the company into new areas of the clothing market including Bar Harbour, leisure and casual wear for a mature consumer; Old Salt, a fashion-led proposition for a younger consumer and Paradigm, a 100 per cent cotton fabric with excellent non-iron, wrinkle-free properties.

Recognition continued to come for their many achievements: in 2007 they received an award for 'Innovation' for their development of the Paradigm range and in 2013 won The Queen's Award for International Trade, with over 42 per cent of production being exported to over forty countries around the world. Upon receiving the award, Richard Donner said: 'We have received many awards over the years but The Queen's Award is our most prestigious one and I thank all of our staff for their hard work and determination.'

The family experienced very little antisemitism in England, although Richard Donner, born in 1939 in England, had some hostile reactions from other schoolchildren who considered him a German. His efforts to explain that his parents were Austrian refugees, the very opposite of the enemy, met with incomprehension and he was beaten up more than once. The Donners made an effort to learn English and to speak it at home. Integration was as essential to them as was their manufacturing prowess. In the same spirit perhaps, the family had decided to make a return visit to Austria in 1945, not a move that many

Jewish refugees took, unable to forget the persecution meted out by neighbours or employees.

In his British Library interview, Richard Donner recalled a childhood spent partly at the family firm and the fun of sliding down the fabric chutes at the top of the Double Two factory. But his decision to join the firm was not a foregone conclusion by any means. Nor was his decision to study Textile at Leeds University. However, a Professor Speake had skilfully shown him round the Leeds textile department with a minimum of commentary but gradually revealing a wealth of state of the art machinery, Donner admitted that he was hooked and he enrolled.

Donner's Harvard Business School training also served him well and he spoke of the company's continuing search for innovation in his interview. He faced different challenges from his father, not for him the war but instead the complexities of mechanisation and the problem of trading in Europe without being part of the Eurozone. Even more challenging was the cost of production in the UK, meaning that Double Two's shirts and their many other lines which now include work uniforms are mainly made in the Far East, although designed, developed and marketed in the UK. Richard Donner certainly embraced the flexibility of the original Double Two enterprise, with the company under his regime being early users of television advertising, of computers and of diversifying into other areas, once the original Double Two shirts had outlived their use.

Now the company is run from comfortable premises in Wakefield. The reception area is decorated with a beautiful collage made from Double Two labels over the decades.

There is also a handsome oil portrait of Mr Isaak painted by his granddaughter. Double Two, in all its forms, continues to flourish all over Britain. No wonder Isaak Donner looks on with pride from his portrait.

Double Two label collage (courtesy of Richard Donner)

Frank Usher and the Frocks

British fashion reaped great benefits from Reimann Schule-trained designers.[124] In 1923, Max Bruh signed up for evening classes in fashion drawing at the Berlin Reimann, while by day he worked as a textile trade apprentice for the firm Friedländer & Zaduk, who paid for his classes. The author of the history of the Reimann school takes Bruh as an example of the great success of these evening classes for businessmen and their employees, because it was this training which enabled Bruh to found his own firm, the internationally known fashion firm Frank Usher in London, to where he emigrated. Bruh had come from a poor Jewish family in Silesia, his obituary recounts, and had left school at fourteen to feed his family.[125] When the Nazis came to power in 1933, he had cause to go to Switzerland on business where he was told to flee Germany for England.

It was in England that he met Anne, his future wife, who had been born in Wuppertal in Germany. As a Jew, she too had fled to Britain for safety in 1939. The two married in 1944 and in that inauspicious year, despite the war, they set up their own fashion company.

As one account from 1961 has it:

> Characteristically, Max and Anne Bruh found the only way round the hampering restrictions. At that time in the war, British fashion manufacturers needed textile trading coupons and these were hard to come by especially for a newly established company – they discovered and bought an existing but almost defunct firm named Frank Usher. 'The name was good, so we kept it,' explained Anne Bruh, 'Besides, it gave us such glorious anonymity.' He bought the existing Frank Usher label because 'British fashion manufacturers needed textile trading coupons to operate and it was hard for a new business to get them'.[126]

And what kind of clothes came from the Frank Usher label? One article from 1961 gives an impression of the affordable and 'sensible' glamour that sounds utterly English:

Frank Usher vintage advertisement (courtesy of Roman Originals)

In our glossy-mag world we were frightfully sniffy about Frank Usher frocks – those spangly things worn to Rotary Club dinners and Guildhall 'dos'. Nevertheless the business, owned and run by Max Bruh, was hugely successful, winning countless awards for export and dressing a swathe of genteel British (and foreign) women with an eye on fashion but neither the budget nor the derring-do to go the whole hog.[127]

The author of the piece explained that Frank Usher took the best of Paris design, a habit that started no doubt back in Berlin. On his trips to the fashion shows in Paris, she elaborated:

> Ready-to-wear manufacturers bought, at vast expense, a 'caution ticket' which not only allowed them to enter the couture show but also entitled them to one garment made up, to two toiles or three to four patterns. Max Bruh usually chose the last.

[A toile is a mock-up of a garment, usually made in a cheaper material, as a model or pattern for the real thing.] She continued to analyse Usher's success:

> The trick of interpreters, like Frank Usher, was not stylistic innovation, for they had the safety-net of haute couture design leads, but to know their rag trade inside out; where to get the best value for money in fabrics, seamstresses and novelty trimmings...Frank Usher preferred to use the patterns to make more classic and one shudders at the very word, 'wearable' – interpretations. He knew his market. His women did not want one-season folderol, they wanted a good, reasonably priced dress that would 'see them through'.

The author of Brüh's obituary noted that it was thanks to his commercial success that Max Bruh became an influential voice in the British fashion industry and on the board of the British Fashion Export Council. 'In 1961 the Bruhs sold Frank Usher to Selincourt, the fashion, manufacturing and retailing conglomerate, but maintained a day-to-day control. However, by 1985 he had tired of this arrangement and bought the company back and it was skilfully revived.'

The final word on the Frank Usher designs goes to the top model of the 1950s, Barbara Goalen, who modelled for Elsbeth Juda and Otto

Frank Usher advertisement, 1989 (courtesy of Roman Originals)

Lucas, whom the author of the account bumped into at the fashion photographer John French's retrospective at the Victoria & Albert Museum in the mid-1980s:

> She cooed with delight at Frank Usher's renaissance as she stood magnificently upholstered in one of Usher's quiet black cocktail

dresses. If one opted for his little black classics and avoided the spangle factor they would serve you long and well and Mrs Goalen was certainly a testament to that.[128]

This could be the end of the story: fashions changed and Frank Usher-type 'mother of the bride' looks went out of style. Max died. A north London newspaper provides the last word on the Bruh story:

> Anne Bruh, ninety, shared her story of how she fled her homeland and went on to build an international fashion empire. The book, called *A Nation of Storytellers*, is the culmination of a competition by publishing company Blurb to find stories people wanted preserved forever. Thousands of people entered and, from all the stories submitted, the top twenty most uplifting tales were chosen by a panel of judges to be featured in the book.
>
> Mrs Bruh was encouraged to submit her story by her grandson, Adam, who wanted to learn more about his family history. Mrs Bruh said: 'It was a wonderful experience to have had the opportunity to tell this story and now my family and I have a wonderful book, a physical record that will be treasured forever.' Sharing her story helped Mrs Bruh to return to her home town earlier this year for the first time since she left Germany all those years ago. She visited her old house and the cemetery where many of her relatives are buried on the emotional trip. Raised near Düsseldorf, in a well-established German Jewish family, Mrs Bruh's blissful childhood was ruined by the Nazis' rise to power. Her family's business and property were confiscated and Mrs Bruh, along with her siblings, were subjected to beatings by children who were once friends.
>
> They left Germany for the Netherlands in 1938 but, without the necessary papers to cross the border, ended up in a refugee camp. The family's fortunes were transformed when Mrs Bruh accepted a job as a typist at a London organisation that hired

Jewish refugees aged under seventeen. Her son Robert, who stepped in to finalise the story when Mrs Bruh fell ill just before publication, said: 'Without knowing a word of English, working with Cockneys was difficult but funny.' She later had to relearn English – that 'piper' was properly pronounced 'paper'. Mrs Bruh met her husband, a fellow refugee from Berlin, and together they set up their own fashion house, Frank Usher, which became an influential force in the British fashion industry and had offices all over the world. When her husband fell ill, Mrs Bruh took over as managing director and remained there until she retired aged eighty.

Ultimately, Frank Usher designs were bought up by Roman Originals, a clothing company based in the Midlands. But as her son said of his mother, Anne Bruh: 'She's not really told anyone her story before and people should know.'[129]

Lord Kagan and Gannex

The refugees from Nazism were not saintly, they were human beings who had been through harsh experiences and some of them fell foul of the law. There was Pringle's Otto Weisz driving along the road with a highland cow on his bonnet. Some managed to break the blackout rules, as did the Brits. There are, however, at least a couple of refugees who attained the peak of their career in textiles and had their achievements recognised by the very highest in the land, only to fall from grace to disgrace and prison. It seems that the same *chutzpah* and drive which allowed them to succeed could overspill into risky territory.

One such was the colourful Joseph Kagan.[130] His life story was tough even by the standards of the victims of Nazi persecution, as he was the victim of both Stalin's and Hitler's murderous regimes. He was born Juozapas Kaganas in Lithuania in 1915 to Jewish parents who manufactured textiles. In particular, they supplied the grey cloth to the Kaiser's army, ideal for camouflaging troops in the Russian winter. Young Joe was destined to follow in this trade and started to learn early on. His parents, however, had higher aspirations for him and it was decided he should go to England, to Leeds University to study textile technology there.

He returned to Kaunas, Lithuania several times during his study period, a fateful mistake as it turned out, because in 1940 he was there when Stalin's forces moved in – and was trapped. The MP Tam Dalyell took up the story of Kagan's return to Lithuania in the obituary he wrote:[131]

> Joseph Kagan took over the family woollen mill, which the Russians allowed him to keep. In later years it was pointed out that it was highly unusual in the circumstances of the Soviet invasion of the Baltic republic for anyone to be allowed to hold on to their factory, least of all if they were Jewish, domiciled in a ghetto. This was interpreted as an indication that Kagan might

at an early stage have had relations with the KGB, if not that he was an actual KGB agent.

Worse was to come, much worse. In 1941 Hitler's armies marched into Lithuania and all Jews were forced into the Kaunas ghetto. Kaganas met his wife during his incarceration there but, not long after, he was arrested and sent as slave labour to a foundry. He realised that the only hope of survival for him and his family was to somehow hide and survive until the end of hostilities. Then his luck changed because he realised that the Catholic foreman of the foundry, Vytantas Rinkevicius, was a humane man, one who might risk his life and those of his own family members to save endangered Jews. An audacious plan was drawn up whereby the Kaganas family (Joseph, his wife and her two parents) would move behind a partition backing onto the foundry. Rinkevicius was to bring them food every day and remove excrement. The space for the family was just six feet long. Today it is hard to even imagine the mental and physical hardship endured during this incredible arrangement which lasted for nine long months. In later life, Rinkevicius was recognised as a 'righteous Gentile' at Yad Vashem in Israel for his outstanding bravery and self-sacrifice.

When the Russian Allies reoccupied Lithuania at the end of the war, Joe Kaganas got permission to move to Romania from where he travelled on further to Israel. From there he was able to return to West Yorkshire where he knew he could make his living from textile manufacture. Ever inventive, his first step was, with borrowed money, to make rough blankets in a shed near Huddersfield. It was in that Yorkshire town that his father now lived, having been out of the country when Lithuania was invaded by Germany. Evidently another spectacular survivor, he became Britain's second-oldest man, living to be 109 years old.

Next came the greatest coup by Kagan (his newly-anglicised name) in the form of a new fabric – Gannex. This textile, created in 1951, combined what one blogger called 'the warming properties of wool with the waterproofing of polyester' [probably nylon]. It was

Lord and Lady Kagan with a Gannex coat (courtesy of Jenny Kagan)

essentially a nylon outer layer bonded to a woollen inner layer, making the coat both warm and rainproof.

Like Tibor Reich's Harris tweed enlivened with Lurex thread from his native Hungary, Gannex serves as a metaphor for the weaving together of two textile cultures: traditional British wool and creative European modern know-how. Gannex was an instant success, chosen by the Bradford police for their uniforms, by the Ministry of Defence, by Arctic and Antarctic explorers and Himalayan climbers.

Kagan started to create Gannex raincoats from larger premises in Elland, Yorkshire; they too leapt off the rails. The Duke of Edinburgh was persuaded to order one from Harrods, 'securing the Royal Warrant and leading to the provision of raincoats for the Queen and even her corgis to wear'.[132] Gannex's biggest fan was, however, the Prime Minister, Harold Wilson, rarely seen without his warm raincoat. Wilson was committed to reviving the Yorkshire textile industry and saw Gannex as a symbol of this revival, it being the major employer in Elland at that time.

The success of the new fabric made Kagan a multi-millionaire, literally a rags to riches story. Kagan was able to show his gratitude for Wilson's patronage by providing Labour Party funding. In return, Kagan

Joseph Kagan with Harold Wilson (courtesy of Jenny Kagan)

was given a knighthood in 1970 and then in 1976 he was made Baron Kagan of Elland. Harold Wilson also gave Gannex raincoats as gifts, one recipient being the Russian premier Nikita Khrushchev. But Russian approval was not a blessing for Kagan, as mentioned above, and again questions were raised about Kagan's loyalty. How had he convinced the Russians back in Lithuania to let him run his father's private factory? And now, in 1970s Britain, why was he so friendly with one Richardas Vaygauskas, a Lithuanian at the Soviet Embassy and known KGB operative? Was it really because they shared a passion for chess? Or was it, as Kagan said, because he wanted to ensure that family members back in Lithuania fared well under the Soviets?

Harold Wilson remained loyal to his colourful friend, but his loyalty was put to a much more severe test. In December 1979 warrants were issued for the arrest of Kagan and his wife. It was alleged that in 1977 Kagan had stolen twenty-three barrels of indigo dye powder from Kagan Textile Ltd, which had been sold to another company and no longer belonged to Kagan. He was alleged to have falsified documents for accounting purposes. In some quarters, however, it was claimed that the real crime had been tax evasion but that this was not an extradictable offence and Kagan was in Israel when the warrant was issued.[133] Only when he made the mistake of visiting Paris was Kagan arrested. In 1980 he was fined, stripped of his knighthood (but not his peerage) and sentenced to ten months in prison. The MP Tam Dalyell noted in Kagan's *Independent* obituary that the prison sentence was not to Kagan what it would have been to others:

> He taught many of his fellow inmates to play chess to a high standard and also won a reputation as a neat and dextrous sewer of materials. Whereas many members of the House of Lords would simply have crumbled in prison, Joe Kagan found it a picnic compared to German concentration camps and the Russian army.

Some opined that it was really his KGB connections which had been responsible for his arrest – a warning to him to keep his distance. Yet another account has it that a 'disgruntled former mistress betrayed him in Paris'.[134] Or was he perhaps a spy?

On his release he appeared in the House of Lords, as was still his right, and he made good use of his time there. 'As an ex-prisoner', continued Tam Dalyell, 'he made uniquely valuable contributions to debate on penal matters and wrote powerful letters to the broadsheet press'. And Dalyell concluded his account of Kagan's life by saying, 'In my opinion Kagan was a man whose contribution to Britain far and away outweighed any of the naughty things which he may have done.' A refugee who contributed a different sort of 'colour' to British life, Joseph Kagan died peacefully at his London home in 1995.

The Fabulous Kroll Dynasty

Natasha (1914–2004) and Alex (1916–2008) Kroll,[135] like Lord Kagan above for one, were double refugees. They were born in Moscow into a Latvian Jewish family but because Alex contracted tuberculosis when a child, he was sent to a sanatorium in Berlin to recover. The whole family were able to follow on, as the father was transferred to the Russian Embassy in Berlin effectively defecting from the Soviet Union in the mid-1930s. Both Natasha and Alex studied at the Reimann Schule. Natasha, who was enrolled from 1933–36, was both a student of Elsa Taterka, the celebrated poster artist and in Natasha's opinion a wonderful teacher, and under Georg Fischer, studying window display, as did her brother Alex. In her final year, she was exempted from paying any fees, being taken on by Reimann as an assistant. However, it cannot have been possible for her to enjoy this recognition of her ability for long, for the meaning of what it was to be a Jewish student in the Third Reich was brought home to her when she was forbidden to participate in an exhibition that she had spent some time preparing for. So when in 1936 Albert Reimann and Elsa Taterka encouraged her to leave, as they were doing, for London where she could become an employee of the school in safety, she agreed. Her brother, who had sneaked into the infamous German degenerate art exhibition of 1937 as an act of defiance against the Nazis and there had fallen for work by Otto Dix,

Natasha and Alex Kroll (courtesy of William Kroll)

Kirchner, Beckmann, Nolde and others, followed her to London in 1938.[136]

Their parents were not so fortunate. Their father, Hermann, was arrested in Berlin 'for allegedly conspiring to spirit money abroad'.[137] It was thought that he had been helping Jews less fortunate than himself to escape from different parts of Central Europe, an accusation which resulted in his being sent to Bergen-Belsen concentration camp. At the end of the war, Hermann Kroll, having survived, was put on a truck by Allied soldiers. However, he was tipped off that he was being returned to Russia and escaped by jumping off the transport lorry. Eventually he and his wife made it to Britain to join their children.

Natasha's first class in London had twenty students; after all the Reimann had its supporters in Britain and word quickly spread that there was now a chance to study at this world-class institution in London, under famous teachers, some of whom had fled from the Berlin school. But the school was forced to close down in 1940 as it proved impossible to run classes during the Blitz in central London, and even the correspondence courses offered were ultimately too much of a challenge. Not daunted, Natasha Kroll found employment at the modern Simpson of Piccadilly menswear store, becoming its display manager in 1942.

It was probably one of the few stores in London where 'state of the art' would have been appreciated. Her obituary takes up the subject of her window display talent while pointing out the great challenge of creating a stylish window for Simpson in the midst of wartime austerity:

> For all their innovation, Kroll's designs were tempered by a practical attitude. In her definitive book *Shop Window Display* (1954), she stressed that 'the windows were essentially settings for the merchandise'. The lighting and objects were there only to enhance the clothes. At that time, it may have been considered perverse to surround or support the smart Simpson clothes with wooden crates, bricks and ladders, but Kroll cleverly deployed such basic objects to enhance, by contrast, the clothes' elegance.

The rough-with-smooth gambit was only one aspect of her stylistic range.[…]

Many of the trends developing in the fields of exhibition and graphic design – such as the use of dramatic photo blow-ups – were echoed in the Simpson windows. Frequently, the displays were minimalist: simple panels, strategic lighting, with the actual lighting units featured as display elements.[138]

In the obituary it is also pointed out that Natasha Kroll knew how to create topical displays, notably marking the end of clothes rationing by featuring a wastepaper basket stuffed with crumpled coupons. In her archive at Brighton University are photographs and sketches of her windows, also her instructions dated 'Summer 1949' for a 'Women's Window: Background painted by Julian Trevelyan'. The theme was 'Holidays' and Julian Trevelyan was given a free hand in the treatment of the theme.' Julian Trevelyan RA was a celebrated painter of the time who had painted camouflage during the war with Roland Penrose, the surrealist painter and husband of Lee Miller. Having no less an artist than Trevelyan paint the store window display was obviously the standard that Natasha Kroll set.

One young textile designer, later also to become famous and who was encouraged by Kroll, was Terence Conran, then just out of art school. Another who came under her wing was the interior designer Kenneth Partridge, as it was noted in his obituary in *The Telegraph* written by the fashion historian Frederick Michael Pick. Kroll obviously was not squeamish when it came to making an arresting display:

> After the war, he was hired by Natasha Kroll, display director of Simpson of Piccadilly, later recalling his horror when she dispatched him to an antiquarian bookseller with an order for large books containing engraved plates, only to rip the books apart so that the plates could be used in window displays.[139]

This job at Simpson was, however, just the start of her career. The Reimann school, like the Bauhaus, produced versatile graduates who could and did turn their hands to more than one discipline. In 1944 she illustrated the children's book *The Princess and the Pea* published by Collins.

Here there was another refugee connection, for the company which produced the book as the first book packagers in Britain was Adprint, created by the Austrian Wolfgang Foges and run by his fellow countryman Walter Neurath, later to co-found Thames & Hudson, the art publishing house.[140] No doubt Natasha Kroll knew Neurath and this is how the commission came about. The frontispiece bears the information 'figures and scenes created by Natasha Kroll' and on the next page the reader learns that the colour photography is by Zoltan Wegner, another refugee photographer who did much work for Adprint. Her archive is full of exquisite sketches and paintings for the book. The story is played out by characters in eighteenth-century costumes, wide sweeping dresses in taffeta trimmed with lace, made by Natasha. Surely her ability to design and realise these tiny costumes was a tribute to her training at the Reimann. Natasha took up a career in 1956 with the BBC at their design department. Later she worked in film, creating sets. Her many talents were recognised when she was elected a Royal Designer for Industry in 1967.

Alex Kroll

While his sister Natasha followed on from display at Simpson with a new career pathway in film and television design, Alex turned to magazine publishing after his studies at the two Reimann schools; Simon Kroll, Professor of Paediatrics at Imperial College London, remembers his father's ability in technical drawing, probably acquired there.[141] Alex Kroll's obituary in *The Times* noted that he had been both an art director on *Vogue* and *House and Garden* in the 1940s and 1950s and also the editor and publisher of Condé Nast Publications, that is to say the book arm of the business. They must have done well, as on his retirement he learned that the company had made 'close to $1 million in revenue and royalties from books he had commissioned and co-partnered around the globe'.¹⁴²

Not all of the books were an unqualified success, however: one on knitting had printing errors which led hundreds of readers to write in, enclosing photos of jumpers with one sleeve longer than the other or dangerously plunging necklines. Kroll apparently found them reminiscent of designs for avant-garde ballet costumes he had seen in Berlin before the war (possibly the Bauhaus ballet, also known as the Mechanical Ballet). The book that gave him the most pleasure was *Fashion Drawing in Vogue*, published by Thames & Hudson whose co-founder, with Walter, was Eva Neurath (née Itzig), a Berlin refugee like himself, and friend.¹⁴³

Natasha, too, had had a book published through this connection. The foreword of Alex Kroll's book whose subject is unusual given the more popular focus on fashion photography, was written by David Hockney and it remains a respected book in the fashion canon. Kroll obviously had a nose for good photographers for his books as it was Mario Testino, then still unknown, who had taken the knitting-pattern book pictures. But Kroll's major coup was in recognising the talent of Lee Miller. His obituary takes up the story:

> He laid out on the pages of *Vogue* several key spreads by the magazine's unlikely war correspondent, the American model turned writer and photographer, Lee Miller. He helped her to choose, from the hundreds she submitted, many of the photographs for which she is now revered and arranged them all with sensitivity.

Alex Kroll's son, Simon, reflected on his father and aunt as people.¹⁴⁴ They present a contrasting picture although it is not possible to say whether their double emigration and troubled childhood was responsible or whether this was simply an inborn personality difference. In any case, while Natasha as known to be 'difficult' and demanding in her work life at least, Alex was optimistic, believing that it was essential to trust people or else life would be impossible. His spine was curved, a result of his childhood tuberculosis, but he was a wonderful, positive person and a warm father. He married a German Jewish refugee, Maria Wolff, who counted the graphic artist Dorrit Dekk among her friends.

The couple spoke Russian and German to each other but to their two sons English, albeit with strong accents. Simon Kroll remembers how, ironically, the one word Alex could never pronounce correctly was 'sewing' which he pronounced 'suing'. Like many of his fellow *Mitteleuropäer*, he played the piano, enjoyed chess and revelled in the company of his family and friends. These included the typographer, Robert Harling, just one of the guests to the Krolls' country house which they used at weekends for socialising.

When asked about their new identity, the German refugees to Britain often said that while they did not feel 'English', they did feel 'British', while others limited the feeling of identity to 'European'. Did Alex Kroll feel English rather than, in his case, Russian? His son said that he felt British. He had burned his Soviet passport as an anti-Stalin gesture, remaining, however, staunchly left of centre by British standards all his life.

Natasha, who never married, had a glamorous social circle too, one which included the Penguin Book designer and Holocaust survivor Germano Facetti and members of the Pasternak family (of *Doctor Zhivago* fame). Her talent and drive were rewarded with a BAFTA for her designs for *The Hireling* film.[145]

The Skype screen comes into focus slowly, revealing a youthful-looking, smiling man with brown curly hair and tortoiseshell-framed glasses. He introduces himself as William Kroll, the founder and CEO of Tender, a denim company which he has run for the past ten years.[146] But he has many other facets to his entrepreneurial life: he designs a range of products too, including ceramics and home goods. His fascination for the way watches are made has led to his involvement in a watch company. He also teaches menswear design at Central Saint Martins and Westminster University. What urges him forward is his abiding love of tradition and quality combined with a keen interest in the way things look. Added to this is a glorying in the construction of objects including garments; this is one reason that Tender clothes have visible tailoring. And, as William pointed out, 'tender' can refer just as much to the coal truck of a train as to an emotive adjective, a less glamorous but pleasingly utilitarian suggestion for the clothes.

This passion for the visual may well be genetic, for not only had his grandfather been an alumnus of the Reimann School in both Berlin and London but William thinks his grandmother, Maria Wolff, may have been too. She certainly worked at the advertising agency Crawfords, just as graphic designer Hans Schleger did, and was chiefly responsible for the fashion label Mary Quant. Maria also worked in various other fields, often fashion related, including cosmetic companies. There is a photograph of her taken by the *Vogue* photographer Clifford Coffin. Both grandparents introduced young William's eyes to the delights of London in a way that was both gentle and open, not inviting judgement. Less expected was William's memory that he got the impression from his grandfather Alex that 'if a thing was worth doing, it was worth doing badly', an openness and have-a-go attitude which encourages experimentation and risk-taking.

William recalled that from the time that he was ten years old, his grandfather Alex would take him out to restaurants for lunch. Then the two of them would stroll around the White Cube galleries or the Hayward, perhaps not places more conventional grandfathers would choose. This was how a Lichtenstein exhibition made its mark on the young Kroll. While Alex worked for Condé Nast and *Vogue*, William's great aunt Natasha, something of a polymath, was certainly interested in clothes and encouraged William to draw 'how you want'. He spent time with the European friends of the Krolls too. One who became a sort of substitute when his real grandmother died was the celebrated designer Dorrit Dekk, whose work had featured extensively at the Festival of Britain. William remembered that these refugees and others lived in studios on the Fulham Road, with the sculptor Anthony Caro next door. This place was part of his childhood too and he remembered the excitement of visiting there. All three of the refugee 'grandparents' were thrilled when William chose to go to Central St Martins and remained positive about his career choice.

As well as inspiring William's choice of the arts, Alex Kroll impressed his grandson as being resolutely against name dropping, despite the glamorous *Vogue* circles he moved in. William remembers Alex at the *Vogue* celebration 'People in Vogue' being singled out by Alexandra Shulman, the then *Vogue* Editor, for a special hug, but he had not put himself forward for such recognition.

William has dipped into the Kroll archive at Brighton University for inspiration for his own designs too. He took Natasha's drawings and worked them into T-shirts, tote bags and mugs. He is one of that third generation springing from creative Continental Jewish refugees, up there with Thomas Heatherwick and Sam Reich, all acknowledging their debt to their grandparents while enriching the current British design scene.

Jerseycraft: Mr Bratman of Wakefield

Swathes of Italian and French luxury silks hang on the walls in 'Chintz Tower', as Adam Sykes playfully nicknames the quietly beautiful showroom of Claremont, his fabric company in Chelsea. Sykes's family have textile in their DNA, but of a different kind and his transition to furnishing silks came about quite through chance.[147]

Frank Bratman as a young man (courtesy of Adam Sykes)

His grandparents were Jewish refugees; his grandfather, Frank Bratman (1905–1984) was actually born in Budapest to Czech parents and was brought up in both Hungary and Czechoslovakia, speaking Hungarian before he did German, the *lingua franca* of the Austro-Hungarian Empire. His parents also paid for him to have English and French lessons, something he was grateful for as an adult.

Having moved to Vienna for study, he found a summer job at a relative's knitting mill, the Julius Otte Gebrüder company (known as Otte) who made knitted sportswear. On the managing director's sudden death, he was invited to take over the management of this company despite being aged only twenty-one years and relatively inexperienced. Rejecting advice to turn down the offer and have some fun, he took on the challenge, throwing himself into the role of running the mill. Otte was similar to Pasolds (who later in Britain made Ladybird clothes), the Czech company who made fleecy stockinette fabrics. Because this was around 1930, a dreadful time for trade and the beginning of the world depression, sales fell and Bratman decided to develop new woollen fabrics, especially worsteds and fancy yarns. However, he came up against opposition to the manufacturing changes this would entail. British workmen obviously were not the only ones to resent change, a story told many times by refugees in the textile trade who had encountered such resistance in Britain. Bratman's new woollen jersey sold well, and the Vienna branch of the company continued to trade until the *Anschluss* in 1938. Having married the boss's daughter, Lucie, in 1930 and now with two daughters, Eleonora and Ingeborg, Bratman concentrated on his career at Otte which exported their sportswear to many countries including Britain.[148]

This was just as well, for when the *Anschluss* came, as was often the case, several of Otte's employees revealed their support for the Nazi party. It was time to leave for safety. Bratman's daughters remembered that they were only allowed to take one doll and one book each with them. Thanks to Bratman's special status as a Czech refugee, it was possible for him to re-enter Vienna and he already had a visa which allowed him to enter and re-enter Britain. This meant that he was able to pack up his knitting machines in boxes and transport them over to

England. His plan was to build up a factory in England that would use British wool as they had done in Vienna.

The family of four arrived in London in 1939 shortly before the outbreak of war, soon moving on to Huddersfield, not the only refugees in the textile trade to settle there. The move had been engineered by a concerned friend of Bratman's from Yorkshire. His Czech nationality had the added advantage that he would not be rounded up and interned in 1940, as were so many of his German and Austrian counterparts. The large Victorian house that the Bratmans rented (and continued to rent, European-style, many years after an Englishman in his situation would have bought the property) served as temporary accommodation for a series of homeless refugees who had arrived under less fortunate circumstances from the 1940s onwards.

In an article he wrote for a trade journal, Bratman expressed his gratitude to the individuals and to the Board of Trade who had helped him: 'Sometimes I have asked myself how it came about that all this help should have been forthcoming, given freely to me, a stranger within your gates.'[149] But he was not one to depend on others for long and he focused all his energy on setting up his own mill, along with a local technician whom he had succeeded in helping to flee to England. The new company was formed just as the war broke out, apparently an inauspicious start, and was named Jerseycraft.

Adam Sykes noted that although Huddersfield was the seat of a centuries-old weaving industry, knitting was a rarity. Bratman, though, pointed out that he had chosen Huddersfield 'because of the high tradition and long tradition of the textile workers in the district. I knew that the best men's fabrics in the world are made in Huddersfield.' Knitted fabric for all sorts of clothes was what Jerseycraft produced. Frank Bratman was a man of vision.

Moreover, he was a Viennese Jew, with all that this implies: cultured, with a love and knowledge of the arts, especially music, and he was cosmopolitan, speaking German, Czech, Hungarian, French and English. The cousin of his wife's grandmother was no less a composer than Gustav Mahler. He was the classic citizen of 'Mitteleuropa' and must have seemed exotic indeed in Huddersfield. His knitted fabrics were stylish and the colours subtle and different from the traditional English palette. At least some of the wool though was sourced from local sheep. Adam Sykes remembers his grandfather's magnificent office, the vast desk covered with piles of swatches. Perhaps this scene was what sowed the seeds of his own future career.

Jerseycraft soon acquired some glamorous clients: the jersey was bought by the *crème de la crème* of Paris couture houses, including Balmain, Givenchy, Yves Saint Laurent and Patou. This coup was thanks to the Anglo-Irish couturier Edward Molyneux.[150] Obviously Molyneux had been more than satisfied with Jerseycraft fabric supplied to him and was keen to help this forward-thinking and creative refugee. Paris couture had survived the war and the German occupation and was again bursting with vitality, thanks in large part to the Dior 'New Look'. Photographs of models wearing his clothes made from his jersey show girls as slender as Audrey Hepburn, apparently in the early 1960s. It seems that Jerseycraft was merged into a larger textile conglomerate which nevertheless kept Mr Bratman on at the helm of his own company until the end of the 1960s.

On the success of Jerseycraft, Bratman pointed to a common feature of Continental design in the postwar period: 'colour and colour combinations were not only different but in many instances most unusual compared to anything shown up to that time'.[151] His experience of colour in Hungary and Czechoslovakia before emigration marked him for life, just as it did Tibor Reich, who brought the vivid colours of Hungarian folk costumes and the luscious trimmings of the Austro-Hungarian military uniforms to his weaves in Britain, bringing exciting change to British consumers after the drab wartime palette.

Also in his printed interview, Bratman talked through his creative process. It was essential, he maintained, to leave the office and go away, abroad even, to avoid the daily concerns of an MD and open one's mind. Not only did he walk the streets and look at other shops and their goods, 'but one should visit exhibitions of art, paintings, drawings, designs or any other object like china, pottery, etc which have nothing to do with our industry'. He had recently visited the Orangerie in Paris where 'I saw one or two paintings which gripped me to such a degree that I felt impelled to use an element of the artist's design structure in one or two of my next season's patterns and I feel they will be a success'.[152] It is perhaps hard to imagine a Huddersfield textile company MD like himself seeking inspiration from French Impressionism. His European peers, though, would have found this a normal and commendable process.

While Bratman refused to return to Austria after the war, never able to forget the vicious antisemitism he experienced there, like many fellow Austrian refugees to Britain he found solace in holidays in Switzerland: it had a familiarly Alpine landscape, in particular the skiing and hiking opportunities, but was devoid of Austrians. When asked if the personal events in his life had contributed to his business success, he replied drily that two Nazi invasions were not essential to success but that such events could generate the necessary dedication to bring about success.

Adam Sykes's brother, Tim, was studying law at the Sorbonne when in 1981 his grandfather told him he was coming to Paris to visit. Together the two men went to one of the couture fashion shows that were on then and the younger man was struck by the fact that his grandfather was treated 'like royalty' by staff behind the scenes after so long. Bratman's daughter Lorle also attended many *défilés*, even meeting Christian Dior whom she pronounced 'a nice little man'. After his retirement Bratman became a senior advisor to the Wool Secretariat, a sign of the establishment respect accorded to him.

Frank Bratman's grandson, Adam Sykes, gives the credit for his own career to another Viennese émigrée, Lily Fleissig, a friend of his mother who had fled to the USA where she had learned to make clothes so that she would no longer to have to work as a domestic there. So good was she at this that she soon found work at Western Costume, making clothes for Hollywood stars such as Joan Crawford, who asked Lily to make her own private clothes also. The dress for the main character in the *King and I* was only one of Fleissig's triumphs. She advised Adam to move into interior design and helped him into this field. From there, he moved to work with the 'king of interiors', Nicky Haslam. But he realised that he enjoyed the furnishing fabrics part of the trade most and from there it was a short step to Claremont which he took over himself in 1997. Now he, like his Viennese grandfather before him, commands a firm whose fabrics delight the senses.

Kultur! Textile Refugees in Opera, Theatre and Visual Arts

What is more quintessentially English than a summer evening at the Glyndebourne opera festival? The guests wander through the gardens of the country house that gives its name to the event, taking in the view of the Sussex Downs beyond before picnicking from wicker hampers on smoked salmon and other English delicacies. And yet, not only was the whole venture inspired by the founder's experience of opera in pre-war Germany but the original producer, the conductor and the manager were all refugees from Nazism. Over the years, many of the singers, too, were German-speaking refugees.[153]

John Christie, the founder, had fallen in love with Mozart's operas in Germany in the 1920s, a time when this work was little performed in Britain and he was determined to recreate the experience in his family home of Glyndebourne. A friend urged him to read all the books there were on German theatre design and he made a trip to Vienna to bring back suitable theatrical equipment. He brought back a singer, Jani Strasser, from that city too.

Three who had fled Nazism and who between them made Glyndebourne a success were Carl Ebert, Fritz Busch and Rudolf Bing. Ebert was the very successful and popular Intendant of the Darmstadt Theatre, both CEO and director of productions, and he had taken on the Viennese-born Rudolf Bing, a singers' agent, as his administrator. Feeling his theatre needed a musical director, he approached the conductor Fritz Busch, then Music Director of the Dresden Opera, who agreed to work with Ebert in Berlin. But by then, the shadow of Nazism was cast on the wall. In March 1933 Busch was booed by Nazi sympathisers at the Berlin State opera. Neither Busch nor Ebert were Jewish but were both committed to freedom, including artistic freedom and equality, refusing to dismiss Jewish or left wing employees, something now required by the new regime. Göring himself tried to threaten Busch into staying, but Busch fled to Switzerland, as did Ebert, never to return to Germany.

A bizarre series of events led the three men to Glyndebourne. Fritz Busch's brother, a violinist, had been performing in Eastbourne and was delayed in returning home by fog. Over-nighting in the area with other musicians, he heard that an eccentric Englishman was trying to set up an opera festival. Busch told his brother, Fritz, who then contacted Ebert. The two men, although hardly convinced of the enterprise, went to England in 1934 to meet Christie. They managed to convince him to put on Mozart, explaining that the English should be helped by Christie to like Mozart's operas. Joined by Rudolf Bing, Ebert and Busch oversaw the first productions, *Le Nozze di Figaro* and *Don Giovanni*. In those early days, Christie went round wearing Lederhosen. The lavatories were labelled 'Damen' and 'Herren' in the unlikely event that any guests had missed the German influence.

The combination of talented Germans (and Austrians) with a beautiful English setting and a sympathetic and generous founder was a marriage made in heaven, something to which Glyndebourne is often compared by guests and musicians alike. And the Austrian émigré, Hans Schneider, who made and later designed costumes for Benjamin Britten's productions (see 'Hans Schneider and the Arts') was not the only Austrian from the 'rag trade' to make his mark at Glyndebourne.

Money was of course a constant preoccupation as opera was not cheap to stage, even given the generous pockets of John Christie. Just as one refugee, Busch, died young so another refugee took up his place in Glyndebourne's history and that was Miki Sekers. In 1951, textile manufacturer Sekers had supplied the company with specially-dyed fabrics for *Don Giovanni* and was a keen patron of the art. Seeing at the Aix en Provence Festival a programme with advertisements, as the house history takes up the story, he had the idea of organising something similar for Glyndebourne. His ambitious target was to enlist 'forty advertisers, who would contribute a total of £20,000'.[154] Although he only achieved £18,000, he had persuaded his business contacts, like Aristoc and Marshall & Snelgrove to advertise in the prestigious programme. Also he had hosted parties to which captains of industry were invited. The author of the history of Glyndebourne opines that it is difficult to see how Glyndebourne would have survived without this support, and referred to Sekers saying that he had pioneered the task of attracting sponsorship and so made Glyndebourne's resurrection of the 1950s possible.[155]

When Mr Francis Steiner was interviewed about Tick-a-Tee in Cumbria, he was asked what the worldly Viennese, Berliners and other cosmopolitan, cultured refugees thought of Cumberland which had offered them a safe haven from the Nazis and also a good living. Luckily, replied Mr Steiner, his own uncle had enjoyed fishing, something one could do in that wet, rather isolated northern landscape. But how on earth did these people come to terms with the distinctly barren cultural scene? The answer was that they made their own amusements. One in particular did so – Miki Sekers. It was not enough to be a patron of far away Glyndebourne, he wanted a local theatre too. He set about acquiring a barn on his own land and turned it into the Rosehill Theatre.

The theatre opened in 1959 in Whitehaven and is still a flourishing hub today, 'offering a diverse range of arts and entertainment from music, theatre, talks, comedy, shows for young people and more'.[156] Described as 'a rose-red, silk-lined jewellery box', the theatre was designed by the artist Oliver Messel, one of those who had produced designs for Seker's brocades. Over the years great names from the world of British show business have appeared on its stage: David Bowie, Jacqueline du Pré, Benjamin Britten and John Gielgud to name but a few. Sekers had hardly recreated his native Budapest with this project, nevertheless he had founded the only theatre for miles around, for which local people remain profoundly grateful.

Djanoglys

Many a refugee was able to ensure their profitability by securing a contract with Marks & Spencer to supply them with clothing. It was a risk for the suppliers in that usually it meant allocating a large share of their production to the store, but until around the new millennium anyway, the demand for M & S products seemed to be inexhaustible and the suppliers were consequently kept busy. Members of the Djanogly family, just such suppliers to M&S, also had a close relationship with the Sieffs. Like for example the Krolls (see 'The Fabulous Kroll Dynasty'), Jonathan Djanogly and his sons Simon and Jack were double refugees having fled their native Russia after the Revolution of 1917, settling in Chemnitz in Germany where they set up a ladies' hosiery business. From there they supplied some of their goods to M & S (as well as to other retailers) well before Hitler came to power. They set up a warehouse in London around 1932 and would travel regularly from Chemnitz to England. They had already learned French and soon picked up English too.

Fortunately, the family were warned against the threat from Nazism by employees from their own factory and acted fast. However, before emigrating definitively to Britain, the Djanoglys first visited Czechoslovakia, planning to settle there. Hearing of a textile business that was going bankrupt, Jonathan and his son Jack set off for Prague, while his other son Simon went to America to buy machinery and ship it back to equip the new enterprise. The bank manager asked them to come on Friday afternoon to conclude the deal, but as observant Jews they refused to break the Sabbath and suggested Monday instead. Before Monday, however, Jonathan, sitting in a coffee house with his son saw a group of Communists rushing in from one side of the square and a Nazi group from the other. He made what was to be his last, but excellent, business decision ever: this was no place for a Jewish business. They hastily arranged for the plant to be sent to Liverpool instead. [157]

Apparently they asked which area was known for its mining industry as such areas always had plenty of female labour which they needed for the work in their textile factories, and were directed to Nottingham, home to coal mining but also lace-making.[158] Arriving in Mansfield, just outside Nottingham, they bought four acres of agricultural land, possibly cow pasture, spending some of their very limited funds that they had been able to bring with them. Years later, Harry asked his father Simon why he had bought such a relatively large plot. So as not to limit his horizons in the future, came the reply. They built their factory, located more machinery and immediately took up where they had left off, creating a vertical factory covering all processes from spinning to finishing.

The war was a tough time for the company as the factory was requisitioned for the manufacture of tank parts. Simon Djanogly volunteered for war work and was sent off on observation, possibly with the Pioneer Corps. It was Harry (later Sir Harry), Simon's son born in 1938, who took their company, Nottingham Manufacturing, from hosiery into knitwear (and much more): 'Djanogly developed two-ply lambswool jumpers and cardigans at less than half the price of branded goods.' This was good news for M & S: now millions of people could buy what had formerly only been sold at the likes of Harrods, in the form of brands such as Pringle. Not content with his hugely successful products leaping off M & S shelves, by the 1960s Harry Djanogly also developed machine-washable lambswool jumpers, yet another great selling point.

While in the early days communication with the Sieffs had been tricky for Jonathan Djanogly who spoke mainly Russian and some German, Harry Djanogly was able to forge a close relationship with Marcus Sieff. The special nature of M & S and their suppliers has been the subject of studies, and the number of Jewish suppliers noted. However, although the Sieffs definitely were ready to support the refugees from Nazism, it was a two-way relationship with both parties benefiting: 'M & S was not jealous of others making money. They wanted us to prosper,' said Sir Harry.[159] What is more, the unethical practice of giving presents to M & S to favour their custom was frowned on by Djanogly: 'If you can't get business in the proper way on value, price and quality, you shouldn't be in business' he said.[160]

(Left to right) Simon Djanogly, Jack Djanogly, Edward Sieff, Moshe Sharett, the second Prime Minister of Israel, c. 1960 (courtesy of Sir Harry Djanogly)

The business was merged with Carrington Viyella in 2005 at which time it had a turnover of around £260 million a year, an annual profit of £26 million and a staff of fourteen and a half thousand employees, not bad for a modest start in a Mansfield cow pasture. They continued to supply M & S. The Djanoglys now turned to the task of donating their huge fortune, thereby culturally enriching the country which had given them refuge in the late 1930s. Sir Harry emphasized that of all the Djanogly philanthropy, in his opinion, the most important was their involvement in education: 1987 had seen the founding of the Djanogly Learning Trust, an inner-city school for 3,000 children. It was opened by Margaret Thatcher in the Djanogly's chosen home of Nottingham. Not a glamorous cause but rightly the one he could be proudest of.[161] The University of Nottingham too was a focal point of their donations, receiving funds for a library and other buildings.

Through establishing these connections and actively contributing to the longevity of both The Playhouse, Lakeside Arts and arts at Nottingham University and Nottingham Trent University, the Djanoglys have had a positive and profound effect on accessibility to the arts for all in their local area. But their giving doesn't stop there.[162]

The author of that article went on to list the Djanoglys' other notable gifts, referring to their understanding of culture 'as a shared treasure and collective asset'.

They made major contributions to both Tate Britain and Tate Modern galleries, indeed were instrumental in the founding of the latter. The Victoria & Albert Museum too benefited from their generosity, where they took a particular interest in aspects of quintessentially British culture, such as British ceramics. Visitors to the Museum have the Djanoglys to thank for the new ceramics gallery there. Finally, the author refers to the other major London galleries and museums where the Djanoglys made a real difference:

> ...the Djanoglys' beneficence continues to be felt at the Royal Academy, National Gallery and National Portrait Gallery. At the National Gallery they provided valuable support for the Gallery's East Wing Capital Project in 2005 with an endowment of £500,000, helping to accommodate the ever-increasing numbers the Gallery welcomes through its doors. They have also been ardent champions of the National Portrait Gallery for many years, donating to numerous acquisition campaigns, as well as capital projects.

Their Jewish heritage was not forgotten either: 'They were also instrumental in the development project which created the Jewish Museum which we enjoy today.' Unlike some émigrés, the Djanoglys kept their strong Jewish faith. They had been fortunate not to lose any members of their family in the Holocaust. Sir Harry said in an interview that his family had never experienced antisemitism in Britain, a country where it was possible to be proud of one's Jewishness.[163] His parents had been enormously grateful to Britain, determined to love everything about British life. However, their antipathy for Germany continued after the war, naturally enough, but within measure: while they would not holiday there nor buy a German car, ever pragmatic, they would buy Germany machinery if it was the best for the company.

The Djanoglys were recognised for their philanthropic activities: Harry Djanogly was appointed a Commander of the British Empire in the 1983 Birthday Honours and knighted in the 1993 New Year Honours for charitable services. In 2014, Sir Harry and Lady Djanogly were awarded the Prince of Wales Medal for Arts Philanthropy. Moreover, their donations made a really staggering change to the Great Ormond Street Hospital, raising the number of outpatients that could be seen there from 14,000 to 120,000 a year.

These days, M & S are experiencing difficulties on the high street and the days when almost every woman in Britain wore a woollen cardigan, almost certainly manufactured by Djanogly, are long gone. However, we can bask instead in the warmth of their generous suppliers, Djanogly, every time we visit the National Portrait Gallery or another museum where this refugee family enriched our cultural lives.

Landsberger: Bags of Ingenuity

Mr Ralph Land (born Landsberger) CBE and his twin brother, Emeritus Professor Frank Land at the LSE, both enjoyed stellar careers in the early days of Information Technology, starting their working life at the forward-thinking Jewish food company J. Lyons, who were the first in Britain to use a computer. However, it was not necessarily on the cards that they would be high-flyers in IT; they might even have become poachers, as Ralph related in an interview.[164]

He and Frank Landsberger were born in 1928 in Berlin where their father Louis had an engineering company. Their mother Sofia (1899–1998), the heroine in this story, was from Vienna where she had studied art and had become a painter. Their Berlin apartment was very large, something they realised when they brought a chandelier from their Berlin flat to UK on their emigration – it was so large that when hung, it touched the floor of their small new living room, a symbol of their reduced circumstances. The family were assimilated Jews, marking Passover and other High Holidays but not otherwise attending synagogue. The boys attended a Jewish primary school. For ten year-old Ralph, *Kristallnacht* was clearly marked in his mind, as a woman covered in blood ran into the school. Outside, people stood outside their smashed shops on the pavement. He also remembers wearing a yellow star on his clothes.

Like many, the Landsberger parents thought the Nazi regime would pass and they delayed emigrating until April 1939. Luckily, there were an uncle and aunt already in Britain. Their uncle guaranteed a payment of £5 a week to the family in case of need and so they were able to enter Britain. In any case, this uncle was the British agent for Louis Landsberger's business although this came to an end when the firm was appropriated by the Nazis, another case of 'Aryanisation'.

Ralph, like so many refugees, adults and children alike, also remembers that his first impression of London was black, sooty and cramped after Berlin with its wide boulevards and monumental buildings. Their first home in London was in Kilburn and the boys were

Landsberger twins in Berlin (courtesy of Ralph Land)

sent off to primary school immediately. Their parents had been advised that English boys wore brown shoes and knickerbockers to school, not the only refugees to get it so badly wrong when it came to the realities of British customs, sartorial and culinary. But the Landsberger boys were bullied for being foreign and for their 'posh' outlandish clothing, by largely working class children at the school. However, this was not the whole picture, and there was kindness from other children too. Ralph and Frank Landsberger missed out on the eleven plus exam and left school at fourteen, only getting a secondary education thanks to the valiant efforts of their mother, who was known as 'Soscha'. She was persuasive with words despite her accent, a very useful skill indeed, as it turned out.

When war broke out, the boys were evacuated to Hertfordshire. The couple who took them had requested two little British girls and were not expecting three German boys (the Landsbergers' cousin had come on the *Kindertransport* and was with them) but the wife relented at the sight of them and took them in, somewhat to the shock of her carpenter husband. They were well looked after by this kind couple.

The German boys learned good carpentry skills which held them in good stead in later life when they needed to help with their parents' new clothing company. The husband also initiated them into the joys of night-time poaching, a good way, albeit illegal, of supplementing the family's food supply.

In return, Ralph feels that the German boys had some influence on the couple's son who later went to university. After graduating, this

'Soscha' Landsberger, self-portrait (courtesy of Ralph Land)

son had a brilliant career with British Airways and the families are still in touch. Louis Landsberger was interned in 1940 and went to the Isle of Man for over six months and the family was left with no breadwinner. There was no state benefit to help them and they had to find a source of income urgently. Mrs Landsberger now called on her artistic skills to make handbags out of felt.

Felt was easy to come by unlike leather which was in short supply during the war. But women still needed bags and there was a high demand for them. How could this German-speaking woman sell her products? She knew only one way and went straight to the top: Soscha took them to stores in Bond Street, for example Meda Sport where they sold well. No doubt her charm and skills of persuasion were a help in selling too. In this way she managed to earn enough to feed her family.

By now, encouraged by her success, Soscha started to make dolls' clothes, still waiting for her husband to be released. When Louis finally returned from internment in late 1940, he found a job with a Jewish-owned company called Printator where he did menial work, helping to make plastic curlers and small objects. Then he bought a shell company called East Surrey Engineering Company which made broom handles. However, this business did not do well; he obviously was less good at sensing market opportunities in England and decided instead to help his wife with her flourishing business. They used his company premises, located in Bloomsbury and the name, but made dolls clothes there, exclusively for Woolworths. In fact, they supplied every single branch of Woolworths in the country. While Mrs Landsberger cut the cloth and designed the clothes, some sixty outworkers were employed to sew the clothes. Then they were packaged up and dispatched. Frank and Ralph made the shelving for the company, taught by their evacuation 'father'. Ralph recalls the lunches at Schmidt's German restaurant on Charlotte Street in return for their help with work.[165]

Like the majority of the Jewish refugees, the Landsberger parents never wanted to return to Germany. They received minimal restitution for the family business. By the end of the war, they all spoke English, albeit with an accent, and made attempts to fit in as much as possible. The brothers, however, who shortened their names to 'Land' in the

1950s, were not against returning to Germany and in fact, Ralph, a successful businessman, worked for some time in Germany. He had the unfortunate task of making some 200 people in one company redundant and feared he might be seen as the 'Avenging Jew', even though in fact the company's problems had arisen from the alcoholism of one manager. Although not a natural linguist, his German was of use to him in his professional life.

Neither of the Land sons has ever forgotten how their mother rose to the challenge of feeding her family by sewing felt handbags with Viennese style and by making tiny but perfect dolls' clothes to delight thousands of little English girls.

Eva Aldbrook: Fashion Illustrator in the Golden Age

'Unfortunately, only a few original illustrations have survived until today. With the need for speed in production and printing, the art of illustration gradually died. Many were destroyed during the printing process, they were actually thrown away as they were considered as useless after they were printed. Those that have survived have become collectible, authentic and historical art works that really illustrate the elegance, attitude and style of each era.'[166]

These thoughts found on a website dedicated to a collector of fashion illustrations are certainly true of the work of one Eva Aldbrook (née Mehl).[167] Her elegant line drawings and paintings are sought after now at specialist auctions. She herself is as beautiful as one of her drawings, and just as elegant, despite her ninety-three years. We sit in her house in Stamford surrounded by her oil paintings of Tuscany and her more recent portraits of her carers. Should we need to refer to it, there is a handsome book chronicling Eva's life but it seems that her memory is as good as her painting.[168]

She was born Eva Mehl in Hamburg in 1925 into an assimilated Jewish family. She was sent to safety in 1938 to Kent to attend the school known as Bunce Court that her sister already attended. (The school was founded in Germany in 1933 by Anna Essinger, who brought the mostly Jewish pupils to England and to safety that same year.) That meant her whole family was now in England. At Bunce Court, aged thirteen, she met Alexander Urbach; and they fell in love despite their young age and vowed they would marry when they could. And so they did, seven years later.

In 1940 she left Bunce Court to train as a ballet dancer but her father (fearing that ballet was an unsuitable career for her) insisted she should have another skill too and she chose art. She enrolled at St Martins Costume and Fashion Department under the celebrated Muriel Pemberton who, according to one obituary 'invented art school training in Britain'.[169] The students learned life drawing and went to see costumes at the Victoria & Albert Museum every week. Eva auditioned for the Anglo-Polish ballet and changed her name to the more Polish-sounding 'Melova'. At eighteen she applied for a dance permit but was told she must either join ENSA (again her father did not approve) or do war work, ending up at Kodak in Whetstone. She and Alexander Urbach married at a synagogue in Dunstan in 1946.

With an introduction by Joseph Karl, Eva Urbach applied for jobs with theatrical costumiers and landed a post with L & H Nathan's, making costumes for West End shows. She was credited with the costumes for a Technicolor film, *The Laughing Lady* 'Costumes by Eva Melova' with Margaret Lockwood. Her book takes up the story:

> While still at Nathan's I was asked by Peter Zadek, who later became a celebrated theatre director in Germany, to design the costumes for a production of Oscar Wilde's *Salomé*. Bernice Rubens, later winner of the Booker Prize for one of her books, danced Salomé, and Joseph Horowitz [sic] composed the music.[170]

From costume design it was but a short step to fashion drawing as she relates:

> In 1949 I started freelance illustrations for magazines and newspapers to which I often brought my own ideas… The first was on children's fashions from Denmark commissioned by Alison Settle of *The Observer* and this led to recommendations to fashion houses like Aquascutum and Simpson. Later on I worked for *Queen* magazine and wrote many articles for the *Evening Standard*'s fashion column for Eileen Ash.
>
> There followed articles for *Vogue* and a trip to Paris to report on the fashion houses for Elsa Garland of *Woman's Journal*. I also covered the London fashion shows for Ernestine Carter of *The Sunday Times* and wrote my own small column called 'A Day in Town' in *The Daily Express*.[171]

Eva Aldbook, sketches of hats (courtesy of Eva Aldbrook)

In 1953 the Urbach couple decided to Anglicise their surname to aid pronunciation, roughly translating each syllable so that Ur – Bach became Ald – brook. When the couple took on a large house in rural Tuscany, Eva turned to fine art, inspired like hundreds before her by the light and the way of life. Back on London she enrolled at the Camden Arts Centre to fine tune her skills. Just one of the highlights of this new interest was the invitation to sketch Henry Moore's portrait from life. Her talent was recognised in the fine arts too and she exhibited at the Royal Festival Hall and at the Ben Uri Gallery in London. Her large archive holds samples of her fashion and costume sketches. In her interview she explained that she had been invited to sketch models in big couture houses like Dior, Lanvin and Molyneux.

They are examples of that golden age of fashion drawing, graceful and suggestive of a shape or texture with just a few lines. Her eyes sparkled as she told how Muriel Pemberton had shown her students how to draw fur or perhaps, how to suggest it. Now, her drawings

Eva Aldbrook sketch of Molyneux outfit (courtesy Eva Aldbrook)

command prices of thousands of pounds on the antiques market, yet more recognition for the outstanding talent of another German refugee to these shores.

Conclusion

In this account of the refugees in Britain working in fashion, there has been a focus on those who succeeded. Naturally, for every one of these, there were many more whose enterprise didn't last long, who foundered or had to diversify, especially in the very difficult circumstances of the wartime. Their stories are kept alive by their families, by scholars and by organisations like the AJR, the Association of Jewish Refugees, who value them all, great or small.

However, in the relatively modest number of refugee stories related here, it is striking how many did not just make a living but who made a name for themselves. Pringle of Scotland were awarded the coveted Royal Warrant to Her Majesty Queen Elizabeth II in 1956, at the time when Otto Weisz was an important member of the company's team. Individual refugee companies too acquired this seal of approval: Ettinger received the Warrant to the Prince of Wales in 1996.

Queen Elizabeth had enjoyed her trip to the Launer works in 1991 and paused to admire the special chocolate cake that had been baked for the occasion. 'Is it made of leather?' she quipped.

She has been buying handbags from Launer since 1968 and granted the company her Royal Warrant which they are rightly proud of. Other forms of favour were expressed for example to Double Two, the Wakefield shirt makers who received the Queen's Award for International Trade in 2013.

In the magnificent Loebl study of 1978 of the refugee companies, many of which were textile-based, in the Northern Trading Estates (see Chapter 3), the author noted:

> Refugee firms received five Queen's Awards for Industry for exports up to our key date, but we are aware that additional Awards have been won since then. The number of such Awards is higher than one would expect from a random sample of the same number of British companies as a whole. Founders or

The Queen visits the Launer factory, cutting cake (courtesy of Launer)

members of their families appeared in the Honours Lists on six occasions. The Honours included two Knighthoods, one CBE, one OBE and two MBEs. Apart from the Knighthoods, the other awards appear all to have been gained for export achievements.[172]

Export revenue, employment, innovation and style: these were the gifts that were given in return for safety in Britain.

Today's refugees to Britain come from all too many war-torn parts of the earth or from countries where they are unable to work, practise their religion or otherwise thrive. How do the refugees from Nazism see these contemporary refugees? In the boardroom, when asked for his advice to present-day refugees to Britain, Mr Richard Donner of Double Two did not hesitate:

> Do come to Britain! We have jobs for you in this time of low unemployment. Put up with problems and just get on with it. Mix with everyone. Intermarriage is good. We need you: you may have to do the hard, dirty jobs at first, you take risks and you will move up. This country is not doing as well in taking in refugees now as HM government did in 1933–39 when it gave refuge to some 80,000 German-speaking refugees.[173]

Notes

1. Other information on Lucas from https://en.wikipedia.org/wiki/Otto_Lucas, accessed 8 March 2018;
   S.Hopkins, *The Century of Hats* (London: Aurum Press, 1999).
2. Interview with Rolf Andersen by the author, 30 August 2017.
3. It is more likely that Wallenberg took them to Sweden.
4. 'Heady Stuff, Pathé (1958).
5. Interview and email correspondence with Susie Hopkins and the author, February 2017.
6. http://fashion-history.lovetoknow.com/fashion-clothing-industry/history-milliners, accessed 6 September 2017.
7. *British Vogue*, October 1968.
8. Museum of London website, https://www.museumoflondon.org.uk/discover/london-open-and-always-has-been, accessed 8 March 2018.
9. On the club, see S. Parkin, *The Colony Room Club* (London: Palmtree Publishers, 2013).
10. https://www.revolvy.com/main/index.php?s=Muriel%20Belcher&m_type=topic, accessed June 2017.

11 Julian Barnes in an interview with the author, June 2017.
12 Richard Balfour-Lynn in a telephone interview with the author, May 2017.
13 Stanley Grant, in a conversation in the shop with the author in 2016.
14 Information on Gerard Ettinger from an interview with the author and Robert Ettinger, his son and CEO of Ettinger on 14 November 2016; from his obituary in *The Telegraph*, 12 August 2002 and from filmed interviews with Robert Ettinger, https://www.ettinger.co.uk/About-Us/The-Ettinger-Story/Ettinger-Films, accessed 31 May 2017.
15 For example, the textile manufacturer and designer Tibor Reich also came from a family of military uniform outfitters.
16 Gerard Ettinger obituary, *The Telegraph*.
17 Recounted by Robert Ettinger in the film *The Foundation Years* in https://www.ettinger.co.uk/About-Us/The-Ettinger-Story/Ettinger-Films, accessed 31 May 2017.
18 I am indebted to Sean Leon, Kangol Global Marketing Director for information provided June 2017 and in particular for sending me the house history by N. Watson, *60 Years of Kangol Quality: 1938–1998*, from which much of the information in this section is derived. I am also indebted to Nadine Meisner for information about her family and Kangol in correspondence in 2021.
19 Herbert Loebl, '*Government-financed factories and the establishment of industries by refugees in the special area of the North of England 1937–1961*', Durham theses, Durham University, 1978, p. 317.
20 N. Watson, *60 years of Kangol Quality 1938–1998*, pp. 6–7.
21 http://www.bbc.co.uk/cumbria/content/articles/2005/12/06/inside_lives_kath_ford_Kangol_feature.shtml, accessed 7 June 2017.
22 N. Watson, *60 years of* Kangol, p. 12.
23 Quoted in N. Watson, *60 years of Kangol*, p. 18.
24 Sean Leon in an email to the author, 7 June 2017.
25 Nic Harris in a phone call with the author, 27 June 2017.
26 On this subject, see U. Walton-Jordan, '"Although he is Jewish, he is M & S",:Jewish Refugees at Marks & Spencer', in A. Grenville (ed.), *Refugees from the Third Reich in Britain, Yearbook of the Research Centre for German and Austrian Exile Studies*, vol. 4 (2016), pp. 117–134.
27 Obituary of Eric Kann, in *Sparks*, 1956, p. 2.
28 U. Walton-Jordan, 'Although he is Jewish', pp. 130–131.

29　On the history of Marks & Spencer see, for example, I. Sieff, *Memoirs* (London: Weidenfeld and Nicolson, 1970); J. Bevan, *The Rise and Fall of Marks and Spencer* (London: Profile Books, 2001).
30　'Paris Inspired', *St Michael's News*, 29 April 1955.
31　Information here from the Marks & Spencer archivist Katie Cameron's notes for a talk 'We actually show the Knee' kindly given to the author 2017.
32　*The Times*, n.d., n.p., 1969.
33　Ibid.
34　'Who is Who', *Sparks*.
35　Information here from N. Hinton, *Silhouette, the Story of Little X*, Shrewsbury: 2009 and from AAD/1994/21, Design archives at the V & A Museum.
36　N. Hinton, *Silhouette*, p. 20.
37　Ibid., p.33.
38　Ibid., pp. 33–34.
39　Peter Lobbenberg in an interview with the author, 2 July 2018.
40　In the interview above.
41　Nick Sigler, in an interview with the author. 2016.
42　On Tibor Reich, see *Tibor Reich: Art of Colour and Texture*, London: 2016 and, for example, A. Nyburg, 'Textile in Exile' in M. Malet, R. Dickson, S. MacDougall, Anna Nyburg (eds), *Applied Arts in Exile: Changing Visual and Material Culture, Yearbook of the Research Centre for German and Austrian Exile Studies,* vol. 19 (2018) pp. 212–228; also R. Sternberg (Director), A. Nyburg, *Refuge Britain; Stories of Émigré Designers,* film (2017).
43　On Tomalin, see R. Dickson, 'Elisabeth Tomalin: Emigrée Designer 1912–2012; 'The only joy in life is being creative. Everything else is more or less pain', in C. Brinson, J. Barbora Buresova, A. Hammel (eds), in *Exile and Gender II: Politics, Education and the Arts, Yearbook of the Research Centre for German and Austrian Exile Studies*, vol. 18, 2017, pp. 154–170.
44　Information in this section from R. Dickson, 'Elisabeth Tomalin'.
45　Ibid., p. 160.
46　Ibid., p. 161.
47　Stefany Tomalin emailed the author 18 July 2017 about the family's connection to Jaeger: 'Meanwhile regarding the Jaeger brand, my entrepreneurial Victorian great-grandfather Lewis Tomalin had fallen in love with all things German, and specially "Dr Jaeger's Sanitary Woollen System" (there's a book that "proves" his theories) so he set up the

company, named it after the good doc. and sold wool yarn, wool underwear, wool bed linen, and splendid outerwear for men, women, and children which evolved from an anti-vegetable fibre health fad to setting high quality fashion trends. Stories say that great-grandfather Tomalin even made a bonfire of his new German bride's hand embroidered cotton and linen trousseau while she watched in distress from the window of their house, wringing her hands! My grandfather Harry Tomalin took over the business, then my uncle Humphrey his eldest son. No other descendants seemed interested. I remember my mum [Elisabeth Tomalin] agitating for discounts on camelhair, and my aunt Liz getting sensible cardigans and tweed skirts. There was a Fullers café inside their store next to Liberty's on Regent St. where you could get wonderful iced walnut cake. The whole store was commandeered in 1953 for a party for the Coronation as it was on the processional route – I was almost 8 and remember leaning out of the first floor changing room windows to watch and wave flags and uncle Humphrey stood in the street and took some marvellous pictures of the Queen in her golden coach – absolute magic! I also remember in the 1960s seeing Jean Muir trying on Jaeger dresses and commenting- "not important enough!"'

48 On refugees at M & S, see U. Walton-Jordan, '"Although he is Jewish he is M & S", Jewish refugees from Nazism and Marks & Spencer from the 1930s to the 1960s', in Anthony Grenville (ed.), *Refugees from the Third Reich: Yearbook of the Research Centre for German and Austrian Exile Studies*, vol. 4, 2002, pp, 117–134.

49 Rachel Dickson, 'Elisabeth Tomalin', p. 167.

50 Information in this section is from R. Chamberlain, G. Rayner, A. Stapleton (eds), *Jacqueline Groag, Textile & Pattern Design: Wiener Werkstätte to American Modern* (Woodbridge, Suffolk: Antique Collectors' Club, 2009).

51 Ibid., p. 22.

52 Ibid.

53 Ibid., p. 217.

54 Ibid., p.48

55 In R.Sternberg (Director), A. Nyburg, *Refuge Britain: Stories of Émigré Designers* (2017).

56 S. Prichard, M. Schoeser, J. Hall, *Tibor Reich: Art of Colour & Texture* (Tibor Ltd, 2016), p. 34.

57 Ibid., p. 50.

58 The Whitworth Gallery, Manchester held an exhibition on Tibor Reich in 2016; Sam Reich produced the only book on Tibor Reich's life and work (see endnote 55); and Tibor Reich is featured in the film 'Refuge Britain: Stories of Émigré Designers', 2017; https://www.ft.com/content/b6a702a8-8a8b-11e4-8e24-00144feabdc0, accessed 23 August 2017.
59 Information on the Aschers here from K. Hlaváčková (ed.), *The Mad Silkman: Zika and Lida Ascher, Textiles and Fashion* (Prague: Museum of Decorative Arts in Prague & Slovart Publishing Ltd, 2019).
60 Ibid. p.36.
61 http://fashion.telegraph.co.uk/news-features/TMG8137062/Ascher-London-is-relaunched.html, accessed 15 June 2018.
62 http://fashion.telegraph.co.uk/news-features/TMG8137062/Ascher-London-is-relaunched.html, accessed 23 August 2017; on Ascher see also Valerie Mendes, Frances Hinchcliffe, *Ascher : fabric, art, fashion : Zika and Lida Ascher* (London: V & A Museum, 1987); K. Hlaváčková (ed.), *The Mad Silkman: Zika and Lida Ascher, Textiles and Fashion* (Prague: Museum of Decorative Arts in Prague & Slovart Publishing Ltd, 2019).
63 G. Rayner, R. Chamberlain, et al., *Artists' Textiles in Britain 1945–1970* (Woodbridge, Suffolk: Antique Collectors Club), 1999, p 34.
64 K. Hlaváčková, *The Mad Silkman*, p. 56.
65 Konstantina Hlaváčková in a conversation with the author in London, June 2019.
66 K. Hlaváčková, *The Mad Silkman*, p. 39.
67 https://www.sekersfabrics.co.uk/timeline/, accessed 5 June 2019.
68 http://www.sekersfabrics,co.uk/about-sekers/sir-nicholas-sekers/, accessed 23 August 2017.
69 https://www.telegraph.co.uk/news/obituaries/10804381/Bernat-Klein-obituary.html, accessed 2 June 2019.
70 https://www.nms.ac.uk/bernatklein, accessed 15 June 2018
71 https://www.selvedge.org/blogs/selvedge/a-life-in-colour-bernat-klein, accessed 15 June 2018
72 Ibid.
73 See A. Nyburg, 'Textile in Exile'.
74 On Otti Berger see, for example, A. Powers, *Bauhaus Goes West: Modern Art and Design in Britain and America* (London: Thames & Hudson, 2019), pp. 167–169.
75 Information on Weisz from Hawick Museum volunteer and former Lyle and Scott knitwear employee Gordon Macdonald; from David Weisz, Otto

Weisz's son; from the Pringle Directors' Minutes book, and from the house magazine, *Pringle Bulletin*.
76 Story from Gordon Macdonald, corroborated by David Weisz.
77 Story from Gordon Macdonald, corroborated by David Weisz.
78 National Archive reference, AZ 12273, and 171/22834.
79 H. Barty-King, *Pringle of Scotland: and the Hawick Knitwear Story* (Shrewsbury, Quiller Press, 2006), p. 116.
80 *Woman in Gold*, Director Simon Curtis (2015).
81 https://en.wikipedia.org/wiki/Maria_Altmann, accessed 2 June 2019.
82 https://en.wikipedia.org/wiki/Maria_Altmann, accessed 14 August 2017.
83 Information in this section from H. Barty-King, *Pringle of Scotland*, p. 121.
84 This information comes from a family memoir and from an interview with Freddie Berdach by the author on 28 September 2016. Arranging to meet the author, he said: 'You'll recognise me, because I'll be the one wearing a bow tie…'.
85 The eminent émigré graphic designer Hans Schleger often sported one.
86 All information here on Hornflowa is from the Loebl thesis, pp. 313–14.
87 Information here on Lucie Rie from E. Cooper, *Lucie Rie: Modernist Potter*, (New Haven and London: Paul Mellon Centre for Studies in British Art, Yale University Press, 2012).
88 Ibid., pp. 130–33.
89 See, for example, the *Omnibus* television programme of 1982 in which Rie was interviewed by David Attenborough.
90 E. Cooper, *Lucie Rie*, p. 251.
91 Ibid.
92 Obituary of Ralf Noskwith, https://www.theguardian.com/world/2017/jan/10/rolf-noskwith-obituary, accessed 9 January 2018.
93 https://www.thejc.com/news/obituaries/obituary-rolf-noskwith-1.431766, accessed 7 May 2018.
94 *The Imitation Game*, Director Morten Tyldum (2015).
95 I am indebted to the John Smedley archivist Jane Middleton-Smith, for her help with the archival research.
96 A. Hillert, *Anny Schröder, Leben und Werk einer Künstlerin zwischen Wiener Werkstätte, drittem Reich und Postmoderne (*Münster: Lit Verlag, 2014*)*, p. 38.
97 Ibid., p. 38.

98   Interview with Francis Steiner by the author, September 2016. Francis Steiner died in 2019 aged 96.
99   Information on Cumberland Childwear from Loebl thesis, pp. 295–296.
100 In an email from Ruth Williams, mother of Hilary Papworth, 19 August 2016.
101 Tate Archives GB70 TGA 200410/1/1/3382.
102 Magdalen College Oxford, Terence Hodgkinson Archive, MC: P174/C2/13.
103 Information here from a conversation between the author and Julian Barnes, 20 June 2017; the story referred to is 'Carcasonne' in *Pulse* (London: Vintage Books, 2011), pp. 190–191.
104 MC: 174, Papers of Terence Hodgkinson.
105 In an email from Neil MacGregor to the author, 22 June 2017.
106 M. Baker, Obituary Terence Hodgkinson, *The Independent*, 13 October 1999.
107 Herschel Feibel Grynszpan assassinated Nazi foreign service officer Ernst vom Rath in Paris on 7 November 1938. The event provided the Nazi establishment with an occasion for *Kristallnacht*, a brutal pogrom launched against Jews and Jewish institutions inside the territory of the Third Reich on the night of 9–10 November 1938.
108 MC/174/p1/6.
109 M. Baker, Obituary Terence Hodgkinson.
110 Inge-Lore Sommerfeld Collection, Wiener Library, London, 1779, Accession 2008/76.
111 Inge-Lore Sommerfeld Collection, Wiener Library, London, 1779, Accession 1775/15.
112 Conversation in Fortnum & Mason with Stanley Grant and the author, November 2016.
113 Information here on Launer from a phone conversation and an interview with Gerald Bodmer by the author in October 2017.
114 Professor Sir Walter Bodmer and Arnold R. Bodmer, respectively.
115 http://www.telegraph.co.uk/fashion/people/queen-elizabeth-whats-inside-her-handbag/, accessed 15 December 2017.
116 Ibid.
117 http://www.dailymail.co.uk/femail/article-3515883/How-Queen-s-handbag-collection-REALLY-worth.html, accessed 15 December 2017.
118 Information here is based on an interview by the author in August 2016 with Richard Donner and John Donner.

119 http://cadensa.bl.uk/uhtbin/cgisirsi/?ps=mPRWmPUzsr/WORKS-FILE/92470024/123, accessed 21 February 2018.
120 In an email to the author from Richard Donner, 27 February 2018.
121 https://www.doubletwo.co.uk/about-us/, accessed 26 February 2018.
122 Richard Donner in an email to the author, 20 August 2017.
123 https://www.doubletwo.co.uk/about-us/, accessed 26 February 2018.
124 S. Kuhfuss-Wickenheiser, *Die Reimann-Schule in Berlin und London 1902–1943: Ein jüdisches Unternehmen zur Kunst- und Designausbildung internationaler Prägung bis zur Vernichtung durch das Hitlerregime* (Aachen: Shaker Medien, 2009), p. 111.
125 http://www.independent.co.uk/news/people/obituary-max-Bruh-1392153.html, accessed 3 August 2017.
126 Anne Barrie, 'They Created Frank Usher' in *Woman and Beauty*, July 1961, p. 53 in https://advantageinvintage.co.uk/2015/11/19/they-created-frank-usher/, accessed 3 February 2018.
127 http://www.independent.co.uk/news/people/obituary-max-Bruh-1392153.html, accessed 38 March 2018.
128 http://www.independent.co.uk/news/people/obituary-max-Bruh-1392153.html, accessed 3 February 2018.
129 http://www.hamhigh.co.uk/news/story-of-hampstead-fashion-house-frank-usher-founder-anne-Bruh-who-escaped-the-nazis-features-in-new-book-a-nation-of-storytellers-1-1698320, accessed 3 February 2018.
130 Information here in Kagan from https://en.wikipedia.org/wiki/Gannex, accessed 5 January 2018; http://ellielaycock.co.uk/2014/01/gannex-granny-lost-yorkshire-mills.html/, accessed 5 January 2018. See also 'Joe Kagan, *Just Another Bump in the Road*, film BFI, 1980.
131 http://www.independent.co.uk/news/people/obituaries-lord-kagan-1568684.html, accessed 5 January 2018.
132 http://ellielaycock.co.uk/2014/01/gannex-granny-lost-yorkshire-mills.html/, accessed 5 January 2018.
133 https://en.wikipedia.org/wiki/Joseph_Kagan,_Baron_Kagan, accessed 5 January 2018.
134 http://ellielaycock.co.uk/2014/01/gannex-granny-lost-yorkshire-mills.html/, accessed 5 January 2018.
135 S. Kuhfuss-Wickenheiser, *Die Reimann-Schule*, pp. 267–8.
136 Obituary Alex Kroll, *The Times*, 27 June 2008.
137 https://www.thetimes.co.uk/article/alex-kroll-magazine-art-director-and-publisher-3pbpfbjvjrt, accessed 29 October 2017.

138 https://www.theguardian.com/media/2004/apr/07/broadcasting.guardianobituaries, accessed 29 October 2017.
139 http://www.telegraph.co.uk/news/obituaries/12062744/Kenneth-Partridge-interior-designer-obituary.html, accessed 30 October 2017.
140 On Adprint and the story of Thames & Hudson, see A. Nyburg, *Émigrés: the Transformation of Art Publishing in Britain* (London: Phaidon, 2014).
141 Prof. Simon Kroll in an interview with the author, 23 November 2017.
142 Obituary of Alex Kroll, *The Times*, 27 June 2008.
143 On Eva Neurath, see *Recollections: Eva Neurath 1908–1999* (London: Thames & Hudson, 2016); A. Nyburg, *Émigrés*.
144 Prof. Simon Kroll in an interview with the author, 23 November 2017.
145 *The Hireling*, Director Alan Bridges (1973).
146 On Tender, see http://www.madebytender.com/, accessed 11 March 2018.
147 Information here from interviews with Adam Sykes by the author in October and November 2017.
148 On Ingeborg's career, see an interview with her, https://www.scotsman.com/lifestyle/interview-ingeborg-bratman-jeweller-1-804506, accessed 12 March 2018.
149 In *Jersey*, July/August 1969, n.p.
150 On Molyneux, see N. Taylor, 'Molyneux', in A. de la Haye, E. Ehrman (eds), *London Couture 1923–1975: British Luxury* (London: V & A Publishing, 2015), pp.100–109.
151 *Jersey*,. n.p.
152 Ibid.
153 Information here from J. Jolliffe, *Glyndebourne: An Operatic Miracle* (London: John Murray, 1999).
154 Ibid., p. 64.
155 Ibid., p. 142.
156 https://www.rosehilltheatre.co.uk/about-us/about-us, accessed 17 June 2018
157 This section from M. Sieff, *Don't ask the Price: Memoirs of the President of Marks & Spencer* (Weidenfeld & Nicolson: London, 1986), pp. 212–213.
158 This section from J. Bevan, *The Rise and Fall of Marks & Spencer* (Profile Books: London, 2001), pp. 108–109.
159 Ibid. p. 105.
160 Ibid. p. 106.

161 In a phone conversation with the author, 25 June 2018.
162 https://artsandbusiness.bitc.org.uk/awards-ab/prince-of-wales-medal-for-arts- philanthropy/2014/djanoglys, accessed 25 June 2018.
163 In a telephone interview with the author, 18 June 2018.
164 Ralph Land, in an interview with the author, 26 September 2016.
165 On Schmidts, see A. Nyburg, 'Food in Exile' in A. Hammel, A. Grenville (eds), *Exile and Everyday Life, Yearbook of the Research Centre for German and Austrian Exile*, vol.16 (2015), pp. 173–190.
166 *www.elenasdiary.gr/en/auctions/114–four-decades-of-style,* accessed January 2018.
167 I am indebted to Sarah MacDougall for the introduction to Eva Aldbrook.
168 A. and E. Aldbrook, *Two Lives Together* (Self-published).
169 https://www.independent.co.uk/news/people/obituary-muriel-pemberton- 1458928.html, accessed 17 June 2019
170 Aldbrook, *Two Lives Together*, p. 52.
171 Ibid.
172 Loebl thesis, p. 170
173 In an interview by the author with Richard Donner, August 2016.

Bibliography

Aldbrook, A., Aldbrook, E., *Two Lives Together* (self published).

Artmonsky, R., Webb, B, *F. H. K. Henrion Design* (Woodbridge: Antique Collectors Club, 2011).

Artmonsky, R., *Showing Off: Fifty Years of London Store Publicity and Display* (London: Artmonsky Arts, 2013).

Backemeyer, S. (ed.), *Making their Mark: Art, Craft and Design at the Central School 1896-1966* (London: Herbert Press, 2000).

Ballard, B., *In my Fashion* (London: Secker & Warburg, 1960).

Barnes, J., *Pulse* (London: Vintage Books, 2011).

Barty-King, H., *Pringle of Scotland: The Hawick Knitwear Story* (Fakenham: J. J. G. Publishing, 2006).

Berkowitz, M., *Jews and Photography in Britain*, (Exploring Art and Culture), (Austin, Texas: University of Texas Press, 2015).

Bevan, Judi, *The Rise and Fall of Marks & Spencer* (London: Profile Books, 2001).

Brandstätter, C., Gregori, D., Metzger, R. (eds), *Vienna 1900 Complete* (London: Thames & Hudson, 2018).

Breward, C., Wilcox, C. (eds), *The Ambassador Magazine: Promoting Post-war Textiles and Fashion* (London: V & A Publishing, 2012).

Chamberlain, R., Rayner, G., Stapleton, A. (eds), *Jacqueline Groag, Textile & Pattern Design: Wiener Werkstätte to American Modern* (Woodbridge, Suffolk: Antique Collectors' Club, 2009).

Chapman, S., https://academic.oup.com/ahr/issue/108/5 *Hosiery and Knitwear: Four Centuries of Small-Scale Industry in Britain c. 1589–2000.* (Pasold Studies in Textile History, number 12.) (New York: Oxford University Press, 2002).

Cooper, E., *Lucie Rie: Modernist Potter*, (New Haven, CT and London: Paul Mellon Centre for Studies in British Art, Yale University Press, 2012).

Cox, C., *Luxury Fashion: A Global History of Heritage Brands* (London: Bloomsbury, 2013).

Crompton, S., Egelnick, T., Friedrichs, H., A., *Best of British: The Stories Behind Britain's Iconic Brands* (Munich: Prestel, 2015).

David, A., *The Patron: A Life of Salman Schocken 1877-1959* (New York: Metropolitan Books, Henry Holt and Company, 2003).

De la Haye, Amy (ed.), *The Cutting Edge: 50 Years of British Fashion 1947-1997* (London: V & A Publications, 1996).

Dickson, R., 'Elisabeth Tomalin: Emigrée Designer 1912-2012, 'The only joy in life is being creative. Everything else is more or less pain.', in C. Brinson, J. Barbora Buresova, A. Hammel (eds), in *Exile and Gender II: Politics, Education and the Arts,Yearbook of the Research Centre for German and Austrian Exile Studies*, vol. 18, 2017, pp. 154-170.

Ehrman, E., *Undressed: A Brief History of Underwear* (London: V & A Publishing, 2015).

Ewing, E., *History of Twentieth Century Fashion*, (London: Batsford, 1985).

Ferber, C. (ed.), *Die Dame:Ein deutsches Journal für den verwöhnten Geschmack 1912-1943* (Berlin: Ullstein, 1980).

Fogg, M., *Vintage Pattern 1950s* (London: Batsford, 2013).

Ganeva, M., *Women in Weimar Fashion* (Rochester, NY: Camden House, 2008).

Gardiner, J., *Wartime Britain 1939-1945* (London: Hodder Headline, 2004).

Greenspoon, Leonard J. (ed.), 'Fashioning Jews: Clothing, Culture and Commerce', *Studies in Jewish Civilisation*, vol. 24 (West Lafayette, IN: Purdue University Press, 2013).

Greiner, M., *Auf Freiheit zugeschnitten. Emilie Flöge – Modeschöpferin und Gefährtin Gustav Klimts* (Vienna: Verlag Kremayr & Scheriau, 2014).

Grenville, A., 'The Kindertransports: an Introduction', in A. Hammel, B. Lewkovicz (eds), *The Kindertransport to Britain 1938/39: New Perspectives, Yearbook of the Research Centre for German and Austrian Exile*, vol. 13 (2012).

Guenther, I., *Nazi Chic? Fashioning Women in the Third Reich* (Oxford/New York: Berg, 2004).

Guenther, I., 'The Destruction of a Culture and in Industry', in Kramer, Roberta S. (ed.), *Broken Threads: The Destruction of the Jewish Fashion Industry in Germany and Austria* (Vancouver: Berg, Vancouver Holocaust Education Centre, 2006).

Hansen-Schaberg, Inge, Thöner, Wolfgang, Feustel, Adriane (eds), *Entfernt: Frauen des Bauhauses während der NS-Zeit - Verfolgung und Exil Frauen und Exil*, Band 5 (Munich: edition text + kritik, 2012).

Hillert, A., *Anny Schröder, Leben und Werk einer Künstlerin zwischen Wiener Werkstätte, drittem Reich und Postmoderne* (Münster: Lit Verlag, 2014).

Hinton, N., *Silhouette, the Story of Little X* (Shrewsbury: 2009).

Hlaváčková, K. (ed.), *The Mad Silkman: Zika and Lida Ascher, Textiles and Fashion* (Prague: Museum of Decorative Arts in Prague & Slovart Publishing Ltd, 2019).

Horwood, C., *Keeping Up Appearances: Fashion and Class Between the Wars* (Stroud: Sutton Publishing, 2005).

Jackson, L., *From Atoms to Patterns: Crystal Structure Designs from the 1951 Festival of Britain:* The Story of the Festival Pattern Group (Shepton Beauchamp: Richard Dennis, 2008).

Jackson, L., *Alistair Morton and Edinburgh Weavers: Visionary Textiles and Modern Art,* (London: V & A Publishing, 2012).

Joliffe, John, *Glyndebourne: An Operatic Miracle* (London: John Murray, 1999).

Jones, S., Cullen, O. (eds), *Hats: An Anthology* (London: V & A Publishing, 2009).

Kanter, T., *Some Girls, Some Hats and Hitler* (London: Virago, 2012).

Kee, R., *The World We Left Behind: A Chronicle of the Year 1939* (London: Weidenfeld, 1993).

Kershen, A. J., *Off the Peg: The Story of the Women's Wholesale Clothing Industry 1880 to the 1960s or The Story of the Jewish Contribution to the Women's Wholesale Clothing Industry 1880 to the 1960s* (London: Jewish Museum London, 1988).

Kremer, R. S. (ed.), *Broken Threads: The Destruction of the Jewish Fashion Industry in Germany and Austria* (Vancouver: Berg, Vancouver Holocaust Education Centre, 2006).

Kuhfuss-Wickenheiser, S., *Die Reimann-Schule in Berlin und London 1902-1943: Ein jüdisches Unternehmen zur Kunst- und Designausbildung internationaler Prägung bis zur Vernichtung durch das Hitlerregime* (Aachen:Shaker Medien, 2009);

Kroll, N., *Window Display* (London: The Studio Publications, 1954).

Lafitte, F., *The Internment of Aliens* (Harmondsworth: Penguin Books, 1940).

Laver, J., *Costume and Fashion* (London: Thames & Hudson, World of Art, 1974).

Lipmann, A., *Divinely Elegant: The World of Ernst Dryden* (London: Pavillion, 1989).

Loschek, I., 'Contributions of Jewish Fashion Designers in Berlin', in R. Kramer, *Broken Threads, The Destruction of the Jewish Fashion Industry in Germany and Austria* (Vancouver: Berg, Vancouver Holocaust Education Centre, 2006).

Mansfield, A., P. Cunningham, *Handbook of English Costume in the Twentieth Century* (London: Faber and Faber, 1973).

March, J., 'Women Exile Photographers', *Applied Arts in Exile: Changing Visual and Material* Culture, *Yearbook for the Research Centre for German and Austrian Exile Studies,* vol. 19 (2018), pp. 49-66.

Medawar, Jean and Pyke, *Hitler's Gift: Scientists who Fled Nazi Germany* (New York: Arcade Publishing, 2001).

Mendes, V., Hinchcliffe, F., *Ascher: Fabric, Art, Fashion: Zika and Lida Ascher*, (London: V & A Museum, 1987).

Moses, Mods, Mr Fish. Jewish Museum Catalogue April 2016.

Nicol, P., *Sucking Eggs: What Your Wartime Granny Could Teach You about Diet, Thrift and Going Green* (London: Random House, 2015).

Nyburg, A., *Émigrés: The Transformation of Art Publishing in Britain* (London: Phaidon, 2014).

Nyburg, A., 'Food in Exile' in A. Hammel, A. Grenville (eds), *Exile and Everyday Life, Yearbook of the Research Centre for German and Austrian Exile*, vol.16 (2015), pp. 173-190.

Nyburg, A., 'Textile in Exile: Refugee Textile Surface Designers', in Malet, M., Dickson, R., MacDougall, S., Nyburg, A. (eds), *Applied Arts in Exile: Changing Visual and Material Culture, Yearbook of the Research Centre for German and Austrian Exile Studies*, vol. 19, (2018), pp. 212-228.

Packer, W., Wilcox, I., Petter, H. M. (after Hans Christian Andersen), Illustrated by Natasha Kroll, *The Princess and the Pea* (London: Collins, 1944).

Packer, W., *Fashion Drawing in Vogue* (London: Thames & Hudson, 1983).

Parkin, S., *The Colony Room Club* (London: Palmtree Publishers, 2013).

Pasold, E., *Ladybird, Ladybird: A Story of Private Enterprise* (Manchester: Manchester University Press, 1977).

Pick, M., *Hardy Amies* (Woodbridge: Antique Collectors Club, 2012).

Powers, A., *Bauhaus Goes West: Modern Art and Design in Britain and America* (London: Thames & Hudson, 2019).

Prichard, S., Schoeser, M., Hall, J., *Tibor Reich: Art of Colour & Texture* (Tibor Ltd, 2016).

Rayner, G., Chamberlain, R., et al., *Artists' Textiles in Britain 1945-1970* (Woodbridge, Suffolk: Antique Collectors Club), 1999

Rayner, G., Stapleton, A., Chamberlain, R. (eds) *Jacqueline Groag: Textile & Pattern Design: Wiener Werkstätte to American Modern* (Woodbridge: Antique Collectors' Club, 2009).

Recollections, Eva Neurath 1908-1999 (London: Thames & Hudson, 2016).

Rees, G., *St Michael: History of Marks and Spencer* (London: Weidenfeld & Nicolson, 1969).

Rennie, Paul, *Festival of Britain Design 1951* (Woodbridge: Antique Collectors' Club, 2007).

Romer, N., 'Photographers, Jews and the Fashioning of Women in the Weimar Republic', in L. Greenspoon (ed.), 'Fashioning Jews, Clothing, Culture and Commerce', *Studies in Jewish Civilisation*, vol. 24, West Lafayette, IN: Purdue University Press, 2013).

Schleger, Pat, *Zero: Hans Schleger, A Life of Design* (London: Lund Humphries, 2001).

Schoeser, M., *World Textiles: A Concise History*, *World of Art* (London: Thames & Hudson, 2003).

Schramm, C., "Architecture of the German Department Store", in R. Kramer, *Broken Threads: The Destruction of the Jewish Fashion Industry in Germany and Austria* (Vancouver: Berg, Vancouver Holocaust Education Centre, 2006).

Secrest, M., *Elsa Schiaparelli: A Biography* (London: Penguin Fig Tree, 2014).

Segal, L., *Other People's Houses* (New York: Fawcett Crest, 1958).

Shepherd, N, *A Refuge from Darkness: Wilfrid Israel and the Rescue of the Jews* (New York: Pantheon Books, 1984).

Sieff, I., *Memoirs* (London: Weidenfeld & Nicolson, 1970).

Sieff, M., *Don't Ask the Price: The Memoirs of the President of Marks & Spencer* (London: Weidenfeld & Nicolson, 1986).

Silverman, L., 'Ela Zirner-Zwieback, Madame d'Ora and Vienna's New Woman' in L. Greenspoon (ed.), 'Fashioning Jews, Clothing, Culture and Commerce', *Studies in Jewish Civilisation*, vol. 24 (West Lafayette, IN: Purdue University Press, 2013), pp.

Suga, Y., *The Reimann School: A Design Diaspora* (London: Artmonsky Arts, 2013).

Taylor, N., 'Frontline Fancy Goods', in *Selvedge: The Fabric of your Life*, Jan/Feb 2010, pp. 49-50.

Taylor, N., 'Molyneux', in A. de la Haye, E. Ehrman (eds), *London Couture 1923-1975: British Luxury* (London: V & A Publishing, 2015), pp.100-109.

Ullstein, H., *The Rise and Fall of the House of Ullstein* (London: Nicholson and Watson, 1944).

Walker, Richard, *Savile Row: An Illustrated History* (New York: Rizzoli, 1989).

Wallach, K., 'Weimar Jewish Chic: Jewish Women and Fashion in 1920s Germany', in Leonard J. Greenspoon (ed.), *Fashioning Jews: Clothing, Culture and Commerce*, Studies in Jewish Civilization, Volume 24 (West Lafayette, IN: Purdue University Press, 2013), pp. 113-135.

Walton-Jordan, U., '"Although he is Jewish, he is M & S": Jewish Refugees at Marks & Spencer', in A. Grenville (ed.), *Refugees from the Third Reich in*

Britain, *Yearbook of the Research Centre for German and Austrian Exile Studies*, vol. 4 (2016).
Watson, N., *60 Years of Kangol Quality: 1938-1998*
Westphal, U., *Berliner Konfektion und Mode: Die Zerstörung einer Tradition 1836-1939* (Berlin: Heinrich & Co, 2009),
Westphal, Uwe, *Ehrenfried und Cohn* (Berlin: Lichtig Verlag, 2015).
Wilcox, C., *The Golden Age of Couture, Paris and London 1947-1957* (London: V & A Publishing, 2008).
Wilson, E., Taylor, L., *Through the Looking Glass: A History of Dress from 1860 to the Present Day* (London: British Broadcasting Corporation, 1989).
Winder, R., *Bloody Foreigners: The Story of Immigration to Britain* (Little, Brown, London: 2004),
Woolman Chase, E. and Chase, I., *Always in Vogue* (London: Victor Gollancz, 1954).
Worth, R., *Fashion for the People: A History of Clothing at Marks & Spencer* (Oxford/Hamburg/New York: Berg, 2006).

Filmography

Man in the White Suit, Director Alexander Mackendrick (1951).
'Heady Stuff, Pathé (1958).
Wilfrid Israel: The Essential Link, Director Yonatan Nir (2016).
Refuge Britain: Stories of Emigré Designers, Director Robert Sternberg, with Anna Nyburg (2017)

Unpublished PhD Thesis

Herbert Loebl, *Government-financed factories and the establishment of industries by refugees in the special area of the North of England 1937-1961*, Durham theses, Durham University, 1978.

Index

A
Adams, Jack, 55, 102, 108. 176
ADEFA (Arbeitsgemeinschaft deutsch-arischer Fabrikanten der Bekleidungsindustrie), 34-36
Aldbrook (née Mehl), Eva, 136, 241, 243-44
Altmann, Bernhard, 146, 153-54
Altmann, Fritz, 154
Altmann, Maria, 153
Ambassador, The, 22, 24, 70, 74-76
Amies, Hardy, 116,144
Andersen, Rolf, 85-86, 91-93
Anderson, Frank, 55, 102, 176
Antisemitism, 9, 10, 27, 39, 41, 45, 51. 92, 110, 200, 226, 234
Arkwright, Richard, 34
Ascher, Lida, 138-140
Ascher, Peter, 140
Ascher, Zika, 138-40
Asprey, 96, 197
Association of Jewish Refuges (AJR) vii, 86, 245
AJR *Journal*, vii
Auerbach, Ellen, 21
Awards, 106,107, 200, 204, 245, 246
Ayars, Anne, 182

B
Bacon, Francis, 93
Balfour-Lynn, Richard, vii, 94
Ballard, Bettina, 64, 69
Balmoral Castle, 155
Barnes, Julian, 93, 111, 181-83
Bauhaus, 17, 21, 23-26, 72, 74, 78, 131, 145, 217, 218, 251, 258, 260
Baum, Vicki, 20
Beaty, Stuart, 155-56
Beckhough, Harry, 197
Belcher, Muriel, 93, 247
Belz, 196
Ben Uri Gallery, 243
Berdach, Freddie, vi, vii, viii, ix, 158-59, 162-63
Berdach, Walter, 158-63
Berger, Otti, 145, 251
Berliner Illustrirte, 20, 77
Berliner Tageblatt, 74
Bezalel Academy of Art and Design, 143
Bing, Rudolf, 181, 228-29
Black, Misha, 72
Bletchley Park, 61, 97, 168-70
Bloch-Bauer, Adele, 154
Blumenau, Emil, 118
Blumenau, Hans, 119-21, 125
Blumenau, Ralph, vii
Blumenfeld, Edwin, 22, 77
Bodmer [Billigheimer], Gerald, vii, 192-94, 253
Bolshoi Ballet, 2, 186
Boy George, 107
Bratman, Frank, vi, x, 222-26
Bregenz, 158
Bressart, Felix, 96
'Britain Can Make It', 69-71, 139
Britten, Benjamin, 2, 180, 185, 229-30

Brno, 176
Brookner, Anita, 187
Bruh, Adam, 207
Bruh, Anne, 203, 207
Bruh, Max, 203-05, 207
Bruh, Robert, 208
Budapest, 11, 12, 132, 133, 135, 141, 223, 230
Budischowsky, Helena (Hello), 14-15
Burlington Arcade, 160
Burlington Magazine, 185
Burton [Bassell], Otto, 28, n. 19
Busch, Fritz, 228-29

C

Calico Printers, 199
Central School of Arts and Crafts, 23, 257
Chamberlain, Neville, 40, 60
Chambre Syndicale de la Haute Couture, 64
Chanel, Coco, 15, 20, 23, 46, 64, 77, 131, 144, 156
Charnos, vi, viii, ix, 168-71
Chemnitz, ix, 7, 11, 110, 124, 125, 169, 231
Chermayeff, Serge, 10
Christie, Agatha, 25
Christie, John, 225, 229
Churchill, Winston, vi, 61, 158, 160-61
Cižek, Frank, 131
Claremont, 222, 227
Cleator Mill, 102-05, 107-08
Colony Room Club, 93, 247, 260
Comme des Garçons, 49, 109, 167
Conran, Terence, 216
Courtaulds, 19
Couture, v, 5, 15, 20, 64, 65, 69, 111, 116-17, 130-31, 133, 135, 140, 144, 166, 205, 225-26, 255, 261-62
Crompton, Samuel, 143
Cross, Joan, 180, 185
Cumberland Childwear, 176-78, 252

D

Dachau concentration camp, 154
Dalyell, Tam, 209, 213
Dan, George, 106
De Carlos, Michael [see Donnellan, Michael], 115
De Gara, Tomi, 141
Debenhams, 47
Dekk, Dorrit, 219-20
Dench, Judi, 193
Designers, see 14-16, 23-25, 78-81
Design, graphic, 4, 27, 33, 78, 216
Diana, Princess of Wales, 107
Die Dame, 29, 19-20, 258
Dior, Christian, vi, 110, 112, 114, 141, 144, 153, 225-26, 243
Dietrich, Marlene, 4, 15, 95-96, 101
Display, 26, 27, 37, 45, 70, 72-73, 82-83, 121, 128-29, 138, 214-15, 216-17, 257, 259, 269
Djanogly, Harry, 232-33
Djanogly, Jack, 231, 233
Djanogly, Jonathan, 231-32
Djanogly, Simon, 231-33
Doc Martens, 1
Donnellan, Michael, 115-17
Donner, Isaak, 196, 199, 200-01
Donner, John, vii, 196, 200, 253,
Donner, Richard, vii, viii, x, 23, 139, 196, 198-99, 200-02, 247, 253, 256

Double Two, vi, x, 19, 29, 139, 196-99, 200-02, 196-202, 245
Dryden [Deutsch], Ernst, 13-15, 19-20, 27, 29, 76, 153, 155, 259
Duchess of Cornwall, 193
Dundee Courier, 155
Düsseldorf, 207

E

Ebert, Carl, 228-29
Ehrenfest [née Drenning], Klothilde, 50, 67-68. 172, 175
Ehrenfest, Oskar, 174
Elegante Welt, 19
Etam, 151
Ettinger, Gerhardt, vi, ix, 2, 82, 96-100, 245, 248
Ettinger, Robert, vii, viii, ix, 2, 91, 98-100, 248,
Ettinger, Trude, 76, 78

F

Farbe und Form, 27
Ferrier, Kathleen, x, 182
Festival of Britain, vi, 71, 83, 132, 220, 259. 261
Fleissen, 44
Fleissig, Lily, 226
Ford, Kath, 103, 108
Forsyth of Regent Street, 81
Fortnum & Mason, 92, 95-96, 107, 192,
Fox, Frederick, 94
Franklin, Caryn, 156
Friedländer & Zaduk, 203

G

Games, Abram, 71

Gannex, vi, x, 82, 209-12, 254
Garbo, Greta, 101-02
Gerson, Hermann, 10, 16
Glasgow School of Art, 156
Glyndebourne, 180-01, 228-29, 302, 255, 259
Goalen, Barbara, 86, 205, 207
Goebbels, Josef, 32, 174
Goebbels, Magda, 37
Goldie, 107
Göring, Hermann, 154, 228
Grant, Stanley, vii, 95, 248, 253
Gregg, Hubert, 96
Greig, Eileen, 106
Groag (née Pick), Jacqueline, 130-33, 135
Groag, Jacques, 131
Grynszpan, Herschel, 253 n. 151
Guenther, Irene, 28, 35, 41, 258

H

Hajek, Ferry, 176-77
Hallé Orchestra. 193-94
Hampstead, 139, 159, 254,
Harella, 79-80
Hargreaves, James, 43
Harper's Bazaar, 77, 79
Harris, Nic, vii, 108, 248
Harrods, 11, 47, 57, 73, 92, 96, 144, 161, 211, 232
Hartnell, Norman, 63, 92, 112, 117
Hawick, viii, 146-47, 151, 153, 155-56, 251-52, 257
Hawick Express, 146-155
Hawick Museum, viii, 151, 251
Heartfield, John [Herzfeld, Helmut], 80
Heatherwick, Thomas, vii, ix, 127-28, 130, 221

Heim, Eric[h], 110-11, 130
Hemmings, David, 94
Henrion, F H K, 79-81, 83-84, 257
Herzl, Theodor, 51
Hinton, Nigel, 126, 249
Hitler, Adolf, 1, 3, 12, 16, 27, 29,
    31-32, 34, 40, 42, 44, 58, 60, 97,
    119, 138, 168-69, 174, 192,
    209-10, 231, 254, 259-60
Hodgkinson, Terence, 181, 184-85,
    253
Holocaust, 41, 53, 124, 133, 188-89,
    219, 234, 258-59, 261
Homosexuality, 5, 27, 92, 168
Hopkins, Susie, vii, 88-89, 92, 87,
    247,
Hornflowa, ix, 57, 76, 164-65
Horst, Horst P., 22, 77
Horthy, Miklós, 41
House & Garden, 92, 132, 217
Höss, Rudolf, 38
Huber, Gustav, 105
Huguenots, 43-44
Huyton Camp, 192

I

Illustration, 4, 19, 21, 77, 79, 80
Immigration, 51, 54, 58, 82, 262
Incorporated Society of London
    Fashion Designers (IncSoc), 63,
    92, 112, 114,
Industry, v, 2, 9, 17, 28, 31, 34, 41,
    44, 58, 105-06, 110, 124, 130,
    169, 176, 205, 208, 211, 217,
    229, 231, 245, 257-59, 261
Internment, 61, 68, 86, 105, 129,
    239, 259
International Textiles, 74-75, 153

Isherwood, Christopher, 4
Israel, Nathan, 6, 11, 35, 37, 47,
Israel, Wilfrid, 5, 26, 27-28, 37, 41,
    262
Isle of Man, 61, 86, 105, 112, 124,
    151, 173, 177, 239

J

Jackson, Samuel, 107
Jacobs, Marc, 109
Jäger, Gustav, 6-7
Jaeger, 6-8, 72, 129, 249-50
John Lewis, 112
John Smedley, vii, viii, ix, 47, 49-50,
    67, 172-73, 252
Juda (née Goldstein), Elsbeth (Jay),
    22, 24, 74-75, 83, 128, 153, 205
Juda, Hans, 33, 74-75, 153

K

Kaczynski, Martin, vii, 12, 38
Kagan [Kaganas], Joseph, vi, x, 82,
    127, 209-14, 254
Kallmus, Dora, 22
Kangol, vi, viii, ix, 82, 101-09, 248
Kann, Eric, 110-11, 130, 248
Kanter, Trude, 13, 16, 39
Karl Marx Hof, 158, 163
Karstadt, 10
Katz, Hans, 74
Kauffer, McKnight, 79
Kaufhof, 11
Kavanagh, Pat, 183
Kelly, Angela, 193
Kelly, Jude, 71
Klappholz, Eugen, 151-52
Klein, Bernat, vi, ix, 127, 135, 137,
    143, 146

Klimt, Gustav, 12, 28, 154, 258
Knighthoods, 57, 212-13, 246
Knitwear, 13, 17, 47-50, 58-59, 67, 111, 146-48, 151, 153-54, 156, 172, 175, 232, 251-52, 257
Knize, 13-15, 29
Kokoschka, Oskar, 13, 174
Kölling, Hildegard, 26
Konfektion, v, 4-5, 8-9, 12, 15-17, 20, 22, 28-29, 31, 33-38, 41, 74, 262
Kraus, Max, 164
Kroll, Alex, x, 65, 68, 80, 214, 217-19, 221, 254-55
Kroll, Natasha, 215-17, 260
Kroll, Simon, vii, 217, 219, 255
Kroll, William, vii, x, 214, 219,
Kunstgewerbeschule, 6, 23, 131, 174,
Kawakubo, Rei, 167

L
Ladybird Clothes, 40, 42, 58, 68, 223, 260
Lampl, Fritz, 166
Land [Landsberger], Frank, 236-37
Land [Landsberger], Ralph, vii, viii, x, 236-38, 256,
Landsberger, Sofia (Soscha), 236, 239
Lanvin, 15, 77, 107, 140, 243
Launer, Sam, vi, viii, x, 192-95, 245, 246, 253
Lauren, Ralph, 14
Leather, 2, 14, 36, 95-96, 98-99, 164, 192-94, 239, 245
Lee, William, 43
Lehr- und Versuchsanstalt, 22

Leischner, Margarete, 24
Lelong, Lucien, 64
Leon, Sean, ix, 104, 107, 248
Lestawear, 57
Lette Verein, 25
Liepa, Maris, 187
Lipmann, Anthony, 14, 19, 29, 83, 259
Lobbenberg, Annemarie, 122
Lobbenberg, Hans, 119
Lobbenberg, Max, 118
Lobbenberg, Otto, 118-19
Lobbenberg, Peter, ix, 122, 249
Loebl, Herbert, 57, 59, 164, 245, 248, 252, 256, 262
London Gazette, 173
Loos, Adolf, 14
Lorant, Stefan, 21
Lucas, Otto, vi, ix, 2, 85-95, 247

M
MacGregor, Neil, 112, 183-84, 253
Macmillan, Harold, 54
Mademoiselle Paule, 87
Magdalen College, Oxford, vii, 181-82, 184-86, 253
Mahler, Marian [Marianne], 23
Manchester, 124, 129, 146, 193, 196, 250
Manchester Guardian, 54
Manheimer, Victor, 10, 16
Mappin & Webb, 193
Marks & Spencer, vii, viii, 2, 34, 46-47, 59, 93, 110-16, 127, 129, 144, 161, 177, 180, 186-88, 191, 231, 248-50, 255, 257, 260, 261, 262
Maryport, 55, 164-65, 176, 178,
Matlock, 47, 49-50, 173, 175

Index

Matlock Bath, 49
Mein Kampf, 31, 119
Meisner, Joseph, 102-04, 106-07
Mendelsohn, Erich, 10, 72
Meyer, Frank, 196
Miller, Lee, 77
Millinery, 86-87, 89, 94
Ministry of Information, 75, 129
Miyake, Issey, 164, 167
Molyneux, Edward, x, 63, 135-36, 139, 141, 225, 244
Moholy-Nagy, László, 24
Moholy-Nagy, Lucia, 24
Montgomery, Bernard, Field Marshall, ix, 105
Moro, Peter, 72
Morton, Digby, 92, 116-17, 135,
Mosely, Oswald, 60
Mülheim an der Ruhr, 85
Museum of London, viii, ix, 85, 89-90, 247

N
Nast, Condé Montrose, 76-77, 217, 220,
National Archives, 151, 173, 252
Nazism, 2, 22, 27, 33, 71, 109-10, 209, 228, 231-32, 247, 250
Neufeld, Rudolf, 166
Neuländer Simon, Else (Yva), 21
Neurath, Eva, 68, 218, 255, 260
Neurath, Walter, 217
Newman, Alice, 6
News Chronicle, 54
Nieper, David, vii, 50
Nieper, Ron, 50, 172
Noskwith [Noskovitch], Rolf, vi, 62, 168-70, 252

P
Palmer, Arnold, 107
Papworth, Hilary, 100, 177, 253
Pasold & Co, 40, 44, 65-66, 105, 223
Pasold, Eric, 42, 45, 58, 65, 68, 260
Patou, Jean, 87, 156, 225
Pears, Peter, 2, 185
Pemberton, Muriel, 241, 243, 256
Perutz, Gisela, 72
Perutz, Max, 72
Peterhans, Walter, 21
Photography, v, 4, 20-22, 25, 26, 74-78, 83, 217, 218, 257
Picture Post, 21
Pioneer Corps, 61, 97, 159, 232
Piper, John, 2, 75, 180-81, 185
Piper, Myfanwy, 181
Poiret, Paul, 8, 15-16, 131
Posen, 95
Prada, 147
Prague, 40, 80, 110, 124, 131, 138, 140, 192, 231
Princess Elizabeth, HRH, 132, 135, 139, 155
Pringle, Elizabeth, 48-49
Pringle, Robert, 146-47
Pringle of Scotland, 146-158, 245, 252, 257

Q
Quant, Mary, 106, 220
Queen Elizabeth, HRH, x, 49, 94, 135, 139, 193, 195, 211, 245-46, 249

R
Rathbone, Eleanor, 54
Rayne, 193
RCA (Royal College of Art), 24, 107

Reich, Sam, vii, 133-34, 221, 250
Reich, Tibor, 127, 132-35, 141, 143, 211, 225, 248 n. 15, 249n. 42, 250 n. 56, 260, 262
Reichskammer für die bildenden Künste, 36
Reimann, Albert, 25
Reimann, Heinz, 25-26
Reimann Schule [School], 25, 128, 203
Rie, Lucie, vi, 23, 164, 166-67, 252
Riederer, Marietta, 33
Rinkevicius, Vytantas, 210
Ringl & pit, 21, 75
Ruskin, John, 45

S
Sander, Bertha, 145
Saunders, Jonathan, 156
Schiaparelli, Elsa, 15, 64, 77, 101, 131, 261
Schleger, Hans, 33, 79-81, 84, 220, 252 n. 85, 261
Schocken, Salman, 10=11, 14, 28, 47, 72, 110, 257
Schneider, Hans, 2, 93, 110-117, 130, 180-87, 229,
Schröder, Anny, 174, 252, 258
Sekers, Nicholas (Miki), ix, 76, 141-43, 229-30
Selfridges, 47, 73, 161, 194,
Shrimpton, Jean, 92
Sieff, Edward, 183, 233
Sieff, Israel, 34
Sieff, Marcus, 232
Sigler, Gerhardt, 124-26
Sigler, Nick, vii, viii, 124-26, 249 n. 41,

Simpson of Piccadilly, 47, 72, 215-17, 242
Smith, Graham, 107
Smith, Maggie, 193
Smith, Paul, 99
Snow, C.P., 168
Snowman, Daniel, 71
Somerville, Philip, 94
Sparks, 110-12, 114-16, 130, 191, 248 n. 27, 249 n. 34
Spreiregen, Jakob (Jacques), 101-06
Stalin, Joseph, 209, 219
Steiner, Francis, 176-180
Steiner, Max, vii, 55, 176-79, 230, 252 n. 98
Steiner, Maya, 177
Stern, Grete, 21
Strnad, Oskar, 174
Stussy, 109
Sudetenland, 40, 44, 65, 131, 138, 177, 192
Summerfield [Sommerfeld], Inge-Lore (Illo), 191
Sussmann, Ella, 158
Swan & Edgar, 161
Sykes, Adam, vii, viii, x, 222, 224-26, 255 n. 147
Synthetics, 5, 19, 29 n. 29, 57, 140

T
Tailoring, 10, 12, 14, 23, 95, 220
Taylor & Penton Gowns, 180
Taylor, Neil, viii, 68 n. 6, 255 n. 150, 261
Textile design, 129, 144, 146
Thatcher, Margaret, 193, 233
Tick-a-Tee, 55, 176-78, 230

Tietz, 10
Tokyo, 99, 167
Tomalin [neé Wallach], Elisabeth, 127-31, 249 n. 43
Tomalin, Lewis, 249 n. 47
Tomalin, Miles, 129
Tomalin, Stefany, 129, 249 n. 47
Tyne Textile, 57

U
Ullstein, 19-20, 29 n. 32, 261
Unemployment, 34, 52, 55, 247
Usher, Frank, 203-208, 254 n. 126

V
Victoria & Albert Museum, vii, 2, 81, 85, 206, 234, 242
Vienna, 11-15, 22-23, 28 n. 19
Vogue, 64-65, 69-70, 76-77, 79-81, 83 n. 16, 84 n.22, 89, 92, 153, 217, 218, 220-21, 242

W
Wabena, ix, 161, 163
Wakefield, 196-97, 199, 201, 222, 245
Wallenberg, Raoul, 85, 247 n. 3
Walsall, 98-99
War, see 60-69
Warburg Institute, 185
Warsaw, 101
Watson, Nigel, 102-04, 106, 248 n. 18

Wedgwood, Josiah, 54
Wegner, Zoltan, 217
Weisz, Otto, 146-157, 245, 251 n. 75
Weisz, David, vii, 251 n. 174, 252 n. 76, 77
Werkbund, Deutscher, 73
Wertheim, 10
Westphal, Uwe, 9, 17, 28 n. 5, 10, 11, 29 n. 26, 28, 41 n. 1
Westwood, Vivienne, 49, 156
Wiener Library, vii, viii, 124, 188, 190,
Wiener Werkstätte, 23, 26, 29 n. 41, 131, 132, 166
Wilson, Harold, 211-13
Windsor, Duchess of, 2, 85
Windsor, Duke of, 50, 101
Winfield, Rex, 199
Winter, H, 164
Winton, Nicholas, 53
Wittkower, Rudolf, 184-85
Wolff, Gisela, 14
Wolff, Fritz, 15
Wolff, Maria, 219-20
Worth, 15
Wuppertal, 203
Würzburg, 192

X Y Z
Zurich, 158-59